LAW AND RESPONSIBILITY IN WARFARE

The Vietnam Experience

Edited by PETER D. TROOBOFF
Foreword by ARTHUR J. GOLDBERG

The University of North Carolina Press
Chapel Hill

Copyright © 1975 by
The University of North Carolina Press
All rights reserved
Manufactured in the United States of America
ISBN 0-8078-1239-0
Library of Congress Catalog Card Number 74-22431

Library of Congress Cataloging in Publication Data
Main entry under title:

Law and responsibility in warfare, the Vietnam
  experience.

  Papers and discussions from a special meeting of the
American Society of International law in Oct. 1971.
  Includes bibliographical references and index.
  1. War (International law) — Addresses, essays,
lectures. 2. Vietnamese Conflict, 1961-   — United
States—Addresses, essays, lectures. I. Trooboff,
Peter D., 1942-   ed. II. American Society of Inter-
national Law.
JX5001.L38   341.6   74-22431
ISBN 0-8078-1239-0

FOR MY PARENTS
who value study and respect diversity

Contents

PART THREE: INDIVIDUAL RESPONSIBILITY IN WARFARE

Foreword

This collection concerns the test during the Vietnam War of the ability of the combatants to conduct hostilities in accordance with international law. The book results from a special meeting of the American Society of International Law in October 1971 in which I participated as chairman of a public forum on the legal responsibility of the individual in wartime.

I find two central themes emerging throughout the book. First, the difficulties of interpreting, and insuring compliance with, the laws of war in Vietnam bear striking parallels to those in some of the previous armed conflicts involving the United States. Second, I am impressed by recent emphasis on individual rights in analyzing the laws of war applicable to both combatants and noncombatants.

Despite the teachings of historians, each generation is inclined—some would say destined—to view its actions and problems as unique. This tendency is particularly apparent with respect to armed conflicts. Science and technology appear to have qualitatively changed the nature of warfare. In Vietnam we saw apparently new strategies—bombing in free-fire zones (or, as they came to be known, specified strike zones) and defoliation-herbicide operations. For Americans engaged in combat, it seemed unprecedented to fight a war against forces, often not in uniform, that at one moment fought and the next moment hid among the civilian population.

As the chapters of this book demonstrate, there is precedent for some of the combat operations and some of the questions relating to the laws of war that arose in Vietnam. In the American Civil War and again in the Philippines at the beginning of this century, the United States fought forces that did not carry their weapons openly and did not wear the trappings of combatants. In each of these conflicts, difficult questions arose in determining whether irregular forces had complied with the laws of war and whether they should be treated as enemy soldiers or civilian outlaws.

The strategies and weapons in Vietnam were also not entirely new. The German bombing of purely civilian centers of population and the retaliatory Allied bombing in World War II of German targets correspond, in some degree, to United States area bombing of Viet Cong sanctuaries in Vietnam. Even napalm, with its awful ability to burn and asphyxiate, was developed and used during World War II by both sides. The indiscriminate killing of civilians by Hanoi and the Viet Cong at Hue is reminiscent of German civilian massacres in World War II.

So, the conduct of the Vietnam conflict was not as unique as some thought. But the American public correctly perceived that United States military actions and those of its adversaries raised many new and troubling issues. And, on a more limited scale, but not to be condoned, what about My Lai? I believe that these concerns arose, in part, out of an increased concern about the rights of combatants and noncombatants.

The contributors discuss the legal and moral issues that arise in fighting guerrilla forces with the high-technology weapons of modern warfare. Identifying the "enemy" and determining how to treat him pose equally difficult legal and moral questions. What is the status of the Vietnamese man who tends rice fields by day and carries food, information, or weapons to guerrilla forces by night? Or of the Vietnamese mother who hides guerrillas in her home, because they demand something under threat of force, or because her son, who was pressed into service, is among those seeking refuge, or because her sympathies are with the Viet Cong? Finally, how does the foot soldier respond to an eleven-year-old who may have a grenade?

The foregoing questions, of course, raise technical issues under the laws of war. But, in addition, they force us to examine the rights to which the suspected combatant or civilian accomplice of the combatant is entitled, as well as the rights of the military in dealing with this type of warfare. The criteria for determining such rights developed during wars in which the distinctions between the soldier and the innocent civilian seemed, and usually were, sharper. These standards arose before we experienced the significant redefinition of individual liberties that the political process and the courts shaped in this country during the 1950s and 1960s. Finally, and possibly of equal significance, traditional laws-of-war provisions were formulated before the advent of television, which brought into our living rooms the terrible impact of war on combatant and noncombatant alike.

This book represents an important inquiry into those grave questions that arose from military conduct by all sides in the Vietnam War. Unlike many publications on these issues, it is a balanced presentation. The book includes contributions from experts whose views differ sharply on the application of the laws of war to the strategies and weapons employed in Vietnam. And they have diverse perspectives on the rights of combatants and noncombatants in that conflict. Together these contributions again demonstrate the importance to this country of what our first Chief Justice called the "free air" of American life. They will help us to understand problems that we hope never to confront again, but that no responsible citizen can regard as only of historical interest.

ARTHUR J. GOLDBERG

Acknowledgments

The precise origins of this book remain uncertain. But I owe a considerable debt to Harold D. Laswell, President of The American Society of International Law during 1971, his successor, William D. Rogers, and Stephen M. Schwebel, then the Society's Executive Director, for entrusting the project to me.

In his customary fashion, Richard R. Baxter offered that combination of advice, encouragement, and discipline that makes him a valued teacher and friend. And throughout the months of organization leading to the meeting at which the chapters were first presented and during the subsequent editing, John Lawrence Hargrove, then the Society's Director of Studies, lent his full support, but preserved my enthusiasm by leaving ultimate responsibility for the book to its editor.

To Justice Goldberg and to the contributors, I can only express the hope that they find in the final work ample reward for their considerable efforts and scholarship. A special word of thanks is due to Covey T. Oliver, who gave of his time and energy by chairing the private sessions at which the contributions were first discussed. As the Society's Fellow in 1971-72, Jay Burgess drew up a summary of those sessions that has been useful in preparing the Introduction and editing the chapters.

I am also indebted to my fellow members of the Society's Panel on Humanitarian Problems and International Law, who taught me so much about international humanitarian law in armed conflicts. On behalf of the Society and the contributors, I wish to thank The Ford Foundation and The Andrew W. Mellon Foundation, whose support for that panel and for the preparation of this volume was most appreciated. Needless to say, neither Foundation nor the Society is responsible for the positions or views expressed by the contributors.

Harry Almond, Waldemar Solf, and Ronald Bettauer, in their personal capacities, and Howard S. Levie reviewed drafts of the Introduction and provided constructive criticism that I have attempted to meet. But, of course, any misstatements there remain my responsibility.

Malcolm MacDonald, Chief Editor of The University of North Carolina Press, imposed severe deadlines and seemed to recognize instinctively that the practicing lawyer, even as editor, works best on a tight schedule. I am also grateful for the final editing by Katharine Cosby at the Press.

My colleagues at Covington & Burling, by their cooperation and, at times, their forbearance, afforded the time and resources to permit work on this project. Several hardworking secretaries, Laverne Peacock, Nancye Mittendorff, Norma Fricker, and Ralph Kivi, typed the countless revisions of chapters and footnotes.

Yet the greatest share of whatever credit this book deserves belongs to my wife, Rhoda. As each contributor knows, she carefully edited each chapter for style so that I could concentrate on substance. She undertook countless administrative tasks and coordinated the contributors' corrections and the index so that I could devote time to the Introduction and additional research for the contributors. And when the pressures of practicing and editing became very great, she was always there in good spirits to bolster morale and encourage greater effort by both of us. This, then, is a part of what we have created together during our first five years.

Law and Responsibility in Warfare

Introduction

Peter D. Trooboff

For the American people the details of the Vietnam War are beginning to fade from memory. The Paris Peace Agreements of January 1973 have been signed; the prisoners of war held by North Vietnam and the Viet Cong have been returned; and United States military action, even air strikes, finally terminated in Southeast Asia during August 1973. The Congress has, over a Presidential veto, enacted legislation to restrict the Executive Branch's war-making powers. [1] And still the armies of the governments in Vietnam continue the fight under the regime of a cease-fire that has never entered fully into force.

Once the domain of politicians, journalists, and editorialists, the Vietnam War in this country has now become the province of historians and political scientists. They have begun to examine in perspective the policies and decisions that led to American involvement and disengagement. In time, their works will shape the collective memory of those who lived through the domestic upheaval caused by Vietnam—and of new generations that did not.

While American military forces were actively engaged in the hostilities, the legality of the methods and weapons used in the war became the subject of a great national debate. Partisans could be found supporting points of view ranging from outright condemnation of American military leaders and troops as war criminals to lengthy defenses of the legality of the actions of United States armed forces in Vietnam. This debate eventually became part of the larger domestic controversy over the wisdom of continued American participation in the war. Ultimately, discussions of American adherence to the laws of war attracted less attention as the scale of United States military activities in Vietnam declined.

If Vietnam were the last counterinsurgent effort involving American or other nations' forces, the legal issues raised by the conduct of American military forces in Vietnam would not be pressing. But that is hardly the case. In an unstable world the United States may again believe itself compelled to assist an ally in combating insurgents. Moreover, other nations now have the capability to deploy high-technology weaponry against insurgents and to pursue the counterinsurgent methods and tactics upon which American forces relied in Vietnam.

The Vietnam War has also left America an unwanted legacy. For what shall be done with the many who fled the United States rather than serve in armed forces whose conduct they believed violated the laws of war? And what is the proper course for dealing with the war's military and civilian leaders? Should they be honored, tried as war criminals, or simply left to be forgotten? Perhaps only time can resolve these questions. But some would grant a total and unconditional amnesty to the young men of conscience who left rather than serve; others would see that as unwarranted acceptance of the most extreme claims made by the war's opponents. The conditional amnesty proclaimed by President Gerald Ford on 16 September 1974 may not satisfy the groups holding either point of view. The former regard it as exacting a penalty from those who committed no wrong other than refuse service in an unjust cause; the latter say that the Proclamation fails to demand a high enough price from draft dodgers and deserters.

This book presents papers by leading American experts concerning the status under the international laws of war and individual responsibility of United States military actions in Vietnam. As Justice Goldberg explains in his Foreword, the chapters in this book (except, of course, those on the 1972 Christmas bombings) were first prepared for a symposium in October 1971 sponsored by the American Society of International Law. The primary emphasis is on the international legal principles and national policies with respect to three subjects—the methods and tactics that American forces pursued in Vietnam; the weapons they used; and the responsibility of individuals who participated in, commanded, or shaped policy for forces using such methods, tactics, and weapons. It does not examine certain related subjects such as the legality under international law of United States entry into the Vietnam War. In short, the focus is on the military conduct of the war and on the persons responsible for that conduct.

Unlike many of the publications that appeared while the United States was still engaged in hostilities in Vietnam, this book seeks to present a balanced account. It contains sharply conflicting points of view. Many of the contributors were themselves active participants in the national debate over the conduct of the war, either as government officials, as leaders in antiwar movements, or as scholarly commentators on the application of the laws of war in Vietnam.

In this introduction, I shall first outline the international laws of war and individual responsibility that underlie the contributors' analyses. It is, of course, not possible to provide a comprehensive statement of these laws here. But this summary will attempt to guide readers who are unfamiliar with the substantial body of treaties, decisions, customary norms, and literature on the legal principles governing military conduct in armed conflict. The second part of this introduction will identify the principal legal and policy questions on which the contributors join issue.

International Laws of War and Individual Responsibility

Reasons for the Laws of War /   Any discussion among lay-men about the laws of war inevitably begins with this question: "Why have rules governing the conduct of war if, by definition, war is a total effort to destroy the enemy?" This issue troubles nonlawyers and lawyers alike. Indeed, its continued reappear-ance after two world wars, Korea, and Vietnam suggests that American political leaders and educators have failed to explain to the citizenry the legal framework within which hostilities among nations take place. The persistence of the inquiry into the rationale for laws of war parallels the difficulties experi-enced by the United States military services in teaching rules of warfare to enlisted men and officers.

The answer to the question is that history has demonstrated, on humanitarian and pragmatic grounds, that laws governing the conduct of war are advantageous to all parties to hostilities. There are numerous illustrations of concern for humanitarian principles in recorded history. In *The Republic*, Socrates com-ments that in the War of the Hellenes the attackers need to spare the innocent men, women, and children of Hellas because "they know that the guilt of war is always confined to a few persons and that the many are their friends."[2] Likewise, although the early Christian Church condoned and even encouraged great brutality in the name of propagating the faith, it required penances of soldiers who had taken a human life.

But humanitarianism alone would probably not have led to the well-developed laws of war that exist today. A second critical reason for seeking to restrain conduct in warfare is pragmatism. Warfare without restriction can lead to retaliation in kind or even to escalation of the brutality. For example, the use of a per-fidious weapon such as poison arrows, which were outlawed early in recorded history, motivates the enemy to use the same in defense. Unless restraints exist, the brutality that neither side desires will take hold. Similarly, killing prisoners taken from among the enemy's troops may cause him to kill his prisoners. And, besides, prisoners can be exchanged for one's own cap-tured forces, possibly during the hostilities, or if that proves im-practical, after their termination.

A second purely pragmatic reason for rules governing warfare is that noncombatants, especially the enemy's civilian popula-tion, have been found to be more valuable if they remain un-harmed and preferably cooperative. They can possibly be forced to work in place for the occupying force. Reconciliation will hardly be easy and its benefits, such as increased trade, will be delayed if abuses to enemy soldiers, or to their families in occupied territory, are widespread during hostilities.

Finally, maintaining military discipline is considerably more difficult among forces bent on destruction of nonmilitary objectives. Discipline is the cornerstone of military forces. Soldiers who carry on unnecessary destruction and violence are unlikely to exhibit the qualities of cooperation and respect for authority that are essential in battle. Maintaining order and a cooperative fighting unit is not possible if each man is out to satisfy only his own secret lusts. Thus restraints on destroying nonmilitary objectives, including both persons and property, promote the creation of a successful army and respect for the orders of its commanders.

History of the Laws of War / The origins of the laws of war can be traced to some of man's earliest recorded history, although the legal principles were obviously not formulated with the same detail that we find in contemporary rules. For example, the Old Testament prescribes the restrictions governing the ancient Hebrews in warfare. In Deuteronomy, the Israelites are told to spare noncombatants and the "trees of the field" of remote enemies. [3] In another early work, written in the fourth century B.C., *The Art of War*, Sun Tzu prohibits injuring a previously wounded enemy or striking elderly men and orders the care and proper treatment of captive soldiers. [4]

In the Middle Ages the Christian Church sought to limit the brutality of warfare by proscribing violence on certain days. Thus, in 1035 the Archbishop of Arles proclaimed a "Truce of God" from "vespers on Wednesday to sunrise on Monday." At the Second Lateran Council in 1139 the Church fathers outlawed "under penalty of anathema" the use of crossbows and arrows "against Christians and Catholics." At the same time, the heraldic courts adopted and refined a code of chivalry that regulated the conduct of knights in battle and was enforced at the courts of Christian princes.

In the late Middle Ages and throughout the Renaissance, scholars, jurists, and theologians refined these restrictions on warfare in learned texts. Among the most notable of them was undoubtedly *On the Law of War and Peace* by the Dutch lawyer who is sometimes called the father of international law, Hugo Grotius (1583-1645). His work contained a comprehensive synthesis of the laws of war based on his prodigious scholarship. And by its publication Grotius helped to formulate principles that until that time could only have been gleaned from the scattered annals of state practice and from the available scholarship.

*Early United States Contributions
to the Laws of War* /   From its very beginning, the United
States demonstrated its commitment to respect the emerging
principles that were to become the international laws of war.
For example, two treaties signed by the new nation contained
express provisions governing the rights of noncombatants at the
outbreak of hostilities. In 1782, the Continental Congress entered into a Treaty of Peace and Commerce with The Netherlands. Article 18 of that accord provided that in the event of war
the citizens of the two countries would have nine months to
return to their respective homelands "with their effects . . . in
all freedom and without any hindrance. . . ."[5]

The Treaty of Amity and Commerce between this country and
Prussia in 1785 stipulated a like period at the onset of war for
"the merchants of either country, then residing in the other,
. . . to collect their debts and settle their affairs, and . . . de-
part freely, carrying off all their effects, without molestation or
hindrance. . . ."[6] In addition, the treaty with Prussia, which
was negotiated by John Adams, Benjamin Franklin, and
Thomas Jefferson, set forth detailed rules concerning the treatment of prisoners of war. Article 24 included a prohibition on
sending prisoners "into distant and inclement countries, or . . .
crouding [*sic*] them into close and noxions [*sic*] places. . . ."
This agreement also required the parties to furnish to each officer who was prisoner "as many rations, and of the same
articles and quality as are allowed . . . [by the capturing
power] to officers of equal rank in their own army. . . ." A
similar provision guaranteed to the "common soldier" in captiv-
ity rations equivalent to those received by his counterpart in the
opposing army. Finally, prisoners were to be permitted to
receive and keep parcels from their friends and "to make . . .
reports, in open letters to those who employ [them]. . . ."

In the American Civil War, the United States undertook an
initiative that was to influence the development of the laws of
war from that time to the present. Faced with an enemy who
sent men "in the garb of peaceful citizens . . . to waylay and
attack . . . troops, to burn bridges and houses, and to destroy
property and persons," Maj. Gen. Henry W. Halleck asked for
advice from Francis Lieber, a German-born immigrant who
was a member of Columbia Law School's first faculty. [7] Professor Lieber had fought in the Prussian Army against Napoleon,
had published a philosophical study in 1839 that included
chapters on warfare and its conduct, and had given lectures in
1861 and 1862 at Columbia on "Laws and Usages in War."

Professor Lieber's reply to General Halleck was published and distributed to the Union Army in a pamphlet entitled "Guerrilla Parties." This led to appointment of a board "to propose . . . a code of regulations for the government of Armies in the field as authorized by the laws and usages of War." While serving as the only civilian member of this board, Professor Lieber drafted the code that bears his name. In April 1863 the United States promulgated the Lieber Code as General Order No. 100, "Instructions for the Government of Armies of the United States in the Field." The Code was, in truth, the first codification of the laws of war. It contained a detailed discussion of the meaning of "military necessity" and provisions governing such diverse issues as the treatment of prisoners of war and noncombatants, the pursuit of certain methods of warfare, and the requirements for protecting civilian property. Perhaps the overall tone of the Code can best be understood from this frequently cited provision from article 15: "Men who take up arms against one another in public war do not cease on this account to be moral beings, responsible to one another and to God."

Codification of International Law Protecting Victims of Warfare / While the United States developed a code of land warfare during its struggle to secure survival as a nation, the great powers of Europe also began to recognize the need to codify certain rules of warfare. As a result of the tragic and widespread neglect of the sick and wounded and the execution of some injured soldiers at Solferino in the Franco-Austrian War of 1859, the Swiss government convened an international conference at Geneva in 1864. This action was prompted by Henri Dunant, the founder of the Red Cross movement, who had been an eyewitness to the death and suffering at Solferino. From the 1864 meeting resulted the Convention for the Amelioration of the Condition of the Wounded in Armies in the Field. [8] In a word, the Geneva Convention of 1864 established the first rudimentary international rules for the protection of sick and wounded soldiers and created certain protections for the persons, hospitals, and ambulances aiding them. The Geneva Convention of 1864 entered into force in 1865, but it was not until 1882 that the United States, which did not take part in the 1864 conference because of its preoccupation with the Civil War, became a party.

As a result of the Swiss role in promoting the 1864 Convention, the International Committee of the Red Cross (ICRC) was organized. The ICRC is a private organization composed exclusively of Swiss citizens. Its statutes make the ICRC responsible for developing, as well as implementing, international law relating to the treatment of victims of warfare. [9] It is interesting that the first Nobel Peace Prize was awarded in 1901 to Henri

Dunant, the person most responsible for Swiss interest in mitigating human suffering in war, and that the ICRC itself
received the Nobel Peace Prize in 1917 for its actions during
World War I.[10]

From this modest beginning with the Geneva Convention of
1864, there developed a comprehensive regime of treaties governing the obligations of belligerents in warfare to treat sick and
wounded soldiers, as well as shipwrecked sailors, prisoners of
war, and, finally, civilians in occupied and unoccupied territories. The European powers and the United States, responding
to a call from Czar Nicholas II of Russia, met at The Hague in
1899. There they adopted an agreement that extended to maritime warfare the principles for protection of sick and wounded
embodied in the 1864 Convention. In 1906 over thirty nations
met at Geneva to lessen "the inherent evils of warfare as far as is
within their power . . . [and] to improve and supplement" the
1864 Convention. They negotiated the Geneva Convention of
1906, which substantially expanded the protections afforded to
the sick, wounded, and shipwrecked and broadened the protection of persons who cared for them during combat. The 1906
Convention also gave official status to the Red Cross emblem for
the "sanitary service of armies" and prohibited its use by
unauthorized persons. The United States ratified both the 1899
and 1906 Geneva Conventions.[11]

Each world war gave further impetus to developing the provisions of the 1899 and 1906 Conventions. Thus, after World
War I, another, more extensive Geneva Convention concerning
the sick and wounded was adopted in 1929.[12] In addition, the
participating nations agreed to a new 1929 Convention on the
Treatment of Prisoners of War.[13] The latter agreement sought
to codify the developing international legal principles governing the conditions for internment of prisoners of war and included provisions relating to their food and clothing, work in
camps, right to communicate with families, and, finally,
release and repatriation after cessation of hostilities. In addition, the Geneva Prisoners of War Convention of 1929 recognized the right of the International Committee of the Red Cross
to undertake humanitarian activity on behalf of prisoners of
war with the consent of the concerned belligerents. Again the
United States ratified these Geneva Conventions.

Finally, in the aftermath of World War II, governments met
again at Geneva and negotiated the four agreements currently
in force, which together are known as the Geneva Conventions
of 1949. Relying on almost a century of experience with regulating the treatment of victims of warfare, the representatives

at the 1949 conference adopted extensive and detailed provisions for the protection of the wounded and sick in armed forces in the field (the First Convention);[14] for wounded, sick, and shipwrecked members of armed forces at sea (the Second Convention);[15] for the treatment of prisoners of war (the Third Convention);[16] and for the protection of civilian persons in time of war (the Fourth Convention).[17] Today 135 nations adhere to the Geneva Conventions of 1949, making them among the most universally accepted agreements in contemporary international affairs. On 2 February 1956, the four Geneva Conventions of 1949 entered into force for the United States. Both South Vietnam and North Vietnam are parties to the Conventions, although the North Vietnamese adherence is subject to an important reservation.[18]

As a number of the contributors to this book emphasize, the Geneva Conventions of 1949 apply, according to article 2, "to all cases of declared war or of any other armed conflict which may arise between two or more of the High Contracting Parties, even if the state of war is not recognized by one of them." This provision is particularly significant because it makes clear that the detailed obligations under the Conventions do not apply in so-called internal conflicts, i.e., those that do not involve at least two of the high contracting parties. But, as discussed below, article 3 of each Convention sets forth certain minimum standards required of parties to conflicts "not of an international character." The Conventions clearly apply in the event of partial or total occupation of the territory of a high contracting party by another party.

Each of the Geneva Conventions carefully defines the persons who are entitled to its protections. The First and Second Conventions protect wounded, sick, and shipwrecked persons who are "members of armed forces of a party to the conflict, as well as members of militias or volunteer corps forming part of such armed forces."[19] The Prisoners of War Convention covers such members of armed forces or militia or volunteer corps who have "fallen into the power of the enemy."[20] In the case of the Vietnam War, one of the most significant provisions of the first three Conventions was that which extends their protection to a party's "other militias and members of other volunteer corps, including those of organized resistance movements."[21] Such "irregular" forces are entitled to protection under these Conventions only if they fulfill four conditions: first, if they are "commanded by a person responsible for his subordinates"; second, if they wear a "fixed distinctive sign recognizable at a distance"; third, if they carry "arms openly"; and, finally, if they conduct their operations in accordance with the laws and customs of war. [22]

As Professor Goldie discusses in his chapter, the first three Conventions also afford their full protection to participants in a so-called *levée en masse*. The Conventions define the persons entitled to protection in such circumstances as "inhabitants of non-occupied territory, who on the approach of the enemy spontaneously take up arms to resist the invading forces, without having had time to form themselves into regular armed units. . . ." [23] But such inhabitants, to receive these protections, are also required to carry arms openly and respect the laws and customs of war.

The Fourth Convention contains two different levels of protection for civilians. The more extensive rights are accorded to "protected persons," who are defined as "those who, at a given moment and in any manner whatsoever, find themselves, in case of a conflict or occupation, in the hands of a party to the conflict or Occupying Power of which they are not nationals." [24] Part II of the Civilians Convention contains a more limited set of obligations applying to the treatment of "the whole of the population of the countries in conflict, without any adverse distinction, based, in particular, on race, nationality, religion or political opinion, and are intended to alleviate the sufferings caused by war." [25] Unlike the higher level of rights for "protected persons," the rights extended by Part II are available to civilians of one state in the hands of armed forces of another regardless of whether the territory is technically occupied. As Mr. Jordan and others discuss, a number of complicated questions arise about the standards of treatment to which the civilians of South Vietnam were entitled by United States forces under the Civilians Convention.

There is one additional feature of the Geneva Conventions of 1949 that relates directly to their application in a civil or internal war. Article 3 of each of the Conventions contains a so-called mini-convention establishing obligations that apply as a minimum to the high contracting parties in the case of "armed conflict not of an international character" within their territory. In general, these minimum standards for internal conflicts establish protections to be applied without discrimination to civilians and to combatants who have "laid down their arms" or are *hors de combat* because they are sick, wounded, or captured or for any other reason. Article 3 specifically proscribes violence to life and person (including murder, mutilation, cruel treatment, and torture), taking of hostages, outrages upon personal dignity (in particular, humiliating and degrading treatment), and sentencing and execution without a fair trial by a regularly constituted court. It also requires that the "wounded and sick shall be collected and cared for."

A complex issue arises over whether a local conflict involving an insurgent force that is supported by foreign states has become an international armed conflict. The question is especially difficult if, as in Vietnam, the defending government is aided by other states. Further, it is unclear, as Mr. Warnke notes in his chapter, whether North Vietnam was a "foreign state" after the 1954 Geneva Accords.

In order to encourage more protection for the victims of internal wars, article 3 of the 1949 Conventions states that the "Parties to the conflict should further endeavor to bring into force, by means of special agreements, all or part of the other provisions" of the Geneva Conventions. It also stipulates that application of the article 3 protections "shall not affect the legal status of the Parties to the conflict." Nations would be most reluctant to agree to grant even article 3 protections to rebels or civilian victims of internal warfare if such action might confer a legal status on the rebels or insurgents that they would not otherwise enjoy. Thus, article 3 precludes affecting the status of insurgent guerrillas, whatever it may be, by a provision whose purpose is solely to protect victims of an internal conflict.

The 1949 Conventions extend an even greater role to the ICRC than it had under earlier conventions. In particular, each of the conventions confers on a "Protecting Power" the responsibility for implementing certain provisions benefiting the "protected persons"—whether they are the sick and wounded, prisoners of war, or civilians. The conventions contain detailed provisions governing the selection of such a power. However, the nation chosen to serve as Protecting Power has to be approved by the parties to the conflict, and obtaining such approval will often be impossible.

The 1949 Conventions make clear that if a Protecting Power cannot be agreed upon, a Detaining Power—for example, a country that holds prisoners of war—"shall request" a neutral state or a humanitarian organization to "undertake the humanitarian functions performed . . . by a Protecting Power. . . ."[26] Moreover, if protection cannot be arranged in either of these ways, the parties are obligated to request or to accept "the offer of the services of a humanitarian organization, such as the International Committee of the Red Cross," to assume such functions.[27] Finally, article 3, the "mini-convention," specifies that the ICRC may offer its services to the parties to an internal conflict. Unlike the case in which the full Conventions apply, in a conflict "not of an international character," which is treated solely in article 3, the parties are not required to request a neutral state or humanitarian organization to fulfill the Protecting Power's functions.

North Vietnam, along with the Soviet Union and a number of other socialist countries, entered a specific reservation to these provisions on Protecting Powers when they ratified the Geneva Conventions. They stated that no recognition would be accorded to a request by a Detaining Power to a humanitarian organization such as the ICRC or a neutral state to undertake the Protecting Power's functions unless the government of the protected persons has consented. In the Vietnam War, North Vietnam and the National Liberation Front refused to request the ICRC to carry out any humanitarian functions with respect to their troops held as prisoners of war in South Vietnam. In addition, North Vietnam and the National Liberation Front failed to honor the request by the United States for the ICRC to perform humanitarian functions for captured American soldiers.

Limitation of the Methods, Means, and
Weapons of Warfare /   Governments have also sought to take limited steps toward codifying restrictions on the methods and means of warfare and the weapons employed in battle. The earliest effort in this direction was the Declaration of Saint Petersburg of 1868, in which the signatories stated that the object of warfare, "to weaken the military force of the enemy" by disabling the greatest possible number of men, "would be exceeded by the employment of arms which uselessly aggravate the sufferings of disabled men, or render their death inevitable. . . ."[28] As a result, they renounced, "in case of war among themselves, the employment, by their military or naval forces, of any projectile of less weight than four hundred grammes, which is explosive, or is charged with fulminating or inflammable substances." This ban on exploding bullets was never signed by the United States and, as Professor Baxter points out in his chapter, has not become part of customary international law. But it was the first formal international agreement restricting the use of a weapon of warfare.

At the Hague Conference of 1899 convened by Czar Nicholas II, the twenty-six participating nations sought to limit certain other weapons. In the Hague Declaration of 1899, the signatories, noting that they were "inspired by the sentiments which found expression" in the 1868 Declaration of Saint Petersburg, stated their intention to abstain from the use of so-called dumdum bullets (i.e., bullets that "expand or flatten easily in the human body, such as bullets with a hard envelope which does not entirely cover the core, or is pierced with incisions"). [29] In two other Hague Declarations of 1899, the contracting parties agreed to prohibit the "use of projectiles the object of which is the diffusion of asphyxiating or deleterious gases" [30] and banned for five years the "launching of projectiles and explosives from balloons, or by other new methods of similar nature." [31] While the United States signed and later ratified the agreement to forego the use of projectiles and bombs launched from balloons, it did not sign the 1899 Declarations on dum-dum bullets or on asphyxiating or deleterious gases. But the United States "has acknowledged that it will abide by the terms of the agreement prohibiting expanding bullets." [32]

Although the prohibitions on specific weapons at the 1899 Hague Conference were important, the most significant result of that meeting was undoubtedly the codification of the Regulations respecting the Laws and Customs of War on Land in the annex to the Second Hague Convention of 1899 on the Laws and Customs of Warfare. This effort had its origins in a conference held by the European powers twenty-five years earlier at Brussels. While the Brussels Declaration of 1874 never entered into force, its provisions, based in many respects on the Lieber Code, had a considerable influence on the nations meeting at The Hague in 1899. The Hague Regulations of 1899, revised and amended again at The Hague in 1907, were incorporated as an annex to the Fourth Hague Convention of 1907. The United States ratified the Hague Regulations after the 1899 Conference [33] and again after the 1907 Conference. [34] They remain in force today and contain many of the most important provisions of contemporary international law governing the methods and means of warfare, as well as the use of weapons. In addition, many of these provisions have now entered into customary international law and, as explained below, are binding on states even if they are not parties to the treaty containing the Hague Regulations.

Although the Hague Regulations include many detailed rules governing warfare, it is possible to identify in them certain essential features. First, article 22 provides, in introducing the chapter "Means of Injuring the Enemy," that "[t]he right of belligerents to adopt means of injuring the enemy is not unlimited."

Second, the Regulations set forth specifically prohibited weapons and methods and means of warfare. For example, article 23 specifies that it is forbidden to "employ poison or poisoned weapons"; to "employ arms, projectiles, or material calculated to cause unnecessary suffering"; to declare that "no quarter will be given"; or to make improper use of the flag of truce, the Red Cross emblem, or the enemy's flag, insignia, or uniform.

Third, the Hague Regulations impose limitations for the protection of noncombatants from the effects of warfare. Article 25 prohibits "[t]he attack or bombardment, by whatever means, of towns, villages, dwellings, or buildings which are undefended. . . ." Pillage of a town or place, "even when taken by assault," is also prohibited by article 28.

While the Hague Regulations appreciably advanced the codified laws of war, the nations taking part in the Hague Conferences of 1899 and 1907 recognized that their actions still left considerable possibility for brutality in warfare. At the urging of the Russian jurist F. F. Martens, the Hague Conventions of 1899 and 1907 to which the Regulations are annexed contain the following so-called Martens clause:

> Until a more complete code of the laws of war has been issued, the High Contracting Parties deem it expedient to declare that, in cases not included in the Regulations adopted by them, the inhabitants and the belligerents remain under the protection and the rule of the principles of the law of nations, as they result from the usages established among civilized peoples, from the laws of humanity, and from the dictates of the public conscience.

Following World War I, nations renewed their effort to codify the laws of war governing the use of weapons and the methods and means of warfare. For example, the United States joined in 1922 with France, Great Britain, Italy, and Japan in a treaty prohibiting "the use of submarines as commerce destroyers." The 1922 treaty included in article 5 a restraint on the "use in war of asphyxiating, poisonous or other gases, and all analogous liquids, materials or devices."[35] Although the United States ratified this treaty, it did not enter into force because of the French refusal to ratify it.

The same five nations also established a commission of jurists to consider new rules for the laws of war to cover "new methods of attack or defense resulting from the introduction or development . . . of new agencies of warfare." The jurists met at The Hague from December 1922 to February 1923 and prepared the Draft Hague Rules of Air Warfare. The carefully drafted 1923 Rules never were formally adopted, nor were they followed in the practice of belligerents during World War II. This was apparently because certain of the Rules did not conform to the practice of states. For example, article 24 provided that if a military objective, which was carefully defined, was situated so that it could not be "bombarded without the indiscriminate bombardment of the civilian population, the aircraft must abstain from bombardment."

The 1923 Rules represent an important step toward defining the laws of war with respect to air warfare. Unfortunately, only theoretical progress has been made to date in this direction, as Professor Hamilton DeSaussure and Robert Glasser emphasize in discussing the 1972 Christmas bombing of North Vietnam. In the United States, a draft manual on rules of air warfare was prepared by the Air Force, but it has never been officially adopted. Professor DeSaussure and Mr. Glasser present a summary of the practice of the United States and other countries during and since World War II in conducting air warfare. They advance an important proposal concerning the future rules governing it, but their analysis and recommendation are, as the contributors in chapters 10 and 11 explain, highly controversial.

Professors Levie and Tucker, and the commentators on their papers, devote considerable attention to the 1925 Protocol for the Prohibition of Poisonous Gases and Bacteriological Methods of Warfare.[36] The Protocol begins with a statement that "the general opinion of the civilized world" has "justly condemned" the use of those gases outlawed by the previously mentioned five-power treaty of 1922. The high contracting parties further agreed in the Protocol that the use of such gases was prohibited and, in addition, agreed "to extend this prohibition to the use of bacteriological methods of warfare. . . ."

The United States signed the Geneva Protocol in 1925, but had not ratified it at the time of the Vietnam War. In August 1970, President Nixon reintroduced the Protocol in the Senate and requested its advice and consent to ratification. In a report accompanying the submission, the Secretary of State said that "[i]t is the United States understanding of the Protocol that it does not prohibit the use in war of riot-control agents and chemical herbicides. Smoke, flame, and napalm are also not covered by the Protocol." In December 1974 the Senate gave its advice and consent to the Protocol after the Administration announced that United States national policy would henceforth preclude use of herbicides or riot-control agents except in certain limited and specified circumstances. The President signed the instruments of ratification for the Protocol in January 1975, and its entry into force should take place in 1975.[37]

An important post-World War II development of the Hague

Regulations was the signing at The Hague in 1954 of the Convention for the Protection of Cultural Property in the Event of Armed Conflict. Article 27 of the 1907 Hague Regulations provided that "all necessary steps must be taken to spare" centers of religion, art, science, and charity, as well as historic monuments not being used for military purposes. Besieged areas were required to notify the enemy of such places in advance of attack and to mark them with distinctive and visible signs.

The 1954 Convention constitutes a substantial elaboration of this article in the 1907 Hague Regulations. Under the Convention, the parties undertake to refrain from using cultural property on their territory or that of other parties for purposes that expose it to destruction or damage and to refrain from launching hostile actions against such property unless "military necessity imperatively requires" an exception to such obligations. If zones of sanctuary for cultural property are registered and situated at "an adequate distance" from large industrial centers or important military objectives, the Convention grants such zones special protection. These protections include immunity from attack and from use for military purposes.

It is interesting to note how the 1954 Convention draws upon the Hague Regulations and Geneva Conventions for the protection of persons. Thus, the 1954 treaty also has in article 19 a mini-convention requiring, at least, "respect for cultural property" in armed conflicts "not of an international character." And article 21 provides for Protecting Powers who are "responsible for safe-guarding the interests of the Parties to the conflict." Finally, the United Nations Educational, Scientific, and Cultural Organization (UNESCO) has a special role like that of the ICRC in the Geneva Conventions. Under the 1954 Convention, the parties may call upon UNESCO "for technical assistance in organizing the protection of their cultural property, or in connection with the application of the . . . Convention or the Regulations for its execution." The United States signed the 1954 Convention but has not ratified it.

Individual Responsibility for War Crimes /   In warfare combatants take action that would unquestionably be criminal if committed in peacetime. What, then, is a "war crime"? It is, as Professor Taylor has concisely explained, "an act that remains criminal even though committed in the course of war, because it lies outside the area of immunity prescribed by the laws of war."[38] In other words, the laws of war regard certain conduct as criminal even if carried out in time of war.

Before World War II there was considerable precedent for the trial and punishment by armed forces of their own or the enemy's troops for committing war crimes. Courts-martial and heraldic courts of medieval times often tried knights for violation of the code of chivalry. The Lieber Code had provided in article 71 that "[w]hoever intentionally inflicts additional wounds on an enemy already wholly disabled, or kills such an enemy, or who orders or encourages soldiers to do so, shall suffer death, if duly convicted, whether he belongs to the Army of the United States, or is an enemy captured after having committed his misdeed." Following the Civil War, the Commandant of the Confederate prison camp at Andersonville, Maj. Henry Wirz, was convicted and executed in 1865 for conspiring "against the laws of war, to impair and injure the health and to destroy the lives of large numbers of Federal prisoners, to-wit: 45,000 at Andersonville." [39]

In the twentieth century, there were also instances prior to World War II of individuals being convicted for war crimes. Atrocities committed by United States troops in the Philippines during the insurrection of 1899-1902 gained considerable national attention at that time and ultimately led to the court-martial of a number of American soldiers. [40] Finally, after World War I, a few of the more than eight hundred accused German war criminals were tried by the Supreme Court of the Reich at Leipzig. Although several of these Germans were convicted, they received particularly light sentences for their war crimes and some even escaped from prison. [41]

During World War II, the question arose among the Allies as to what action should be taken after the hostilities against those Germans who had planned and waged the aggressive war or committed acts in violation of the traditional laws of war. In the 1942 Declaration of Saint James, the Allies stated that they would punish those responsible for war crimes "through the channel of organized justice." A year later, in the Moscow Declaration, the Allies announced their intention to bring those accused of war crimes "back to the scene of their crimes" to be "judged on the spot by the peoples whom they have outraged." As for those accused of criminal acts that had no particular location, the Moscow Declaration provided that they would be punished by the joint decision of the governments of the Allies.

The idea alluded to in the Moscow Declaration of creating an international criminal tribunal to try offenses that affect more than one nation was not new, but there was also not much precedent for it. In 1474 a court composed of Swiss, German, and Alsatian judges tried Peter von Hagenbach, governor of a German territory that included the Upper Rhine, for atrocities

against the citizens of Breisach that he had ordered as the commander of that city. [42] After World War I, the Commission on
the Responsibility of the Authors of the War and on Enforce-
ment of Penalties, which was appointed by the Allies, recommended creation of a "high tribunal" of three judges appointed
by each of the five major powers and one judge appointed by
each of the other seven Allies. This international tribunal was to
have tried enemy soldiers accused of violations of the laws of
war and the laws of humanity, as well as officials who "ordered
or abstained from preventing violations of the laws or customs
of war." [43]

Despite the objections of the American Secretary of State and of
the noted international lawyer James Brown Scott, the Versailles Treaty incorporated a provision calling for trial of the
German Kaiser before an international tribunal, and of other
Germans accused of violating the laws of war before mixed
military tribunals, for crimes committed against nationals of
two or more of the Allied nations. [44] But the international and
mixed tribunals were never convened and, as previously indicated, only a few Germans were tried at Leipzig for war crimes
committed during World War I.

Two international tribunals for the trial of war criminals were
convened after World War II. In addition, military tribunals
under the jurisdiction of each of the Allies tried thousands of
individuals as war criminals.

Perhaps the best known of the post-World War II war crimes
trials was the one conducted at Nuremberg, Germany, by the
International Military Tribunal (IMT). From November 1945
to August 1946 the Nuremberg IMT heard charges against
twenty-two leading members of the Third Reich. Under the
London Charter of August 1945, which established the Nuremberg IMT, each of the major powers—the United States,
France, Great Britain, and the Soviet Union—had a representative on the four-man tribunal. [45] Associate Supreme Court
Justice Robert H. Jackson served as chief United States prosecu-
tor against the accused German war criminals. The Nuremberg
IMT found nineteen of the German defendants guilty of one or
more counts; twelve were sentenced to hanging.

An International Military Tribunal for the Far East was established in January 1946 by General Douglas MacArthur as
supreme commander for the Allied powers. [46] The Far East IMT
tried twenty-eight major Japanese political and military leaders
from June 1946 to April 1948 and rendered its judgment in
November 1948. It was composed of judges from eleven na-

tions, including the four major powers represented on the Nuremberg IMT. The Far East IMT found twenty-three of the defendants guilty and sentenced seven to hanging, sixteen to life imprisonment, and the others to lesser terms of imprisonment.

At Nuremberg, pursuant to the Allied Control Council's Law No. 10, the United States, under the able direction of then Brig. Gen. Telford Taylor, conducted twelve trials of German military officers, government officials, and business leaders before military tribunals, each composed of three American civilian judges. Among these trials were the *Hostages, Einsatzgruppen,* and *High Command* cases, which are discussed extensively in several of the contributors' chapters.

The Nuremberg and Far East International Military Tribunals and the Allied military tribunals applied some legal principles that could be traced to their predecessors, but they also relied on some unique principles. Article 6 of the charter of the Nuremberg IMT defined three distinct crimes for which there was to be individual responsibility:[47]

1. *"War crimes:* namely, violations of the laws or customs of war. Such violations shall include, but not be limited to, murder, ill-treatment or deportation to slave labor or for any other purpose of civilian population of or in occupied territory, murder or ill-treatment of prisoners of war or persons on the seas, killing of hostages, plunder of public or private property, wanton destruction of cities, towns or villages, or devastation not justified by military necessity."

2. *"Crimes against humanity:* namely, murder, extermination, enslavement, deportation, and other inhumane acts committed against any civilian populations, before or during the war, or persecutions on political, racial or religious grounds in execution of or in connection with any crime within the jurisdiction of the Tribunal, whether or not in violation of the domestic law of the country where perpetrated."

3. *"Crimes against peace:* namely, planning, preparation, initiation or waging of a war of aggression, or a war in violation of international treaties, agreements or assurance, or participation in a common plan or conspiracy for the accomplishment of any of the foregoing."

As to the first offense, war crimes, we have already seen the long historical development of rules limiting methods and means of warfare and protecting the rights and property of noncombatants in times of war. In a number of the earlier war crimes cases, the defendants sought to excuse their conduct on the ground that they had been ordered by an officer or other higher authority to commit an act that violated the laws of war.

This so-called superior orders defense was put forward in 1474 by von Hagenbach, who argued that Duke Charles of Burgundy had commanded the atrocities at Breisach; by Major Wirz in his famous trial concerning the Andersonville prison camp; and, finally, by some of the German defendants at the post-World War I Leipzig trials.

In each of these cases the defense of superior orders was rejected. The grounds for the refusal to allow this defense can be found in the statement by the Judge Advocate in the Andersonville trial. After conceding for the purpose of argument that Major Wirz had acted pursuant to the orders of his commander, General Winder, in carrying out and permitting violence against and death to Union prisoners, the Judge Advocate said:

> A superior cannot order a subordinate to do an illegal act, and if a subordinate obey such an order and disasterous consequences result, both the superior and the subordinate must answer for it. General Winder could no more command . . . [Major Wirz] to violate the laws of war than could . . . [Major Wirz] do so without orders. The conclusion is plain, that where such orders exist both are guilty, and *a fortiori* where . . . [Major Wirz] acted upon his own motion he was guilty.[48]

The London IMT Charter explicitly rejected the defense of superior orders but gave it new importance in determining the punishment for war criminals. Article 8 of the Charter provides that "[t]he fact that Defendant acted pursuant to order of his Government or of a superior shall not free him from responsibility, but may be considered in mitigation of punishment if the Tribunal determines that justice so requires." The principle of allowing superior orders to mitigate punishment has been carried forward and today appears in article 509 of the United States Army Field Manual entitled *The Law of Land Warfare.*[49] That provision makes clear that the superior orders defense is available to an accused only if he "did not know and could not reasonably have been expected to know that the act ordered was unlawful." Article 509 specifies those considerations that the court should take into account in deciding whether to allow such a defense.[50] Even if the defense is rejected, the Army Manual provides that the fact that action was taken "pursuant to orders may be considered in mitigation of punishment."

It is important to distinguish war crimes, as defined in the London Charter, from crimes against peace and crimes against humanity. Some texts use the term "war crimes" in a broad sense to include not only those considered as such under the

Nuremberg IMT Charter, but also crimes against peace and crimes against humanity. This confuses concepts with different meanings. Unlike the war crimes elaborated in the London Charter definition, there was considerably less precedent after World War II for holding individuals criminally liable for their participation in the planning, preparation, initiation, or waging of an aggressive war or a war in violation of a nation's international obligations. The contributors to this book are not concerned with the substantive legal principles involved in determining whether the United States or its military or civilian leaders were guilty of engaging in an aggressive war in Vietnam. As described below, there is sharp debate between Paul Warnke and Tom Farer over whether there is any continuing viability for determining by the judicial process whether a nation engaged in an aggressive war. In any event, the conduct of the United States and its leaders is analyzed exclusively in connection with whether they have any responsibility for alleged war crimes in the narrow sense in which that term is used in the London IMT Charter.

With respect to crimes against humanity, it is important to note that such offenses came within the Nuremberg IMT's jurisdiction only if they had been committed in execution of or in connection with a crime against peace or a war crime. Since the post-World War II trials, the United Nations has adopted a resolution affirming that genocide—the "denial of the right of existence of entire human groups"—is "a crime under international law which the civilized world condemns, and for the commission of which principals and accomplices . . . are punishable. . . ." In addition, the Convention on Genocide has been prepared by the United Nations and adhered to by a number of states, but the United States has, to date, refused to ratify this agreement.

None of the contributors to this book makes allegations of the commission of genocide by any of the parties to the Vietnam War, although Professor Falk detects "genocidal patterns of thought" among American civilian and military leaders and among troops serving in Vietnam. There is discussion of the commission of ecocide, the meaning of which is apparently based on genocide. Although there is no accepted definition of ecocide and certainly no agreed basis for punishing an individual for committing ecocide, the term is used to mean, in substance, the denial of life to areas of plants and vegetation or total destruction of other features of the natural environment. Whether such conduct actually occurred in Vietnam by the use of herbicides or Rome plows, and if so, what legal consequences should result, is discussed in several of the chapters.

Customary International Law of War / In the above discussion, the emphasis has been on the international laws of war and individual responsibility as codified in treaties among states. Many of those international agreements originated from the practices and shared standards of conduct that states had developed over time. When states have followed "a clear and continuous habit of doing certain actions" and have accepted, either expressly or tacitly, but not necessarily in writing, that such actions are "obligatory or right," international lawyers say that a rule of customary international law has developed. [51]

We have seen that a number of rules of the laws of war developed from practices stretching over several centuries. Publicists like Hugo Grotius and Professor Lieber interpreted these practices and began to generalize them as rules, which in some cases became part of treaties and in others were accepted as binding customary obligations. Thus, even if a rule of warfare is not embodied in a treaty, it may still be binding on states under customary international law.

The difficulty with such customary rules is that one can never be certain at what point a practice of states, sometimes called usage, has ripened into a rule of international law. For example, it is clear that by the time of the 1899 Hague Convention, the prohibition in article 23(a) of the Hague Regulations against "poison and poisoned weapons" had already become a rule of customary international law. The 1899 Convention reaffirmed this rule, which was already binding on states, even if they chose not to adhere to the new international agreement.

On the other hand, many provisions of treaties relate to matters that are not part of customary international law. In the absence of the treaty provision, a state would be under no obligation to limit its conduct with respect to the activity in question. For example, most of the detailed rules in the 1929 Geneva Prisoners of War Convention were certainly not then part of customary international law. Indeed, many such provisions are still binding only on parties to the 1929 or 1949 Geneva Prisoners of War Convention. On the other hand, in some cases, a treaty provision becomes a rule of customary international law some time after the agreement containing the rule is signed and enters into force. Often the status under customary law of rules embodied in treaties is uncertain. There is, for example, considerable controversy over the extent to which the obligations of states under the 1925 Geneva Protocol, which the United States has just recently ratified, have become rules of customary international law binding on all states.

In short, the methods and means of warfare employed by the United States in Vietnam and the weapons used there should be considered in the light of all the laws of war—both codified and customary rules, which collectively comprise what some authors term the law of war. As the book's contributors indicate, there is much disagreement over what restrictions, if any, have become customary obligations binding on the United States even though such restrictions are not part of treaties to which it is a party.

Principal Issues Raised Concerning Application of the Laws of War in Vietnam

This book contains three parts, which treat methods and means of warfare, weapons of warfare, and responsibility of the individual in warfare. But there is inevitably considerable overlap among these parts because of the absence of clear categories into which to place the related issues raised under the laws of war by the conflict in Vietnam. The reader will notice that a number of critical questions recur. It is on these questions that the contributors engage in heated debate. Thus it is useful to summarize them.

May a high-technology counterinsurgent lawfully deploy its advanced weapons and means of warfare against a low-technology insurgent? / In Vietnam there was little doubt that United States forces possessed weapons and equipment that were in many respects technologically superior to those of the indigenous guerrillas—the Viet Cong. Moreover, this advantage usually meant that American troops could pursue methods and means of warfare that were technologically beyond the capabilities of the insurgents. Perhaps the best known high-technology weapons in Vietnam were napalm, lachrymatories (especially CS gas), and herbicides. Their legality is analyzed in considerable detail by Professors Levie and Tucker and by the commentators on those chapters. Professor Falk also examines the legality of cluster-bomb units (CBUs) and other so-called antipersonnel weapons. Among the methods and means of warfare that the United States, as a high-technology power, pursued in Vietnam, probably the most controversial were air warfare and herbicidal crop destruction.

The question posed by the contributors is this: Under the laws of war does this technological superiority affect the legality of

United States military activities in Vietnam? Professor Falk argues that "the methods and tactics of a large-scale counter-insurgent effort, especially if carried out with high-technology weaponry, necessarily violate" the customary and treaty rules of the laws of war. In his view, either counterinsurgency, "if carried beyond certain magnitudes," is ipso facto illegal, or the traditional laws of war "must be virtually, or even totally, suspended under these new sets of circumstances." His paper seeks to demonstrate the "massive scale" of United States violation of the laws of war by the weapons and by the methods and tactics pursued in Vietnam.

To Professor Falk the other contributors offer responses based on policy, fact, perspective on fact, and law. L. F. E. Goldie and Hamilton DeSaussure take strong issue with the view that technologically superior armed forces must deny to themselves the weapons and strategies at their disposal because the enemy lacks similarly advanced military capability. Professor DeSaussure says that the view advanced by Professor Falk "would reduce internal armed conflict to a game of sport in which the sides must be equal in size and capability." Professor Goldie adds that Professor Falk's weighing of environmental issues, once there has been a decision to use force or enter a field of operations, is "irrelevant and inhuman" when "lives are in the scales. . . ." But Professor Goldie regards environmental issues as legitimate and important concerns in the initial evaluation of whether to enter combat in a particular locale.

Robert Komer challenges the factual premises for Professor Falk's analysis. He argues that Professor Falk's theses of the responsibility of United States military leaders for violations of the laws of war "fail on two key grounds—evidence and intent." Ambassador Komer seeks to show that the Vietnam War was not carried on by the United States with an intent to produce the consequences in terms of civilian casualties, ecological damage, and the like that Professor Falk says occurred and on which his analysis heavily relies. Moreover, Ambassador Komer puts forward detailed figures and other factual data that he interprets to demonstrate that, in fact, the effects of United States policies in the Vietnam War were not as Professor Falk describes them.

The most extensive criticism of Professor Falk's discussion relates to his interpretation of the laws of war as they applied to the situation in Vietnam. Beginning with some perceptive general observations about the nature of warfare, Robert Jordan III proceeds to analyze the three most controversial aspects of the United States methods and means of warfare in

Vietnam—the use of firepower against inhabited villages, relocation and resettlement, and, finally, "free-fire" or, as they were later called, specified strike zones. In each case Mr. Jordan relies on the relevant treaty law and post-World War II war crimes decisions to show the basis for finding that these United States practices in Vietnam were not in violation of the laws of war.

To Mr. Jordan's legal analysis Richard Baxter adds the important consideration of whether "there is already a wide range of customary and conventional international law applicable to internal armed conflicts." Professor Baxter explains that "in the absence of a recognition of belligerency or of insurgency, there is no customary international law governing civil wars." Professor Baxter proceeds to describe the difficulties encountered by the United States in seeking to apply the Geneva Conventions *ex gratia* in their relations with the Viet Cong and with civilians. These problems arose, in his view, because of the civil-war character of the Vietnam War.

In commenting on Professor Falk's chapter, Professors Goldie and DeSaussure provide detailed examinations of the applicability of the laws of war to particular United States military conduct in Vietnam. Both challenge the accuracy of Professor Falk's definition of what he calls the "[f]our general principles of limitation [that] form the basis of specific legal norms" in the laws of war. They also consider in detail the specific rules in the Hague Regulations, the Geneva Conventions, and other relevant international legal norms applicable to United States methods and means of warfare and reach conclusions that are contrary in significant respects to those of Professor Falk.

Professor Falk replies to Mr. Komer and his other critics in chapter 7. Mr. Komer offers his surrebuttal in chapter 8. This exchange affords the reader an opportunity to weigh the relative merits of the arguments by some of the leading participants in the controversy surrounding United States goals and actions during the Vietnam War.

In their chapter on the 1972 Christmas bombings, Professor DeSaussure and Robert Glasser trace the evolution of United States policy regarding the bombing of North Vietnam. They present considerable evidence in support of their thesis that the Christmas air attacks were not, and could not have been, for the purpose of achieving a military advantage against the North Vietnamese armed forces or the Viet Cong. It is their view that international law now prohibits bombing for such nonmilitary purposes as forcing the enemy to agree to renewal of negotiations for ending a war. They propose that nations adopt an amendment to the Geneva Conventions of 1949 that would expressly prohibit bombing for "immediate and pre-dominantly political purposes."

Commenting on the chapter by Messrs. DeSaussure and Glas-ser, Townsend Hoopes questions whether state practice as ex-emplified by the Allied air warfare over Germany and Japan in World War II or over Korea supports the international legal rule that they regard as "settled." But Mr. Hoopes supports their proposal for amending the Geneva Convention. He argues that an advanced society, "if logical and . . . governed by a sense of proportion, . . . would, upon entering into a future insurgent situation, find its political and military actions more effective if it deliberately refrained from using weapons of large-scale de-struction, such as bomber aircraft, artillery, and naval gun-fire."

Lt. Col. Norman R. Thorpe and Maj. James R. Miles join with Mr. Hoopes in disagreeing with what DeSaussure and Glasser contend are the contemporary rules of international law gov-erning aerial bombardment of military objectives. Unlike Mr. Hoopes, Lieutenant Colonel Thorpe and Major Miles vig-orously oppose the proposal to outlaw bombing such objectives for immediate and predominantly political purposes. Citing Clausewitz to the effect that war is a continuation of politics by other means, they characterize the proposal as "extreme and unrealistic" and warn that it could "weaken the entire structure of international humanitarian law." Lieutenant Colonel Thorpe and Major Miles fear that adoption of the proposed rule might, in effect, authorize nations for the first time to initiate bombing of military objectives for only military ends without regard to the overall political goals of parties to an armed conflict.

Does customary or conventional international law prohibit the use of lachrymatories (especially CS gas), napalm, and herbi-cides? /   Howard Levie and Richard Tucker analyze care-fully the treaties and customary law governing the status of the three weapons whose use in Vietnam by the United States generated considerable controversy. In addition, Profes-sor Tucker discusses the legality of antipersonnel bombs.

Both contributors conclude that the 1925 Geneva Protocol would not have prohibited the American use of tear gas in Viet-nam even if the United States had been a party to the treaty at that time. But has a rule of customary law developed since the 1925 Protocol was prepared that would prohibit the use of tear gas? Professor Levie believes that no such rule had developed by the time of United States entry into the Vietnam conflict in 1965. But he thinks that "[m]orally and politically the United States would be well advised to adopt and follow a policy of self-denial" under which American forces would be pledged to no first use of tear gas, such as CS.

Following a somewhat different approach, Professor Tucker concludes that "by the time of Vietnam, customary law prohibited the use of all chemical weapons with either lethal or lastingly injurious effects." Thus, the relevant issue for him is whether CS gas has such effects. He explains that the illegality of CS would not be established solely by showing that the gas could have lethal effects in high concentrations, unless there was no way to control its use in such concentrations. It appears that such control is possible. On the other hand, it has been argued that there is a high incidence of deaths among babies and children exposed to CS. Professor Tucker finds that any routine and nondiscriminatory use of such gas in which babies and children were exposed would violate customary law, assuming the gas actually has this lethal effect. But he adds that "[p]resumably, the [tear] gases may be used, and predominantly were used, in a discriminating manner against combatants, where their direct effect is neither destructive of life nor injurious to health." Having said this, Professor Tucker states that "[i]n the broader political context" the use of CS "has to be regarded as deplorable in its apparent disregard of a reaction that was surely predictable."

With respect to napalm, Professor Levie again finds "no rule of international law that prohibits [its] . . . use . . . upon selected targets." Professor Tucker agrees. It is Professor Levie's view that napalm should be totally prohibited in international armed conflict. Doubting whether such a prohibition is practical, Professor Levie proposes a United Nations study to determine whether it is necessary to limit or prohibit the use of napalm. Such a report has now been prepared by a group of government experts appointed by the U.N. Secretary-General; the group included no United States representative. The report confirms Professor Levie's and Professor Tucker's conclusion as to the legal status of napalm. [52]

Finally, Professor Levie concludes that neither conventional nor customary law prohibits the use of herbicides against a valid military target, such as food crops for the military. On the other hand, Professor Tucker finds that herbicides used for crop destruction caused lethal or injurious effects to the health of both combatants and the civilian population. As a result, this use of these chemicals violated the customary international law rule that Professor Tucker believes had developed by 1965. Both authors, however, agree that the unpredictability of the effects of these chemicals and their possibly harmful consequences for the local population provided sound support for the United States decision to phase out their use in Vietnam.

In addressing himself to the issues raised by Professors Levie and Tucker, George Aldrich emphasizes that legal authorities need greater technical information about the uses and operation of various weapons. Mr. Aldrich believes that it will be difficult to obtain agreement on limitations for a militarily effective weapon such as napalm, whose use he also believes is legal. On the other hand, Mr. Aldrich predicts an "extremely limited" future for tear gas and herbicides. But he thinks that even these weapons may continue to have some lawful uses, such as defoliation in the case of herbicides and riot control for prisoner-of-war camps in the case of tear gas.

Exploring the relationships of policy, international legal obligations, and international war crimes for individuals, Anthony d'Amato argues that Professors Levie and Tucker have failed to bring law and policy into harmony. This failure results, in Professor d'Amato's view, from regarding the international legal obligations of states and those of individuals as the same. He explains that states may have obligations under the law of nations even though individuals may not be liable for breaching those obligations. Viewed in this way, the law applicable to states can better conform to a policy on which Professors Levie and Tucker agree—i.e., the prohibition of CS gas or napalm. In Professor d'Amato's framework, no individual would be guilty of a war crime while the law is uncertain about what weapons are prohibited. Thus, the law restraining the destruction that states may lawfully inflict during warfare could be broadened without creating, at the same time, fear that individuals would be prosecuted as war criminals when they exceed the bounds of an imprecise rule.

Approaching still another aspect of Professors Levie's and Tucker's papers, Professor d'Amato suggests that the customary law governing the use of tear gas, napalm, and herbicides "may not have been given its due in this collection or even in any published book or article to date." Contrary to Professor Tucker's position, he maintains that the 1925 Geneva Protocol may "have created a goodly amount of customary law relating to the use in warfare of gases and analogous liquids and materials." Perhaps even more significantly, Professor d'Amato urges a careful review of state practice since 1925 to determine the precise content of customary international law with respect to the use of gases. In his opinion, it may be found that customary law "might just possibly have evolved in such a way as to be more immediately relevant and more prohibitory of the use of tear gas and herbicides than any interpretation, broad or narrow, of the [1925 Geneva] Protocol."

What is the responsibility under international law of individuals who were in command during the Vietnam War? / In any military force, as Robert Jordan elaborates, individuals perceive their level of authority in relation to those above and below in the chain of command. Thus, everyone but the President has a commander over him; only the lowliest private has no one below his rank. It is, therefore, confusing to speak without further clarification of the legal responsibility under the laws of war of those "in command."

In the third part, the contributors generally treat as a person in command any officer who directs or controls in some respect the action of soldiers engaging the enemy on the front line. Such an officer may be at or near the front, as, for example, Lieutenant Calley and Captain Medina were at My Lai in 1968. Or he may be farther from the battle lines, as General Westmoreland was in his Saigon headquarters during the Vietnam War or as the Chief of Staff of the Army is in the Pentagon. In addition, the contributors regard as being in command the principal civilian officials in the Department of Defense, such as the Secretary of Defense and the Secretaries of the Army, Navy, and Air Force.

All of the military officers under consideration here, regardless of their actual proximity to the Vietnam battlefield, shared two characteristics. First, they had the authority to order men—whether a company or several divisions—into combat against Viet Cong guerrillas and North Vietnamese regulars. Although officers possess authority for giving orders, they are not permitted by the laws of war to issue an unlawful order. Both the officer who gives such an order and the soldier, knowing it to be unlawful, who carries it out would be held criminally liable.

Along with the authority, each officer has a corresponding responsibility to his superiors in the military hierarchy for the conduct of his men. This command responsibility of an officer lies at the heart of the American military's operation and is the key to an effective armed force. It is an officer's responsibility for the conduct of his troops that concerns a number of the contributors in part three. They focus on the extent to which the laws of war impose liability on the commander for the wrongful conduct of his troops.

With respect to those troops, imposing "criminal responsibility [on them] for personal conduct that transgresses recognized standards," in Paul Warnke's view, raises none of the difficult problems involved in holding civilian leaders liable for "crimes against peace." He believes that "[r]easonable and decent minds should not differ on atrocities." The only injustice in the Calley case, according to Mr. Warnke, was that "far too little effort was made to convict all those who directed, participated in, or excused the particular conduct."

Focusing on the special plight and training of the front-line soldier in Vietnam, Richard Wasserstrom challenges Mr. Warnke's conclusion. Professor Wasserstrom seeks to show that front-line troops may not have the necessary *mens rea*—state of mind—to be convicted of a criminal act. He argues that they may have been trained to follow orders to do that which is unlawful. Even if the soldier is not so trained or commits atrocities that are not ordered, he may yet, in Professor Wasserstrom's opinion, have grounds to avoid criminal responsibility for his actions. This is because the laws of war are themselves "not a rational, coherent scheme of rules and principles" and their application in specific instances is often uncertain. He also regards modern warfare as "extraordinarily corruptive of the capacity to behave morally" and, hence, conducive to immoral action to which criminal liability should, in his view, not attach.

To these arguments Professor Farer responds by asserting that the laws of war, despite their flaws, are worthy of preservation. And those who violate them should be prosecuted in order to preserve the "net saving of life" that those laws have undoubtedly permitted. Professor Farer emphasizes the divergent values that are reconciled within the existing rules of warfare. He also points to similar compromises of values in our domestic legal system.

On the issue of responsibility of military and civilian leaders for violations of the laws of war, two different, but related, controversies become apparent. First, Paul Warnke joins issue with Tom Farer and Richard Wasserstrom over whether there is any continuing viability to the offense of crimes against peace, for which the major war criminals were tried before the Nuremberg IMT under article 6 of the London Charter. Second, Telford Taylor and Robert Gard present conflicting views on the standard of criminal responsibility that officers bear for the unlawful actions of their men.

With respect to crimes against peace, it is Mr. Warnke's position that "[i]n a world of autonomous national states, this can only be a crime reserved for losers." While he does not necessarily welcome this state of affairs, Mr. Warnke regards whether a nation has launched an aggressive war to be a nonjusticiable question. It is an issue that, in his view, history alone can judge, along with the wisdom of engaging in hostilities.

Professor Farer takes strong exception to Mr. Warnke's views. It is Professor Farer's belief that the obligation to refrain from aggressive war is fundamental to contemporary international life. Hence, holding individuals liable for crimes against peace remains not just viable, but an essential element of today's world order. Professor Farer also believes that Mr. Warnke's attack on crimes against peace raises the issue of whether trials for war crimes are also reserved for losers. Mr. Warnke maintains that the two concepts are not comparable—whatever ambiguity there may be about what is an aggressive war, there can be little doubt that the slaughter of innocent women and children at My Lai was a massacre. To these points Professor Wasserstrom adds a series of perceptive questions concerning the precise motive, purpose, and knowledge of civilian or military leaders that should be proved in order to hold them liable for crimes against peace.

It is My Lai that raises most directly the issue of when the officer in command becomes responsible for his troops' violation of the laws of war. Lieutenant Calley, a platoon leader in Company C of the First Batallion, 20th Infantry, was tried and convicted for the murders he committed at My Lai in 1968. Captain Medina, who was commander of Company C at the time of My Lai, was tried for culpable negligence in failing to exercise control over his men, including Lieutenant Calley, while they proceeded to kill noncombatants in violation of the laws of war. Captain Medina was acquitted.

As with other aspects of the Vietnam War, the trial of Captain Medina for failure to control his men paralleled similar cases that had arisen during previous conflicts involving the United States. After World War II, the United States convicted the Japanese General Yamashita for the atrocities committed by his men in the Philippines. The *Yamashita* case stands for the proposition that a commanding officer is responsible for failure to control his men and prevent their actions in contravention of the laws of war. But there is, as Robert Gard discusses, much controversy over whether General Yamashita was found to have actual knowledge of his troops' atrocities or whether, instead, he was held liable for actions of his men of which he should have been aware, but of which he had no actual knowledge. General Gard thinks the former interpretation is correct; many others take the latter view.

The Army Field Manual 27-10 provides expressly, as Telford Taylor emphasizes, that a military commander is not only responsible for criminal acts that he orders, but also liable for actions within his command of which he has actual knowledge, or should have knowledge." This "should have known" standard is called constructive knowledge. It is, needless to say, a far more severe standard than the "actual knowledge" test. But it is the one that the Army chose to adopt in the light of the United States participation in the prosecution of German and Japanese war criminals after World War II.

In view of the foregoing, it comes as a considerable surprise to most that the jury in Captain Medina's case was told three times to convict him only if they found he had actual knowledge of the actions taking place at My Lai while he was in command. Leonard Boudin quotes the complete text of the relevant portion of the charge.

Captain Medina was acquitted on the basis of the charge to the military court. Citing the *High Command* case, General Gard argues that the charge to Captain Medina's trial court was correct. Relying on the Army Field Manual and his own analysis of the relevant policies at stake, Professor Taylor raises the issue of whether true command responsibility can be maintained if, in the future, officers are held only to the less rigorous standard contained in the Medina charge.

Mr. Boudin asserts that the handling of the *Medina* case and the treatment of Lt. Col. Anthony Herbert provide ample grounds for condemning the Army's conduct with respect to war crimes in Vietnam. And, in Mr. Boudin's view, both the problem of soldiers not prosecuted for alleged war crimes and that of young men who left the country to avoid the Vietnam War should be considered together. He proposes a general amnesty for all—military and civilian leaders, deserting soldiers, and draft dodgers—to cleanse the domestic conscience in a single stroke of the remaining political and moral vestiges of the Vietnam War. In Mr. Boudin's view, President Gerald Ford's Proclamation of 16 September 1974 of a conditional amnesty for draft dodgers and deserters fails to solve the problem because it implies wrongdoing on the part of those who refused to serve and none by those who participated. [53]

Part One

METHODS AND MEANS OF WARFARE

Counterinsurgency, Tactics, and the Law

1   Richard A. Falk

This chapter considers some of the methods and tactics relied upon by the United States to conduct counterinsurgent warfare in Vietnam during the period 1962 to 1973. It is my contention that these methods and tactics cannot be reconciled with customary law or the treaty rules governing the conduct of international warfare. It is my further contention that the methods and tactics of a large-scale counterinsurgent effort, especially if carried out with high-technology weaponry, necessarily violate these rules of law and amount to crimes under international law. And it is my final contention that such a prima facie showing of criminality imposes primary responsibility upon those civilian and military leaders who devised, approved, and carried out these war policies.

Nevertheless, I would at the same time acknowledge that the traditional laws of war did not contemplate the doctrinal interaction of an insurgent challenge and a counterinsurgent response. Neither did they foresee the tactical interaction of low-technology methods of warfare aimed at disguising military identity and high-technology methods aimed at preventing the immersion of guerrilla soldiers in the general population. Such a belligerent setting can lead to the conclusion either that the law must be virtually, or even totally, suspended under these new sets of circumstances or that a counterinsurgent war is ipso facto illegal if carried beyond certain magnitudes.

A leading American theologian, Paul Ramsey, who has done significant writing on the doctrine of just war under modern conditions, argues elaborately that the insurgents, by their prior choice of tactics— especially selective terror against civilian officials and their refusal to separate themselves from the civilian population—bear full moral and legal responsibility for any indiscriminate counterinsurgent response. According to Ramsey, it is permissible to attack as much of the civilian population as necessary in order to complete the counterinsurgent mission successfully.[1]

I would not accept this analysis, which seems to impose total responsibility on those who have the least means at their disposal to select the methods and tactics of struggle, given predominant state control over instruments of violence under modern conditions, as well as governmental repression of opposition politics in many of the more deplorable circumstances of misrule in the Third World.[2] Furthermore, the technology gap tends to produce very unequal destruction. Our best information is that in Vietnam most of the death and destruction can be attributed to the United States/Saigon side and that there was a high ratio of civilian-to-military casualties (estimated at 10 to 1) and an extraordinary edge in firepower (estimated as high as 450 to 1). [3]

These factors explain the emphasis upon counterinsurgent terrorism in the war crimes literature of the last several years. [4] The concern with such terrorism was aptly summarized by a sociologist, Phillip Slater, some time ago: "What most disturbs thoughtful Americans about Vietnam is the prevalence of genocidal thought patterns in our approach to the conflict." [5] These genocidal patterns of thought were exemplified in Vietnam by the "the Dink complex," by kill ratios as measures of military performance and progress, and by the evident belief of many of our soldiers that even Vietnamese babies were enemies who would eventually grow up to serve the Viet Cong. In essence, then, the entire civilian population became the military enemy—because of their sympathies or activities, because of their status as potential recruits, or even because they were visually indistinguishable from insurgent soldiers. Such a tendency in counterinsurgent warfare is particularly grotesque, since military action against guerrillas is supposedly undertaken for the benefit and protection of the population as a whole.

These issues are underscored by the political circumstances that exist in South Vietnam in particular, but generally throughout Indochina. In the Vietnamese conflict the main supply of military capability and guidance on the counterinsurgent side came from sources external to the state in which the struggle for control was taking place. Central to this analysis is the conviction that the United States was an external actor in decisively different respects from those in which North Vietnam was an external actor. I believe this distinction is sustained in the Paris Agreements of 1973, which oblige the United States to refrain from intervention in the affairs of South Vietnam but omit reference to any similar undertaking by North Vietnam. This American externality strengthened the genocidal tendencies of counterinsurgent warfare by weakening the bonds of empathy between actor and victim.

Vietnam was only one example of the experience of a high-technology power intervening to support a counterinsurgent war in a distant land. The external actor values its own lives far more than it does those of its supposed ally—the government of the society in which the struggle ensues. The war becomes an abstraction except for its domestic reverberations. Methods and tactics of war that are more indiscriminate so far as the enemy is concerned are preferred so as to minimize the loss of life for the forces of the external actor. Because

such a war is not normally related to the defense of the national homeland, the intervening side has difficulty maintaining its war effort if
high casualties and financial outlays occur over a long period of years.
For this reason there are strong supplemental pressures to maximize the
covertness of the interventionary policies or to use more expendable
troops to carry out the counterinsurgent mission.[6]

The Nixon era policies of Vietnamization in the period prior to
American disengagement essentially returned the war to its early stages,
when the military policy making remained centered in Washington,
but the dying was largely reserved for the Vietnamese. Those tactics
and methods that involved minimum American bloodshed—air strikes
and long-range artillery—were maintained at high intensity despite in-
sistent Presidential proclamations about "winding down the war."[7] Indeed, the Nixon Doctrine tends to generalize Vietnamization as the
essence of future American involvement in counterinsurgent warfare.
Thus, the political lessons learned from the Vietnam War are to obtain
combat soldiers from the regional combat theater and to supplement
their efforts, as necessary, with heavy air support and a major role in
training, equipping, and advising.[8]

Against this background, concerned Americans and especially international lawyers must deal with two kinds of issues: To what extent
can soldiers and leaders be held accountable for violations of international law? And to what extent can international law be made more
responsive to the specific belligerent contexts of large-scale counterinsurgent warfare?

When these broad legal issues are connected with the facts of the
Vietnam War and with the categories of offenses punished at Nuremberg, there emerge three kinds of basic, interdependent concerns regarding potential or hypothetical individual responsibility:

1. Under what conditions does an externally centered counterinsurgent effort amount to a war of aggression that constitutes a crime
against peace?[9]

2. Under what conditions do the tactics and methods of counterinsurgent warfare amount to war crimes?[10]

3. Under what conditions do the tactics and methods of counterinsurgency amount to crimes against humanity?[11]

In connection with the third concern, it is important to recognize
that "crimes against humanity" are defined so that actions or persecutions constitute such crimes only if "carried on in execution of or in
connection with any crime against peace or any war crime." For purposes of this discussion, I have assumed that the civilians of Vietnam

were, at the time of United States military involvement there, protected persons within the context of the "crimes against humanity" definition.

Four general principles of limitation form the basis of specific legal norms. Those principles are:

> —a prohibition upon methods, tactics, and weapons calculated to inflict unnecessary suffering (principle of necessity);

> —a requirement that methods, tactics, and weapons generally discriminate between military and nonmilitary targets and between combatants and civilians (principle of discrimination);

> —a requirement that the military means used bear a proportional relationship to the military end pursued (principle of proportionality); and

> —an absolute prohibition upon methods, tactics, and weapons that are inherently cruel in their effects and violate minimal notions of humanity (principle of humanity). [12]

In certain contexts, such as, for instance, the treatment of prisoners of war or of the sick and wounded, these principles are spelled out in some detail by positive international law. Nevertheless, ambiguity regarding the laws of war pervades any operational test of necessity, discrimination, proportionality, and humanity. Does application of these principles depend mainly upon the good faith of field commanders and political leaders? Does demonstrating good faith require some showing of an effort to assess collateral damage, to mitigate the suffering of civilians incident to the war, to punish flagrant violations of the rules of warfare, and to exercise reasonable diligence in acting to negotiate a settlement of the war? [13]

The full protection of the laws of war in Vietnam could be denied to combatants on the basis of a variety of contentions. First, it could be argued that the Vietnam War, even at the time of direct United States military participation, did not possess an international character and that therefore the combatants and Vietnamese civilians were entitled only to the minimal protections of article 3 of the 1949 Geneva Conventions. Such a contention seems unconvincing in the context of the Vietnam War, where the combat theater generally embraced more than a single country and where each side alleged that its principal adversary was the government of a foreign state.

A second ground for alleging that the laws of war were inapplicable in Vietnam was that the guerrilla fighters there were entitled to prisoner-of-war status and to the overall protection of the laws of war only if they complied with requirements embodied in the Geneva Conventions, and derived from article 1 of the Hague Regulations—namely, being commanded by a person responsible for his subordinates, having a fixed, distinctive sign recognizable at a distance, carrying arms openly, and conducting their operations in accordance with the laws and customs of war. Such requirements seem to be weighted heavily in favor of the constituted power of governments and to carry over into the laws of war the statist bias of the overall system of world order. [14] Even if the insurgents did not meet these requirements, they concerned only rights that could be claimed on behalf of National Liberation Front (NLF) soldiers; failure by the NLF to satisfy them did not diminish the duty of United States or Vietnamese military forces vis-à-vis Vietnamese civilian war victims. [15]

On the basis of this background it is now possible to examine some of the more controversial methods and tactics used to wage counterinsurgent warfare in Vietnam. It will also be possible to assess the relationship of such methods and tactics to the traditional legal concepts of limitation. I will emphasize those methods and tactics that appear to violate most directly the general mandates of the law of war: discrimination, proportionality, necessity, and humanity.

The facts are not always clear as to the character of the counterinsurgent methods and tactics employed in Vietnam, nor as to their relationship to overall military objectives, their impact on the civilian population, or their origins in policy-making procedures. It is also difficult to distinguish between authorized practices and goals, and their unauthorized extension on the battlefield. However, these difficulties of inquiry and appraisal tend to be exaggerated by those who are not disposed to question the policies put into operation.

It is my contention that the United States government, in order to demonstrate a good-faith effort in upholding the laws of war in a counterinsurgent setting, has a duty to undertake three significant measures. First, it should institute a policy review function, to assess proposed methods and tactics by reference to the four underlying principles of the laws of war and to substantive rules of a more specific character. Second, it should maintain an oversight function to assess the military and nonmilitary consequences of policies put into operation. And, finally, it should carry out a compliance function to encourage military personnel to have respect for the limiting notions of the laws of war, to report and investigate abuses, and to apprehend and punish those who exceed authorized patterns of battlefield conduct.

One final observation will serve as background. The methods and tactics relied upon by the counterinsurgent effort in Vietnam concentrated upon "drying up the sea," that is, making civilians come to the cities (forced-draft urbanization) or else live under conditions of surveillance amounting to direct government control (strategic hamlets or refugee camps). Part of this effort to destroy the value of the countryside as a sanctuary and political base was to destroy the food supply (crop denial program) and to take away the protective cover of nature (defoliation). A major counterinsurgent policy was to destroy, in a very literal sense, any area "liberated" by the insurgents, especially through the massive use of air power and long-range artillery. Such policies took account of the high degree of asymmetry in weapons of long-range and automated destructivity possessed by the two sides. [16] These kinds of objectives, which prevailed during the period of active United States participation in the Vietnam War, underlie the delimitation here of the legal status of the methods and tactics of counterinsurgent warfare. [17]

Air Warfare

In Vietnam the most characteristic method of large-scale counterinsurgent warfare was massive reliance on air power. This was the case because the United States, the counterinsurgent, possessed an air-power monopoly, because air strikes, costing few American lives, were politically cheap domestically, and because air power was highly destructive.

The government generally contended that air power was used to disrupt insurgent supply lines and troop concentrations and to provide close-in logistic support under combat conditions. But many observers claim a far wider use, including the targeting of places for religious observance and of medical facilities such as hospitals. [18] On national television then Vice-president Spiro Agnew described one purpose of the 1970 invasion of Cambodia to be the destruction of NLF "hospital complexes."

There have been many eyewitness accounts of patterns of targeting that covered nonmilitary objectives. [19] Congressman Paul McCloskey and Jacques Decornoy of *Le Monde* reported the extensive bomb damage done in Laos by American air power, which obliterated many villages in the northern part of the country. [20] Fred Branfman, who lived in Laos for several years and interviewed many people in refugee camps, reports that most civilian refugees were fleeing from American air power. [21] The writing of Jonathan Schell and others shows that the bombardment of villages involved a deliberate policy of generating refugees in order to separate the people from the insurgents. The bombardment led to terror and destruction of such magnitude that peasants were forced to abandon ancestral homes of many generations. [22]

In rural societies of Indochina there are relatively few targets that have any direct military or industrial value. Therefore, aside from interdiction bombing, the main function of air power was to clear the countryside of civilians. The so-called free-fire zones (renamed "specified strike zones" to neutralize adverse publicity) were expressions of this tactic. [23] In extensive areas of South Vietnam, presumed to be under hostile control, everything that moved was made subject to slaughter from the air. Civilians, evidently even animals, remained at their extreme peril and were treated as "the enemy." Such uses of air power faithfully embodied the logic of the counterinsurgent military mission— to break the link between the insurgent armed forces and the general population. It is difficult to assess the full impact of these policies, but it has been estimated that in Laos, Cambodia, and South Vietnam between one-fifth and one-third of the population became refugees at some point during hostilities and that extensive civilian death and destruction also resulted. [24]

In these contexts air power was often used without discrimination as to target or military objective, without any sense of proportion in relation to the military end sought, and without regard for the resultant human suffering. A single sniper bullet shot from a village, or less, was deemed sufficient basis to warrant that village's obliteration. The civilian population was rarely consulted and seldom spared.

Antipersonnel Weaponry

In carrying out air attacks in Vietnam, the United States placed heavy reliance upon so-called antipersonnel bombs. These did relatively little damage to property, but maimed and killed people and animals. [25] A great arsenal of antipersonnel bombs was used in massive quantities throughout Indochina, but especially in South Vietnam. These weapons, with their flesh-piercing pellets and flechettes, maimed and disfigured, as well as killed. Delayed-action fuses caused explosions after people had left places of safety. Their deployment against civilian targets appears to imply an acceptance of these horrendous results by military planners. The use of such antipersonnel weaponry contravened the spirit of one of the earliest modern efforts to limit the conduct of war—the Declaration of St. Petersburg of 1868, which sought to outlaw bullets that caused particularly severe injury to life because they were explosive or contained fulminating or inflammable substances.

Why have such weapons been developed, and why were they used? The most convincing answer would seem to involve a desire to kill, wound, and terrorize as many people as possible with the smallest investment of money and effort, and thereby to influence the population as a whole. The large CBU cluster bombs, for instance, sprayed an area of over half a mile. These weapons created wounds that were difficult to treat under any circumstances, but especially difficult given the primitive medical facilities characteristic of Vietnam. [26] This antipersonnel weaponry thus helped break the political link between the insurgents and the population and otherwise contributed to the kill totals that were used to measure progress in the war.

Kill Ratios and Body Counts

It is well known by now that this emphasis on killing people was developed at a staff and command level as one of the major criteria of military progress during the period of heavy American involvement in ground combat (1965 to 1968). Casualty figures are always important in a war, but when there are no fixed territories and few major battles, then there is a search for other ways to determine whether the war is being prosecuted successfully. Body counts and kill ratios received great emphasis because they placed a premium on the sheer magnitude of death and on the statistical comparison between enemy and Allied dead. Because of the difficulty in telling civilians and combatants apart, there was a natural tendency to treat all dead Vietnamese as Viet Cong, as well as a natural incentive to employ tactics that increased the kill totals.

This overall pressure received reinforcement from military commanders who rated the efficiency of units in terms of their body counts. Such an attitude fostered lethal competition among military units of brigade (or smaller) size and eroded still further the inhibitions against killing civilians or attacking civilian target areas after minimum provocation. In the *Duffy* case it became clear, and has been confirmed by many sworn statements of veterans, that body-count competition led to a disposition to kill civilian prisoners, a policy approved of by many field commanders. [27] The high ratio in Vietnam of civilian to military casualties—estimated, as previously indicated, at 10 to 1—emphasizes the extent to which such policies are inconsistent with adherence to the principles of discrimination and proportionality.

Again, these measures of progress were logical, given the prevailing view of counterinsurgent struggle during the Vietnam War. If the people could not be induced to leave areas of suspected enemy strength and if the enemy could not be isolated for discriminate destruction, then the only way to destroy the insurgent was the indiscriminate destruction of any Vietnamese in the target area.

The Phoenix Program

During the last years of American involvement in Vietnam prior to the Paris Agreements, the United States administered a program designed to destroy the political infrastructure of the NLF. The main tactic was the capture and assassination of civilian suspects. Rewards were given. The Phoenix Program set monthly quotas for "eliminations"; in 1970, for instance, the target was 1,800 eliminations a month; 22,341 individuals were killed, captured, or "rallied" in 1970.[28] Ivor Peterson of *The New York Times* wrote in 1971 that "it is impossible to know for sure" who the dead are. He goes on:

They are supposed to be the enemy tax collectors, the political cadre and propaganda teams, the spies and the communications agents who make up the enemy underground.

The Americans acknowledged that, inevitably, some of the dead were also in no way connected with the Viet Cong, but were merely the personal enemies of a province chief or some other influential official. Others, like many of the "nurses," were probably wives or children caught in the crossfire.

As with other aspects of the counterinsurgent program in South Vietnam, much of the killing had little military impact.[29]

Crop Destruction and Well Poisoning

The logic of counterinsurgency entailed making the countryside as unlivable as possible for the insurgents, which usually meant for the population as a whole. The massive use of lethal herbicides illustrated the human consequences of these military pressures. The available figures are incomplete, and in some instances controversial. But even "official sources agree that the diets of more than half a million civilians

. . . [were] chemically destroyed [between the years] 1962-70." [30]

There is evidence to suggest that one widely used herbicide, Agent Orange, caused genetic abnormalities in new-born babies and that its heavy use in an area was accompanied by high rates of miscarriage and stillbirth. Even when such evidence became available, it did not lead to a termination of the use of Agent Orange, at least not until prominent American scientists engaged in a successful public demonstration in the United States. And even after use was officially repudiated, there were disturbing indications that new chemicals, such as Agent Blue, with unknown propensities to injure human beings, were being used by American forces and that large quantities of Agent Orange were to be left behind for use by the South Vietnamese. [31]

To destroy food in an Asian country, where problems of widespread, chronic starvation and malnutrition already exist, is an extreme example of an indiscriminate method of waging war that is likely to inflict cruel suffering almost totally on the noncombatant population. In wartime, soldiers tend to be the last segment of the population to feel the impact of local food shortages. This is just as true of insurgent forces in a rural setting as it is of traditional armies on a conventional battlefield. Thus, the tactic of crop denial inflicts most of its damage on civilians.

To some extent, the outcry against herbicides led to new tactics of warfare designed to achieve the same results. Large earth-moving plows (so-called Rome plows because they were developed in Rome, Georgia) had taken vegetation off 750,000 acres of Vietnamese land as of 1971. They removed the topsoil in such a way that nothing could grow back, and the prospect of serious flooding was greatly increased. One specialist, E. W. Pfeiffer, reported that "every day from dawn to dusk, between 100 and 150 huge plows . . . [were] making flat wastelands, while severely upsetting the environment." [32]

Of a similar character were the frequent reports of efforts to poison or destroy wells in the Vietnamese countryside so as to deny their use to insurgent forces. Such a tactic, in violation of the spirit of the earliest Biblical injunctions, was routinely described in Lt. William Calley's account of the experiences that led up to My Lai:

Our mission then was to blow up Vietnamese wells. Or try to. I think that a 500-pounder could do it, could anyhow make the water taste bad. But twenty tons of TNT would make the well deeper, that's all. Our colonel, though, had a thing about wells: a bag about wells, and he wasn't about to tell a lieutenant or listen to a lieutenant tell him "Sir, you can't destroy wells with TNT. A bulldozer, maybe—" [33]

This tactic, too, illustrates the tendency to inflict indiscriminate damage by selecting a privileged target. The primary effect of its destruction, because of priorities favoring combatants on the insurgent side, was on the very young, the very old, and the sick.

Atrocities and Torture

The dehumanization of the soldier confronted by such military directives has been painfully and abundantly documented. Col. Oran Henderson's comment that "every unit of brigade size has its My Lai hidden somewhere" does not seem fanciful in view of the testimony of many returning Vietnam veterans. It is clear that My Lai as a publicly condemned massacre was artificially isolated from the overall framework of the war.

The story of Lt. Col. Anthony Herbert provides insight into the pervasiveness of atrocities and into the refusal of the military command to act in such a way as to discourage their commission.[34] Lieutenant Colonel Herbert was virtually repudiated by the Army because he dared to report to his field commanders atrocities that he witnessed. It is one thing to cover up an atrocity that has occurred. But it is quite another to indulge their commission, fail to prevent their occurrence, and convey the message to military personnel that it will ruin their careers to seek a conscientious application of the laws of war. In this regard the Herbert case remains both disturbing and revealing. It warrants serious public attention, even if the allegations concerning Lieutenant Colonel Herbert's inadequacy as a military commander are eventually vindicated.

I would emphasize Lieutenant Colonel Herbert's contention, evidently fully accurate, that he witnessed and reported flagrant abuses of captured Vietnamese suspects and was still unable to obtain any effective response from his military superiors other than to secure his own dismissal from command responsibility. A remarkable feature of his personal misfortune is that despite his extraordinary military record—Lieutenant Colonel Herbert was the most decorated soldier in the Korean War and received a steady stream of commendations in his various assignments—no one high in the military or civilian structure intervened on his behalf.

Lieutenant Colonel Herbert seems unusual in the sense that he was able to maintain some feeling for limits under the dehumanizing and brutalizing pressures of combat duty in Vietnam. Lieutenant Calley gives us a more typical, if perhaps extreme, rendering of the American soldier's sensibility in Vietnam, provided he had not opted out via drugs or opted against by accepting an antiwar position:

> . . . if those people weren't all VC then prove it to me. Show me that someone was for the American forces there. Show me that someone helped us and fought the VC. Show me that someone wanted us: one example only! I didn't see any. . . . Our task force commander—well, the Colonel's dead and I'd rather not say. His staff, though, said it's a VC area and everyone there was a VC or a VC sympathizer. "And that's because he just isn't young enough or old enough to do anything but sympathize." I even heard a brigadier general say, "My god! There isn't a Vietnamese in this goddamn area! They all are VC!" I believed it. And as soon as I understood it, I wasn't frustrated anymore. [35]

Such sentiments, to be sure, carry the logic of counterinsurgency beyond the scope of normal perceptions. Yet, without some strenuous interventions at the command level to impose limits, the extreme tactics of My Lai were virtually certain to occur. They did, frequently, especially in low-visibility contexts.

The climate for atrocity was also set by other tactics and methods of war that seemed hardly less indiscriminate and total. This was the case especially with such military actions as obliteration of villages by air or artillery attack; random or computer firing of long-distance artillery and bombing missions; harrassment-and-interdiction patterns of firepower deployment; and naval bombardments that were set by computers to saturate wide areas with a rain of destructive explosives. [36]

Under such circumstances of technological and ethnic distance, it is easy to understand how "the enemy" became the entire civilian population and how the most extreme tactics of abuse gained high levels of combat acceptance. The atrocity in counterinsurgent contexts had a poignant irony. Often the high-level theory of combating the insurgent was directed toward winning "the hearts and minds" of the civilian population—what came to be called "the other war" or "pacification." In a tragic distortion of military logic and overall political strategy, the civilians who were the main focus of "the other war" became the principal victims of methods and tactics designed to benefit them. [37]

Additional counterinsurgent tactics and methods could be described, but they would merely reinforce the overall analysis. Maximum technological ingenuity was used to inflict pain on "the enemy"; it relied on targeting that was necessarily indiscriminate, and it placed upon the civilian population the heaviest burden of the cruelest tactics.

The Vietnamese insurgents contributed to the belligerent setting, of course, by intermingling their soldiers with the general population. They conducted their own extensive programs of persuasion, intimidation, and assassination in relation to the civilian population. In many respects, the combat behavior of the insurgent faction was similar to that of the counterinsurgent. But this was true of the Viet Cong at a far more modest level of technological capability than that of the American counterinsurgent forces. And the insurgents in Vietnam had far more authentic links with the land and the people than did the American soldiers. [38] In this regard, the foreign-directed counterinsurgents in Vietnam and Laos were particularly extreme in their tendency to subordinate the interests of the civilian population to considerations of military effectiveness.

Wherever the political and geographical terrain is supportive of insurgency and whenever the insurgent goals include the liberation of the country from foreign rule, then it is very difficult to avoid combat tendencies of the sort that were disclosed by the NLF during the war in Vietnam. Under these circumstances the foreign supplier of counterinsurgent weaponry is almost certain to be aligned with the most regressive forces in the state in which the struggle is going on, that is, with those forces that identify their interests with the continuation of dependence on foreign rule and on the maintenance of oppressive structures of economic and political exploitation. This analysis of the struggle situation is important because it shows why the population as a whole becomes "the enemy" of the governing groups and why only the most extreme military tactics and methods can offset the relation of forces within the country. It is this imbalance that leads the incumbent, despite its inherent advantages in a world-order system of statist organization, to turn over its own war effort to a foreign government and thereby to relinquish both the symbols and the actualities of self-determination and national sovereignty in order to maintain the appearance of ascendancy for its particular ruling group.

What can international law achieve in such a setting? There is some temptation to accept the genocidal view of counterinsurgent warfare and pronounce the entire enterprise as criminal. But international lawyers have long been reconciled to the pursuit of modest ends. To forbid counterinsurgency is not to prevent it. [39] The most persuasive interpretation of political trends suggests that many wars of this kind will occur in the years ahead. As matters now stand, the foreign policy of most principal governments involves military commitments to governments facing insurgent challenges. This pattern of commitments is partly statism, partly quasi-imperialism, and partly a reflection of alliance policies in a world of rival coalitions. Reorientations of policy in major countries will have to be brought about, if at all, by domestic political movements. [40]

With respect to issues of individual responsibility, the United States already seems to have compromised gravely the expectations it helped to create at Nuremberg. [41] There is no realistic prospect that the Nuremberg approach will be applied in the Vietnam context. Individual responsibility has been imposed, reluctantly and conservatively, upon a few combat soldiers who participated directly in highly publicized killings or abuses of helpless civilians. The official policies have not been scrutinized by Congress in relation to the laws of war; judicial redress has been denied in a number of the court cases; and private action had been taken to discredit the main war planners in any way. The official endorsement of the means and ends of large-scale, externally financed and directed counterinsurgent operations in Vietnam persisted to the very end of American involvement.

In analyzing this situation we find five main characteristics:

1. Counterinsurgent methods and tactics of the kind used in Vietnam violate on a massive scale both specific legal prohibitions and the general principles of the laws of war.

2. There is no organized, influential international effort to condemn these methods and tactics; indeed, many principal governments in the world depend on counterinsurgent capabilities to maintain rule at home and to pursue interests abroad.

3. There is a considerable prospect of continued counterinsurgent warfare throughout the world in the years ahead.

4. Individual responsibility for war crimes in a counterinsurgent context is likely to remain narrowly confined to participants in face-to-face atrocities. [42]

5. The Nuremberg ethos, however, is likely to motivate the assumption of individual responsibility in defiance of governmental directive. The militant antiwar resistance movement in the United States was profoundly influenced by what I have elsewhere called "the wider logic" of Nuremberg. [43]

The fundamental legal challenge, however, involves the basic dynamics of large-scale counterinsurgent warfare in those situations in which a substantial segment of the population voluntarily provides, as it did in Vietnam, a shield for the insurgent cause. The concern here is not with legal reform in the sense of establishing workable standards of conduct, but with the practical and normative issues of individual responsibility. There are a number of background reasons why large-scale counterinsurgent warfare like that in Vietnam does not appear to be aggression in the Nuremberg sense. The locus of struggle is centered in a single country. There is no border crossing except for purposes incidental to the war itself. The external actor's role is usually provided with a veil of legitimacy by its receipt or engineering of an invitation to enter the struggle. Indeed, the insurgent actor may have initiated the struggle, possibly even at the behest of an external actor. [44] Also, the statist bias of the world-order system heavily favors the claims of the constituted regime as compared with those of the insurgent regime.

For a number of reasons it is equally complicated to apply the laws of war to the conduct of a large-scale counterinsurgent war. The virtually inevitable illegality of insurgent methods and tactics tends to vindicate recourse to effective responses. Governments generally maintain the right to request external help to defeat such internal armed struggles. In addition, counterinsurgent weaponry and tactics are a somewhat recent development. International law is generally accorded a very limited sphere of applicability in relation to a largely internal war. [45] Finally, modern warfare has come to be characterized by technological, bureaucratic, and geographical distance between the policy makers and the battlefield soldiers. [46] As a result of these considerations, there was only a very weak effort in the United States during the Vietnam War to shift the appraisal of the war beyond the sphere of imprudence to that of individual accountability for immoral, illegal, and criminal methods and tactics of warfare.

What should be done about this apparent suspension of the laws of war in relation to the most pervasive form of conflict in the latter portion of this century? There is obviously an urgent educational need to bridge the gap between the cool rhetoric of policy making and the awful horror of battlefield execution. But beyond this, there is a need for more formal action, the barest outlines of which I will indicate here in the spirit of identifying fruitful pathways for thought and action:

1. A wise undertaking would be an international effort to clarify the conditions under which an externally based insurgency or counterinsurgency would qualify as an instance of aggressive war in the Nuremburg sense.

2. A world conference of governments under United Nations auspices might seek to establish some limits on methods and tactics that can lawfully be used by all actors, especially external participants, in counterinsurgent wars. A topic, perhaps, might be the threshold limits involving troops, but not equipment. [47] Such a conference might follow

the Hague model of public visibility rather than the Geneva model of technical working sessions of experts. This public event would serve to bring to light the interplay of legal, political, and moral factors involved in governing the conduct of war.

3. A domestic reassessment of the methods and tactics of large-scale counterinsurgency is in order. This might address the overall moral and legal traditions dealing with warfare, including the costs of brutalizing and demoralizing American soldiers.

4. It is necessary to exert a greater effort within the military establishment at all levels to inculcate knowledge of, and respect for, the laws of war and a duty to report, investigate, and prosecute apparent violations.

5. I suggest that this country initiate a series of domestic reforms designed to lift the veil of secrecy covering United States interventionary diplomacy, including counterinsurgent operations. Such reforms would enable the Congress, the courts, and the public to exercise greater review function in relation to Executive Branch initiatives affecting war and peace.

6. It would be desirable to initiate a series of structural reforms at the international level designed to improve impartial fact finding in relation to externally abetted insurgency and counterinsurgency.

These initiatives are not likely to be effective without a fundamental reappraisal of worldwide counterinsurgent activities. This reappraisal can proceed from many angles. One issue specifically needing such reconsideration is the inability to confine high-technology counterinsurgency within the limiting principles of discrimination, proportionality, necessity, and humanity, the serious application of which underlies the entire effort to apply law to the conduct of war.

America, with a new political conscience activated by the bitter experience of the Vietnam War, may seem less prone to engage in such a brutal quest for victory. But beleaguered leaders all over the world are likely to make maximum use of counterinsurgent methods and the more they do, the more indiscriminate their repression of insurgency is likely to be. Pakistan's treatment of the Bangladesh uprisings in 1971 was certainly an ugly foretaste of internally centered counterinsurgency and its tendency to generate international warfare. Unless international society organizes its sentiments and capabilities to oppose these crimes carried out against the innocent, the prospects for a just world order are virtually nonexistent. In this sense, the low profile of the issue of individual responsibility in relation to large-scale counterinsurgency may yet turn out to be a critical indication of the decay and disintegration of the present world-order system, based as it is upon the absolutist prerogatives of national sovereignty with respect to internal military and paramilitary challenges.

In my view, certain reforms can be made on a domestic and on an international level to mitigate the character of large-scale counterinsurgent war. However, the fundamental challenge involves the extent to which high-technology weaponry can be used against a civilian population or a low-technology insurgent in order to maintain a friendly foreign government in power. The legal traditions of limitation and accountability are virtually meaningless so long as these statist prerogatives go unquestioned.

I should emphasize that although much of my discussion is couched in general language, it is primarily a reflection upon the American involvement in the Vietnam War. More broadly based comparative studies of counterinsurgent operations are needed. [48] Also, my focus has purposely been put on the primary impacts of belligerent operations rather than on a technical interpretation of the scope of positive rules and the prospects for their extension or revision. [49] Furthermore, it seems clear that the law of war embodies the homocentric bias present in all legal and political thought in the pre-ecological age. Thus, it fails totally to deal with issues of environmental warfare and ecocide, or, more restrainedly, with obligatory aspects of man's relation to nature during a war. [50] And finally, much more thought needs to be given to the development of constructive proposals that will make the notions of individual responsibility in relation to the initiation and conduct of counterinsurgent warfare relevant to present patterns of public consciousness and to procedural possibilities for legal testing and enforcing. As matters now stand, the Nuremberg idea has been repudiated, but its essential claims remain as valid as most Americans regarded them to be after World War II. [51]

2   *Robert E. Jordan III*

Some general observations about the nature of warfare should precede a discussion of the specific legalities or illegalities of particular new forms of warfare experienced in Vietnam. If they are neglected, one's chances of producing any rational analysis of war—in Vietnam or elsewhere—are greatly reduced.

First of all, war is without a doubt an unpleasant, dirty, cruel business. There is an increasing tendency to think of things that are unpleasant, dirty, and cruel as necessarily illegal. But it is not so with war. Neither the Hague nor the Geneva Conventions, the principal formal guidelines for the conduct of warfare, were designed to make warfare nice. As the preamble to the Hague Convention No. IV of 1907 states, wording of the provisions had been "inspired by the desire to diminish the evils of war, as far as military requirements permit." [1] The term "military requirements" is hardly a term of precision. It allows for much interpretation and leaves room for much deplorable, but nonetheless legal, death and destruction. One of the greatest mistakes that lawyers can make in analyzing the Vietnam War is to brand as illegal all that they consider unwise, unjust, or unattractive.

Second, one must keep in mind that the nations engaging in warfare seldom do so with indifference toward the results. They want to win. It may be possible to convince young men in their early teens that "it is not whether you win or lose, but how you play the game," but nothing, history least of all, can persuade governments that such principles should control their activities in time of warfare. Governments may limit themselves within certain rules of wartime conduct, but they are unlikely to go far beyond what is required of them by custom or convention if they consider their vital interests to be adversely affected.

Third, war involves human beings equipped with normal human reactions to stress, conflict, and difficulty. Military commanders are trained in a tradition that respects aggressiveness. Commanders, like nations, are unlikely to believe that losing is compatible with their best interest. They wish to be promoted, to move from company to battalion to brigade to division commands. They have perfectly normal human ambitions to advance their careers, just as assistant professors wish to become tenured associate professors and ultimately full professors, and businessmen seek to advance up corporate ladders. And, while officers seek to demonstrate their fitness for greater responsibilities, they also must demonstrate an almost universal sense of deep responsibility for the safety of their men. They tend to resolve doubtful cases in favor of the course of action that will afford the maximum protection to the men under their command. And what of these? I would be the last to disparage the motives of patriotism, duty, and sacrifice that have led men into battle for their country for generations. However, I am inclined to believe that the dominating thought of most men committed to active combat in the field is the desire to remain alive.

These are factors that are common to all wars. There may have been variations in Vietnam, but men have been guided by similar considerations in every conflict.

One more ingredient should be added to this potpourri—the nature of the individual infantryman, who, more than any other person in the military hierarchy, faces situations that permit resistance to, or commission of, violations of the laws of war. The infantry may be the queen of battle, as many say, but few would argue that the men of the infantry represent the cream of American youth. The infantryman is likely to be a conscript; he may have had some brushes with the law prior to his entry into military service; he is not likely to be among the best educated of his generation.

And what of the inhabitants of the country of Vietnam? Again I do not wish to discount the motives of patriotism and sacrifice that have no doubt motivated many Vietnamese. But Vietnamese, too, wish to stay alive. As individuals, they are probably far less concerned about the badges and titles worn by one side or the other than they are about keeping themselves and their families alive and being left alone to enjoy some small measure of peace and quiet.

The conflict in Vietnam involved forms of warfare that were different from those of recent American experience. If allowance is made for the exceptions that always exist, it is fair to say that World War I, World War II, and the Korean War basically involved relatively conventional forms of warfare of the type contemplated by the Geneva and Hague Conventions. Battle lines were relatively fixed. Normally, it was possible to identify the persons who constituted the enemy by their uniform or other distinctive insignia.

The Vietnam War was clearly different. Recognizing the enemy was often impossible. Fixed battle lines were more the exception than the rule. The enemy appeared to fight and then melt away. Combatant and noncombatant looked alike to the trained, as well as the untrained, eye. The entire course of conducting the war constituted a different form of warfare, and it evoked some different responses. Many of these responses were controversial; some have been characterized as illegal.

Against this background, let us take a look at some of the methods of warfare used in Vietnam that have become the subject of controversy.

Using Firepower against Inhabited Villages / Some would say that the use of firepower—including aerial bombing—against villages constitutes a war crime. This charge deserves examination, because there were without doubt thousands of examples of the use of firepower against inhabited villages in Vietnam.

It could be a rule of customary or conventional international law that one may not attack a village containing noncombatant civilians. But it is not, and never has been, the rule. The prevailing restriction is that of article 25 of the Regulations in the Hague Convention No. IV of 1907, which states: "It is forbidden to attack or bombard, by any means whatever, towns, villages, dwellings or buildings that are not defended." [2]

The three wars of this century in which the United States took part prior to Vietnam all involved the use of military force against villages or towns. And in those villages noncombatants were interspersed with combatants who were attempting either to deny the town to attacking forces or to harass those forces from within the town's confines. The legality of such attacks depends upon a case-by-case assessment of the undefended status of each area.

Undoubtedly in Vietnam there were violations, even willful violations, of this Hague Convention provision, as there are in every war. But I question the competence of remote observers to determine that an individual village involved in an action in Vietnam was undefended. If, in fact, a military commander reasonably believes that a village is defended, normal application of the doctrine of military necessity permits him to attack the village. We may deplore his judgment in specific cases; we may be certain that under our command it would have been otherwise. But we cannot, according to the laws of war as they are written, characterize such conduct as a war crime.

Difficulties arise, of course, in applying the doctrine of military necessity to specific circumstances. Furthermore, its application must be accompanied by the limiting doctrine of proportionality, which requires that the suffering of noncombatants not be disproportionate to the military advantage to be gained.

Is it permissible to attack a village from which sniper or other fire is being received, if the anticipated ratio of civilian casualties to friendly-force casualties is a hundred to one? How about ten to one or three to one? Were Allied forces permitted to attack a village in which Viet Cong forces sought refuge only temporarily? Was it relevant that they sought refuge there only periodically?

Further, how reliable should one's information be concerning the presence of guerrilla forces in a village? Does the standard of probable cause apply, as in the issuance of a search or arrest warrant? Or is the standard higher or lower than probable cause? Those who have fought in combat will say that a military commander never has all the information he wants, or needs, and that he frequently must act on information from sources whose reliability is at best speculative. But if he waits for certainty or demands unimpeachable sources, he will never act at all. And, remember, his nation is there to win—and he is there to support his nation's objectives while showing his superiors the kind of results that mark him as promotable material.

Whether actions against a village exceed the allowable limits of the necessity-proportionality doctrine is a matter to be determined only by reference to the specific circumstances. Those circumstances are evaluated as they appeared to the military officials involved at the time, not with the special acuity available after the fact. Perhaps the best discussion of the doctrine in a particular case is found in the judgment of the Nuremberg tribunal in that portion of the *Hostages* case dealing with the German General Lothar Rendulic. The court said, in part:

> The evidence shows that the Russians had very excellent troops in pursuit of the Germans. . . . The information obtained concerning the intentions of the Russians was limited. The extreme cold and the short days made air reconnaissance almost impossible. It was with this situation confronting him that he [General Rendulic] carried out the "scorched earth" policy in the Norwegian province of Finmark which provided the basis for this charge of the indictment. . . .
> There is evidence in the record that there was no military necessity for this destruction and devastation. An examination of the facts in retrospect can well sustain this conclusion. But we are obliged to judge the situation as it appeared to the defendant at the time. If the facts were such as would justify the action by the exercise of judgment, after giving consideration to all the factors and existing possibilities, even though the conclusion reached may have been faulty, it cannot be said to be criminal. . . .
> . . . It is our considered opinion that the conditions, as they appeared to the defendant at the time, were sufficient upon which he could honestly conclude that urgent military necessity warranted the decision made. This being true, the defendant may have erred in the exercise of his judgment but he was guilty of no criminal act.[3]

Relocation and Resettlement

Some commentators, including Professor Taylor, have questioned the legality of what is sometimes referred to as a "new" practice arising in Vietnam—the relocation of reluctant civilians from their homes to resettlement areas or refugee centers. The practice was hardly original in Vietnam. The British carried it out widely in Malaya, apparently with some success. But it was somewhat different from normal wartime procedures and deserves analysis.

What are the options available to a commander faced with a guerrilla enemy flitting in and out among the civilian inhabitants of an area? Three come to mind:

> 1. The commander may continue military operations in the area, limited only by the doctrines of necessity and proportionality, with the incidental death and injury to noncombatants that always attends such operations. While civilians may not be attacked as such, they have no immunity to military operations conducted against combatants in their midst.

> 2. The commander may suspend military operations in order to avoid the death of civilians. But this runs counter to the notion that nations pursue victory, that military forces seek to destroy the enemy, and that commanders will not allow their men to become the victims of operations conducted from a haven.

> 3. The commander may seek a way to segregate combatant from noncombatant, pursuing the former militarily and affording the latter protection.

I perhaps display my bias in saying that no military commander is likely to let the enemy immunize himself from attack by mixing among noncombatants. The enemy would be quick to capitalize upon the advantages flowing from such a policy of restraint. Is it inhumane, or immoral, or illegal for a commander to relocate civilians, even at the expense of uprooting them from their homes, if the objective is to spare their lives?

There is no basis for condemning such relocations as war crimes, whatever may be their wisdom or efficacy. For these purposes, I leave aside several relatively esoteric questions that have been the source of much learned analysis. These include whether the conflict in Vietnam was of an international character, thus invoking all the provisions of the 1949 Geneva Convention Relative to the Protection of Civilian Persons in Time of War. [4] If the war in Vietnam was a conflict not of an international character, only article 3 of the Geneva Civilians Convention applies, and it contains no specific prohibition on relocation, provided that the action entails "no violence to life and person" or "outrages upon personal dignity." I will also pass over the argument that, even if the conflict in Vietnam was of an international character, relocations by

United States military forces were nonetheless lawful because they took place within the territory of South Vietnam with the approval of its government.

If one assumes that the Geneva Civilians Convention was applicable to Vietnam, its article 49, while generally prohibiting mass transfers from occupied territory to that of the occupying power, specifically recognizes that "the Occupying Power may undertake total or partial evacuation of a given area if the security of the population or imperative military reasons so demand."[5] In most cases in Vietnam, one could assert with some force that both the security of the population and military necessity supported the practice of relocation. The relocations in Vietnam certainly involved none of the practices of Nazi forces that were condemned by the Nuremberg International Military Tribunal.

In the post-World War II precedents, there is acknowledgment of the validity of relocations, not to mention other practices. Addressing the requirement for exhausting less severe measures prior to taking or executing hostages, the tribunal in the *Hostages* case[6] said:

Hostages may not be taken or executed as a matter of military expediency. The occupant is required to use every available method to secure order and tranquility before resort may be had to the taking and execution of hostages. Regulations of all kinds must be imposed to secure peace and tranquility before the shooting of hostages may be indulged.[7]

The tribunal then set forth the measures that might be taken by an occupying power to "secure peace and tranquility" in the civilian population. These included steps ranging from less drastic procedures such as registering of inhabitants or the establishment of restricted areas to such drastic ones as "compulsory labor to repair damage from sabotage" and destruction of property "in proximity to the place of the crime."

Professor Hersh Lauterpacht also acknowledges the validity of evacuation, with related devastation, when the necessities of war so require.

It is impossible to define once for all the circumstances which make general devastation necessary, since everything depends upon the merits of the special case. But the fact that general devastation can be lawful must be admitted. It is, for instance, lawful in case of a levy *en masse* on already occupied territory, when self-preservation obliges a belligerent to resort to the most severe measures. It is also lawful when, after the defeat of his main forces and occupation of his territory, an enemy disperses his remaining forces into small bands which carry on guerrilla tactics and receive food and information, so that there is no hope of ending the war except by general devastation which cuts off supplies of every kind from the guerrilla bands. But it must be specially observed that general devastation is only justified by imperative necessity and by the fact that there is no better and less severe way open to a belligerent.[8]

Compared to the extreme remedies allowed as alternatives to the taking of hostages, or to limited devastation as a means of controlling a civilian population, the relocation in Vietnam seems a reasonable and humane procedure. Those who would condemn it overlook the drastic measures authorized by the laws of war for an occupying military force.

Free-Fire Zones and Specified Strike Zones

Perhaps the most frequently criticized "new" practice generated by the Vietnam War was the establishment of the so-called free-fire zones. In the minds of many Americans, the term connotes total obliteration of life within a designated area. It is probably fair to say that, while the theory of such zones was consistent with the laws of war, the practices associated with them may not have been. The zones were a predictable military response to the peculiar conditions of warfare in Vietnam, and they are the closest thing to a genuinely "new" practice one can find. Once again, however, the British had used similar restricted areas in Malaya.

In 1965 the United States military command developed rules of engagement to regulate the conduct in combat of its forces. [9] These rules, both originally and in their subsequent revisions and elaborations, were probably the most comprehensive effort ever undertaken by a nation fighting abroad to protect noncombatants in the country at war. In addition to laying down regulations governing the use of firepower, the rules also called for elaborate checks or clearances with local officials prior to firing. These checks worked reasonably well in inhabited areas. In more sparsely populated areas, however, they involved an element of delay that often permitted the enemy to escape. Accordingly, for such areas, a system was developed for getting prior clearance for undertaking military operations at a specified time and in a designated geographic area. These procedures, known as preclearances, obviated the need for further "political" approval from local Vietnamese officials before undertaking operations. Preclearance did not suspend the other elements of the rules of engagement, which continued in force.

The original term used to describe such precleared areas was "free-fire zones" or "free-strike zones." The choice of words was unfortunate, for outside and, some would say, inside the military as well, it tended to be loosely understood to mean "anything goes" so far as the use of firepower was concerned. The United States command recognized the problem, however, and in 1965 changed the designation to the more neutral term "specified strike zone." But there is considerable evidence that the education of military personnel in the name change was not effective. I found military personnel using the "free-fire zone" terminology several years after it had been dropped from the official vocabulary.

So long as a reasonable belief in the enemy's presence was the basis for making a specified strike zone the target of military operations, and so long as undefended towns were not attacked, the doctrine of military necessity clearly justified the use of firepower. Ironically, if the United States command had never sought to impose strict firepower controls countrywide in 1965, there probably would never have been an occasion to develop the term "free-fire zone."

It is difficult to specify just what war crimes may have been committed through misapplication of the precleared-zone concept. Certainly there is some evidence that such zones were used for target practice without regard to the limitations of the Hague Regulations. Individual noncombatants may indeed have been shot without justification. One of the clearest lessons of Vietnam is that special zones of this kind must be clearly defined and the definitions monitored thereafter, if violations of the laws of war are to be prevented.

The Destruction of Property

In the Vietnam conflict, as in all others, property apparently belonging to noncombatants was destroyed. Without going into the herbicide thicket, one can note that crops were destroyed. And domestic animals. And food. And homes. Are these acts war crimes?

Article 23 of the annex to the Hague Convention No. IV of 1907 states that it is forbidden, among other things, "[t]o destroy or seize the enemy's property, unless such destruction or seizure be imperatively demanded by the necessities of war." [10] Is the "imperatively demanded" test something more stringent than the doctrine of military necessity alone? We must assume so, for to assume otherwise requires reading the language as surplusage.

Both the portion of the *Hostages* case cited above and Lauterpacht's comment on evacuation and devastation suggest the lawfulness of devastation in some cases. But just what constitutes "imperative necessity"? And when is there "no better or less severe way," in the language of Lauterpacht?

Where villagers, presumably noncombatants, were interspersed with the Viet Cong, and the property in question was being used to support the military activities of the Viet Cong, what better way was there to deal with the problem than to destroy the property that contributed to the enemy's strength? One could, of course, simply have destroyed the entire village—inhabitants, property, and all—if the enemy was "defending" the village. But that is hardly a less severe way of proceeding. Or one could simply have accepted the continued support being furnished to the enemy in this fashion. But this runs counter to the desire of the nation to win, and of the commander to succeed in his area of operations. The attractiveness of destruction to the commander is obvious. And yet one wonders about the words "imperatively demanded by the necessities of war."

I conclude that what was done in Vietnam generally made military sense—that the destruction usually, but not always, related to a real-world military problem and served a legitimate military objective. And I believe what was done is probably consistent with the precedents from Nuremberg and the other war crimes trials of the 1940s. But the term "imperative necessity" is bothersome. It seems a restrictive test. On further reflection, it appears that the law may be that the constraints on destroying property are more confining than those on killing people. This obviously illogical result finally leads me to conclude that the law must be that gratuitous destruction of property is *verboten*, but that any reasonably well-thought-out relationship between its destruction and diminished support for the enemy satisfies the standard.

3   Comments

Richard R. Baxter *

Much of what Professor Falk has to say proceeds on a completely mistaken assumption—that there is already a wide range of customary and conventional international law applicable to internal armed conflicts. The fact is that, in the absence of a recognition of belligerency or of insurgency, there is no customary international law governing civil wars. The Hague Regulations governing the conduct of war are applicable only to international conflicts. And in the Geneva Conventions of 1949, which protect the victims of war, only article 3, common to the four treaties, deals with noninternational armed conflicts. That article, incorporating a bill of rights in miniature, was thought in 1949 to be a radical innovation by reason of the fact that international law had not previously concerned itself with internal conflicts.

Mr. Jordan has called the question of the character of the conflict in Vietnam an "esoteric" one, and Professor Falk seems implicitly to consider it a matter of little consequence. In many aspects, the conflict in Vietnam was a civil one. The very kinds of conduct that Professor Falk finds so reprehensible in Vietnam normally involved relations between forces of the United States or of the Republic of Vietnam on the one hand and the Viet Cong and the civilian population on the other. Those relations are in strict law governed only by article 3 of the Geneva Conventions of 1949.

It is, of course, true that the United States and the Republic of Vietnam attempted to apply the Geneva Conventions in their relations with the Viet Cong and with civilians. However, much of the Geneva Civilians Convention simply cannot be applied in civil conflicts because its operation turns on notions of belligerent occupation of territory and enemy nationality, concepts that are alien to civil conflicts. And although members of Viet Cong main-force units were treated as prisoners of war, other residents of South Vietnam who engaged in hostile or subversive activities found themselves subjected to the ordinary civil law of the Republic of Vietnam. This practice was in full conformity with the existing international law.

*The views expressed in this chapter are those of Mr. Baxter and do not necessarily reflect those of the United States delegation to the Conference of Government Experts on the International Humanitarian Law Applicable in Armed Conflicts, of which he was a member.

In the "third world" of Charlottesville, Virginia, or Princeton, New Jersey, or New Haven, Connecticut, or Cambridge, Massachusetts, the participation of another state in what was initially a civil conflict may be thought to bring to bear the whole of the international law of war. But this view is not shared by developing countries themselves. At the Conference of Government Experts on the International Humanitarian Law Applicable in Armed Conflicts in Geneva in 1971, the experts from developing countries who spoke to this issue were strongly opposed to the notion that foreign participation in effect turned a civil conflict into an international one for the purposes of the law of war. They saw this theory for the dangerous threat to stability and the inducement to escalation that it is.

But, whether a conflict is civil or international, the protection of the civilian population has become ever more difficult. The safeguards that the law extends to civilians are premised upon their refraining from participation in belligerent activities and upon their identifiability as noncombatants. In these days, when wars are fought for principles and ideologies, civilians have increasingly taken an active part in the support of hostilities or in the hostilities themselves. At the same time, combatants, especially those who fight as irregulars, have found it convenient to conceal themselves among the civilian population and to pass themselves off as civilians. Even temples and hospitals have been used as refuges for troops or places from which to fight.

In the confusion and urgency of combat, where split-second decisions must be made on the basis of inadequate information, the intermingling of combatants and noncombatants has made it difficult and sometimes impossible for a belligerent to direct its fire only against those who are clearly identifiable as combatants. The result is that civilians—not a few of whom have taken no part in hostilities—inevitably get hurt.

A certain mixture of ethics, political philosophy, political theory, morals, international relations, and domestic and international law has been employed in support of what is—to the surprise of no one—Professor Falk's strong hostility to United States military conduct in the Vietnam War. What he has written and what he has said fail to distinguish the law as it is from the law as it might be. This circumstance makes it difficult to comment on the validity of the propositions that he advances. Two instances suffice to show the way in which he has approached questions.

From rules of general international law applicable to international armed conflict, Professor Falk has extracted the four governing principles of necessity (which is actually the converse—a principle forbidding unnecessary suffering), of discrimination, of proportionality, and of humanity. These principles, having been derived largely from rules found in treaties applicable to international armed conflict, such as the Hague Regulations of 1907, are then regarded as giving rise to further precise rules of customary international law having application to noninternational armed conflicts as well. The treaty rules, according to Professor Falk's theory, assume a law-generating force, which was, in fact, not in the minds of the draftsmen of the conventions or of international lawyers who subsequently concerned themselves with the laws of war. According to the prevailing view, the rules in the treaties are, on the contrary, to be taken in their literal sense and to have no wider a range of operation than is permitted by the existing law of treaty interpretation.

If treaty rules generate new rules of customary international law by analogy—not simply by way of incorporation of the treaties themselves into the corpus of customary international law—states will quickly perceive the danger of writing new treaty rules to restrain conduct in warfare. Governments like to think that the treaties they negotiate are the measure of their obligation as to the subject matter dealt with. They will be deeply alarmed if new customary rules are created by analogy with the conventional ones through the mediation of general principles of the law.

We also learn from Professor Falk that some American antipersonnel weaponry "contravened the spirit of one of the earliest modern efforts to limit the conduct of war—the Declaration of St. Petersburg of 1868." It is well that he invokes only the spirit of the Declaration, because the Declaration, by which seventeen states renounced the use in war of explosive projectiles weighing less than fourteen ounces, does not number the United States among its parties. The instrument has not passed into customary international law. And so it remains an interesting historical landmark—a primitive attempt at weapons control. To argue that the "spirit" of this century-old instrument proscribes certain conduct as part of customary international law is really to argue by analogy. And to create new obligations—and thus new crimes as well, to the extent that individual responsibility is involved—in this manner is to revert to a form of legal reasoning that one would have thought had been thoroughly discredited by its perversions in the 1930s.

One can only echo the sense of concern for the future development of the law that is reflected in both Mr. Jordan's and Professor Falk's papers. It would have been helpful if more had been said about what can and should be done to strengthen legal controls over international violence. Under the auspices of the International Committee of the Red Cross, the Conference of Government Experts has engaged in the preparation of new protocols to expand the legal protection of war victims, and a diplomatic conference was convened in 1974 and will reconvene in 1975 to consider these proposals. Substantial progress has been made by the government experts on a new protocol to article 3 (noninternational armed conflicts) of the Geneva Conventions of 1949, which would very materially increase the law governing civil conflicts; on a protocol broadening the range of persons entitled to protection as prisoners of war; and on a protocol that would benefit the wounded and sick in internal and international armed conflicts. There is reason to hope that something may yet be done about the matter of implementation of the Conventions, including improved procedures for the selection of Protecting Powers, wider training in the law, inspection of the state of compliance with the law, and like measures. This is the task for the future, and it is here that the real hope for the laws of war lies.

4   **Comments**

Hamilton DeSaussure

Professor Falk's discussion seems logically to fall into several main contentions, or propositions, that I shall examine one at a time.

Proposition One

*The methods and tactics of a large-scale counterinsurgent effort, espe-
cially if carried out with high-technology weaponry, necessarily violate
the laws of war.*

Professor Falk would reduce internal armed conflict to a game of
sport in which the sides must be equal in size and capability. This is erroneous on legal, logical, and pragmatic grounds.

Article 22 of the Hague Regulations of 1907 provides that "the right
of belligerents to adopt means of injuring the enemy is not unlimited."
This rule cannot, however, be read to mean that technological superiority in weapons, guidance systems, or manpower mobility is per se unlawful. It is totally unrealistic to expect the armed forces of any government to forego the use of any methods, tactics, or weaponry available
and not specifically prohibited by the laws of war. As Professor Baxter
has explained, the international law of war is prohibitive rather than
positive law. The law of war "forbids rather than authorizes certain
manifestations of force."[1] That which is not forbidden by the laws of
war is permitted.

Indeed, a government whose very existence is endangered by
armed attack from within or without must have the right to the full use
of its superior forces and capability to defend itself. The defense of one's
homeland is the most serious matter a government and its citizenry can
undertake. All concerned seek victory in the shortest possible time with
the least loss of life and human resources.

One technical correction is appropriate here. Professor Falk refers
to random or computer firing of long-distance artillery and bombing
missions as indiscriminate and unlawful. All long-distance terrestrial
firing weapons are computer-controlled in a modern armed force in
order to facilitate preplanning and increase accuracy. Such weapons

are random only as to timing and not as to objective. This prevents the enemy from calculating, and thus avoiding, the periods of fire. And computerized and electronically controlled weapons do not inflict pain on the enemy any more than less sophisticated weaponry with the same firepower. It is the use to which such weapons are put, and the intent of the user, that must be assessed rather than the degree of technological sophistication.

Proposition Two

Intervention by a foreign force leads to indiscriminate slaughter of innocent civilians by the external forces.

It is unfair to infer that the external actor, the foreign state coming to the aid of an ally, has any less regard for the laws of war than does the principal defender. No competent evidence establishes that the civilian population became the military enemy in the eyes of the United States armed forces. Any regional security arrangement implies the external assistance of one or more partners in the event of an armed attack, and "genocidal patterns of thought" cannot be said to follow axiomatically.

The callous disregard of the native Vietnamese population referred to as the "Dink complex" undoubtedly existed in the minds of some American soldiers. The trial of Lieutenant Calley and others has documented it. The United States Army recognized this and made necessary changes in its training and indoctrination of combat-bound soldiers. Our military identified this source of bias, discouraged it, and has prosecuted men who were motivated to kill innocent Vietnamese because of it.

At the same time, body counts and the establishment of kill ratios are neither unlawful nor necessarily inspired by callous motives. In addition to establishing the effect of a military engagement and the accuracy of its firepower, body counts can bring to light the commission of possible war crimes. By comparing the number of weapons captured after a battle with the number of dead and wounded left by the enemy, the military commanders not in the field can sometimes identify evidence of possible war crimes. Obviously a high enemy body count in relation to the number of weapons found nearby tends to show that there has been needless killing of unarmed civilians. This would generate an inquiry into the lawfulness of the attack or the conduct of individuals who took part in it. Surely Professor Falk would not oppose that use of body counts.

The charge of genocide, or even genocidal patterns of thought, is a serious one. The United Nations defined genocide as killing or injuring or otherwise attempting "to destroy, in whole or in part, a national, ethnical, racial or religious group."[2] No competent evidence indicates that the United States or its leaders resorted to genocide in Vietnam. It is manifest that far more devastation than occurred anywhere could have been visited upon the Vietnamese and would have been by a nation bent on committing genocide. Deputy Assistant Secretary of Defense Goulding, in his letter of 30 December 1966 to Congressman Ogden Reid, best summed this up by stating: "In view of the great strength of United States air power, it is patently obvious that the damage would be very much greater, and, indeed, unmistakable had the U.S. deliberately attacked any civilian targets in Vietnam."[3]

Our armed forces in Vietnam, both individually and as units, helped establish orphanages, rebuilt homes, served in hospitals, participated in civic relief, and gave generously of their food and comfort items to the indigenous population. Such actions can hardly be viewed as genocidal patterns of thought.

Proposition Three

The principles of necessity, discrimination, proportionality, and humanity, as defined by Professor Falk, constitute the four great fundamental rules regulating armed conflict.

Professor Falk defines "necessity" as a prohibition upon methods, tactics, and weapons calculated to inflict unnecessary suffering; "discrimination" as the requirement that methods, tactics, and weapons discriminate between military and nonmilitary targets and between combatants and civilians; "proportionality" as the requirement that the military means used bear a proportional relationship to the military end pursued; and "humanity" as the absolute prohibition upon methods, tactics, and weapons that are inherently cruel in their effects and violate minimal notions of humanity. Necessity has a twofold connotation in the laws of war. On the one hand it signifies military necessity, which entitles a belligerent to apply such forces as will produce the submission of the enemy's military forces as early as possible and at the least cost in men and matériel.[4] On the other hand, the principle of humanity prohibits any kind or degree of violence beyond what is absolutely necessary to produce such submission.

The principles of military necessity and of humanity constitute two of the basic principles underlying all the other rules or laws of civilized warfare, both written and unwritten.[5] Methods and tactics that are planned and executed to produce unnecessary suffering violate the principle of humanity. Causing such unnecessary suffering also runs counter to military necessity by definition, for only that force needed to defeat the enemy in the least possible time at the cheapest cost is permitted.

Professor Falk's first and fourth principles state the obvious point that any "calculated," that is, planned, effort (methods or tactics) to cause unnecessary suffering to the enemy or to civilians is militarily wasteful and uselessly aggravates human suffering. Such conduct would, of course, violate the principles of both humanity and military necessity.

Professor Falk's second cardinal principle, that of discrimination, involves a most unfortunate choice of terminology and a distortion of the laws of war. Weapons do not discriminate. Rather the combatants who employ them make the conscious determination between military and nonmilitary targets. Particular methods and tactics can be used indiscriminately or selectively. But it is not the attacker alone who must bear the responsibility for the unnecessary suffering of the civilian population. General Assembly Resolution No. 2444 on the Respect for Human Rights in Armed Conflicts, which was adopted unanimously, places on the defender—the forces attacked—an equal duty to safeguard the distinction between the armed forces and the civilian population.[6] That resolution states not only that "it is prohibited to launch attacks against the civilian populations as such," but also "that *distinction* must be made at all times between persons taking part in the hostilities and members of the civilian population to the effect that the latter be spared as much as possible" (emphasis added).

Professor Falk's principle of discrimination is really one of distinction. The insurgents may not use the civilian population as a shield.[7] To be entitled to treatment as belligerents and prisoners of war, they must identify their armed forces or combatants and carry arms openly.[8] Finally, insurgents must not use protected areas and the dwellings, towns, and villages of innocent civilians for military purposes.[9] Clearly, less discrimination is possible by the attacking force when the insurgents themselves disregard the laws of war, dress their combatant forces in civilian or peasant clothes, and merge indistinguishably with the populace.

Colonel G. I. A. D. Draper, the British delegate to the twenty-first ICRC conference in Istanbul in 1969, stated there:

Those who framed the Law of War and who came before us in the long line of the development of that branch of Law knew well the essential value of distinguishing those who fight wars as regular combatants "openly and overtly," to use the old medieval expression, i.e., "in Public and Open Wars." They also knew as they showed quite clearly in the Hague Conventions of 1907, time and again, that once you allow the irregular combatant, the peasant by day and the soldier by night, the man without a uniform but with a bomb in his pocket, the civilian in the street who throws a bomb through a cafe window and runs—once you allow such people to be brought within the proper ambit of *jus in bello*, then you open "Pandora's Box," and you make unmitigated misery for every civilian, who loses what precious legal protection he has under the Law of War.[10]

It is this failure to maintain a separation between military and civilian that General Assembly Resolution No. 2444 seeks to correct. It provides that a distinction between the two groups should be maintained at all times. Distinction and discrimination are two sides of the same coin. The civilian population becomes the helpless victim when either side fails in its duty to preserve this separation of the individuals vulnerable to attack.

Professor Falk's third principle is proportionality. Proportionality, in my view, does not mean a weighing of the military means used against the military objective, but rather assessing the advantage to be gained against the probable casualties that will occur. This is really the principle of humanity stated differently. If the loss in life and resources unnecessarily outweighs the military objective, the military forces must refrain from the particular attack. As stated by the Committee of Experts to the ICRC at its twenty-first conference, "[a]n act of destruction shall not involve harm to the civilian population disproportionate to the importance of the military objective under attack."[11]

I must agree that the doctrine of proportionality in the decisive stage rests within the judgment of the attacking forces. Indiscriminate attack upon civilians can occur if methods and tactics are not soberly and carefully assessed prior to their implementation. However, the fundamental lesson of Nuremberg and of the major and minor war crimes trials after World War II is that those who plan and carry out military operations in a reckless and wanton manner, to the end that unnecessary suffering and devastation are brought upon the enemy, will have to answer for their alleged crimes before a military or international tribunal.

Whether the destruction and death caused by a particular military operation are proportional to the objective is not a hindsight assessment. Rather, it is a question of whether the responsible commander knew, or should have known, of the disparity between the military objective and the probable loss of life and property that would ensue. In providing time for his forces to evade advancing Russian contingents in

Norway, Gen. Lothar Rendulic adopted a scorched-earth policy in the province of Finmark. The inhabitants of the area were evacuated and all villages, housing, communications, and transport facilities were destroyed. The General was charged with wanton destruction not justified by military necessity. As Mr. Jordan discusses in greater detail in chapter 2, the court found him not guilty because it held that the destruction was reasonably judged to be militarily necessary at the time that it was undertaken.

Proposition Four

The use of air power in the context of the Vietnam War was indiscriminate and violated international law.

Apart from the instance of the Christmas 1972 bombings of North Vietnam, which were different in kind from prior United States air attacks and which are examined in chapter 9, this proposition is clearly untenable. The laws of war contain "no prohibition of general application against bombardment from the air of combatant troops, defended places, or other legitimate military objectives."[12] Certainly it is incorrect to say that in rural societies of Indochina there are relatively few targets that have any direct military value. Any place the insurgent quarters his troops, stores his weapons and supplies, establishes his base camp, or conceals his men for ambush and surprise becomes a proper military target.

The conventional laws of war are replete with admonitions that protected persons and places lose their immunity from attack when used by the enemy for military purposes. For example, the Geneva Civilians Convention provides that civilian hospitals lose their immunity when "used to commit, outside their humanitarian duties, acts harmful to the enemy"[13] and that "protected persons may not be used to render certain points or areas immune from military objectives."[14] The Hague Cultural Convention of 1954 reflects customary international law in its provision for the safeguard of cultural property provided it is "situated at an adequate distance from any large industrial centre or from any important military objective constituting a vulnerable point, such as, for example, an aerodrome, broadcasting station, establishment engaged upon work of national defense, a port or railway station of relative importance or a main line of communication" and is "not used for military purposes."[15] While the United States has signed, but not yet ratified, this convention, it does, I believe, reflect customary law by illustrating the types of important military objectives, by warning belligerents to keep their cultural refuges at a distance from them, and by forbidding the use of cultural property for military purposes.

American military operations in the Vietnamese conflict emphasized driving the enemy's combatants from the cities and the populated areas into the rural, thinly populated regions so that the civilian population and their property could be spared as much as possible. Neither the use of specified strike zones nor target-area bombing is a tactic that, by itself, violates the laws of war. The principles of humanity and proportionality apply in these areas and zones as much as they do elsewhere. Professor Stone has stated that "[t]he capital starting point . . . is to recognise 'target area' bombing not as a mere barbarous belligerent whim, but a policy adopted under certain pressures." [16] The same applies to the establishment of specified strike zones. Each of these tactics was adopted as one of the most effective means of getting at the enemy in his jungle lair. Given his failure to properly identify his combatant forces, and his use of civilians, their structures, and their towns for combatant operations, it was inevitable that civilian casualties would occur.

The Military Assistance Command, Vietnam (MACV), adopted specific instructions for American forces in order to limit civilian casualties as far as possible. For example, all targets selected for air attack in South Vietnam had to be approved by the province chief directly or through higher Republic of Vietnam authority, and all pilots were instructed to minimize noncombatant casualties and property damage. In-flight procedures called for constant communication of pilots with air liaison officers and forward air controllers, who cleared the air attack only after identification of the enemy forces. United States Air Force pilots were directed to exercise caution when operating in populated areas, and when the identity of friendly forces was in doubt, the commander of United States MACV would instruct that a strike not be executed. Inhabitants of preplanned strategic military target areas were given warning and adequate time to evacuate their hamlets or villages. Every effort was made to clear specified strike zones of innocent civilians, and strikes within these areas were conducted only after clearance was received from the South Vietnamese and after opportunity was given to evacuate. An exception to the requirement for warning was made for areas in which enemy ground fire had been sighted and for situations in which prior warning would jeopardize the success of the mission.

Summarizing the policy of American forces with respect to bombing in Vietnam, Deputy Assistant Secretary of Defense Goulding said in December 1966 in a letter to Congressman Ogden Reid:

No United States aircraft have been ordered to strike any civilian targets in North Vietnam at any time.

United States policy is to target military targets only. There has been no deviation from this policy.

All reasonable care is taken to avoid civilian casualties. . . .

The United States has not targeted such installations as textile plants, fruit canning plants, silk factories and thread cooperatives.

No dikes have been targeted in North Vietnam, in Nam Dinh or elsewhere. . . .

It is impossible to avoid all damage to civilian areas, particularly in view of the concerted effort of the North Vietnamese to emplace anti-aircraft and critical military targets among the civilian population. [17]

Hospitals and buildings used for cultural and religious purposes were hit during air attacks because the insurgent failed to comply with article 27 of the 1907 Hague Regulations and articles 18 and 19 of the Geneva Civilians Convention. These articles impose a duty upon the parties to a conflict to mark such buildings and places properly with distinctive and visible signs and to place them, so far as possible, in an area that is either remote from a military objective or neutralized by arrangement with the enemy. [18] Certain hospital complexes hit in Cambodia were unmarked and in the very center of military installations defended by antiaircraft and missiles.

In the *Einsatzgruppen* case, the tribunal discussed in the following terms the use of air power in armed conflicts and the inevitable resulting loss of civilian life:

A city is bombed for tactical purposes, communications are destroyed, railroads wrecked, ammunition plants demolished, factories razed, all for the purpose of impeding the military. In these operations it inevitably happens that nonmilitary persons are killed. This is an incident, a grave incident to be sure, but an unavoidable corollary of battle action. The civilians are not individualized. The bomb falls, it is aimed at the railroad yards, houses along the track are hit and many of their occupants killed. But that is entirely different, both in fact and in law, from an armed force marching up to these same railroad tracks, entering those houses abutting thereon, dragging out the men, women, and children and shooting them. [19]

Strategic and tactical air attacks, the establishment of specified strike zones, and area bombing all can be considered as counterbalancing the enemy's policies of concealment, surprise, and treachery. Such air attacks fall within the established principle of military necessity. Debate over their legality ignores the actualities of military engagement in the Vietnamese setting.

Proposition Five

Antipersonnel weaponry causes unnecessary suffering and violates the principle of humanity.

Article 23(e) of the Hague Regulations forbids the employment of "arms, projectiles, or material calculated to cause unnecessary suffering." However, this does not foreclose the use of explosives contained in artillery projectiles, mines, rockets, or hand grenades. Nor does it preclude the use of weapons that employ fire such as flamethrowers, napalm, and other incendiary agents. [20]

Weapons are not to be used to cause unnecessary suffering; but antipersonnel devices, properly employed, destroy enemy artillery emplacements or scatter his combat forces. They reduce his capability for retaliation with greater efficiency than do attacks on his matériel and physical installations. Repairs to gun emplacements, to fortifications, and to means of communication and transportation can be accomplished with amazing speed in combat. The dispersal of, and injury to, the enemy's combatant forces causes much greater confusion, brings his forces into the open where they can be captured or destroyed, and reduces the level of his combat capability through the loss of trained and experienced personnel.

As Professor Stone says, it may be lamentable that the role of law concerning the modes and means of violence has been to define the prohibited rather than the permitted means. [21] But armed conflict is too serious a matter to expect any nation to forego its most effective and advanced weaponry when it can be useful in eliminating enemy forces. It is not the objective of antipersonnel weaponry to kill as many people as possible, but to kill or wound the enemy and destroy his combatant force. To the extent that this is accomplished by bomb clusters, fragmenting explosives, and other antipersonnel weapons, the greater will be the claim by the opposing side that their use breaks the laws of war.

Proposition Six

The Phoenix Program, designed to destroy the political infrastructure of the Viet Cong, operated by assassination and capture, and such a program was prohibited as a permissible method of combating insurgency.

The Hague Regulations prohibit the treacherous killing or wounding of individuals belonging to the hostile nation or army. [22] This prohibition outlaws assassination or putting a price on the enemy's capture "dead or alive." Greenspan has stated that perpetrators of such acts should be tried as war criminals and that belligerents should do all in their power to prevent such acts of treachery. [23]

Whether the Phoenix Program involved such prohibited assassination or treachery by United States military forces is a much-disputed question. One writer, David Welsh, referred to the administrators of the program as "the assassination bureau." He makes the charge that the program, administered by the provincial reconnaissance units, was under the direct control of the CIA. [24] Army authorities disagree with these claims. They state that the program was under the direct supervision and control of the South Vietnamese government itself and that its purpose was to arrest and control those who preyed upon the peaceful population in aid of the enemy. While assassination is clearly an unlawful method of fighting an insurgent force, control of one's own countryside and the arrest of persons who seek to overthrow the established regime certainly are not. The validity of Professor Falk's proposition depends, then, on one's understanding of the facts. If assassination was a central part of the program, that would make it clearly unlawful; but if arrests and detention were its hallmarks, then it would appear a legitimate exercise of civil authority. Ambassador Komer persuasively contends in chapter 6 that the facts do not support the indictment advanced by Professor Falk.

Proposition Seven

Certain types of destruction of enemy-held countryside violated the laws of war.

Lumped into this category are defoliation, crop destruction, well poisoning and obliteration, and deforestation by bulldozing tactics. The Hague Regulations state that "it is especially forbidden . . . [t]o destroy or seize the enemy's property unless such destruction or seizure be imperatively demanded by the necessities of war." [25] The Army Field Manual interprets this provision to mean that the "measure of permissible devastation is found in the strict necessities of war" and cannot be sanctioned as an end in itself. The Manual also states that there must be "some reasonably close connection between the destruction of property and the overcoming of the enemy's army." Devastation for the purpose of intimidating the civilian population or deliberately damaging the territory permanently or for a long period cannot be justified on the ground of military necessity. Widespread crop destruction would seem to be unlawful under such principles. [26]

The Army Field Manual explains that such prohibitions do not outlaw the destruction of "crops intended solely for consumption by the armed forces (if that fact can be determined)." [27] But it is an ironic truism that the enemy's armies are the last to starve and that the general destruction of crops invariably seems to cause unnecessary suffering for the civilian population. Destruction of enemy stores and provisions specifically set aside for the enemy's use would not, however, be such a violation. General Sherman's march of devastation through the Georgia countryside and Sheridan's similar tactics in the Shenandoah during the American Civil War may have been viewed as lawful tactics at the time, but it is very questionable whether they could meet today's test of imperative military necessity.

Siege also denies supplies and food to the invaded locality, and the civilian populace within the invaded area inevitably suffers. However, a siege is combined with attacks. Its goal is to take the besieged location by assault without having to wait, as in a blockade, for the defenders to surrender by reason of famine. [28] In addition, the Geneva Civilians Convention places a duty on the combatant forces to "endeavor" to enter into "local agreements" permitting the evacuation of children, pregnant women, and the sick, wounded, aged, and infirm. However, there are too many prohibitions concerning devastation in the Hague Regulations and Geneva Conventions to have permitted any planned, widespread destruction of the food-producing areas of the Vietnamese countryside that would have been lawful.

Deliberate use of poison or poisoned weapons to contaminate food and water intended to be used by the enemy is a violation of international law. The British *Manual of Military Law* states that water "in wells, pumps, reservoirs . . . and the like from which the enemy may draw drinking water must not be poisoned or contaminated." It has been said that the contamination of sources of water by throwing human corpses and dead animals into them is "a practice confined to savage tribes." [29] Diversion of aqueducts and the drying up of springs and rivers are permitted by international law if their purpose is to deprive the enemy combatants of a source of supply. The doctrine of proportionality plays an important role in crop destruction and water diversion. Such tactics must be carefully considered to insure that the loss of life and damage to property are not out of proportion to the military advantage to be gained. [30]

On the other hand, defoliation by herbicides and deforestation by plowing have an obvious military purpose in jungle combat. These methods force the enemy into the open where he can be attacked. They prevent ambush and the effective use of concealed land mines. They forestall the concentration of men and materials from which to launch an extensive insurgent strike. They interdict the enemy's lines of communication and reduce his intelligence-gathering capability. However much of the Vietnamese countryside was destroyed by these tactics, there had to be an imperative military necessity for employing them.[31] But where that standard could be met in Vietnam, the legality of such defoliation and deforestation cannot, in my view, be denied.

The United States military has stated that the use of the Rome plows was generally limited to clearing jungle areas of the highlands. They were not, it is claimed, employed to raze the crop-producing deltas. The Army has explained that the Rome plows were used only to cut swaths two hundred yards wide on each side of their transportation and communication routes, a minimal part of the total area of South Vietnam. Such clearing prevented enemy ambush and the concealment of land mines. Rome plows were also used to clear base-camp areas. They were not used, according to Army spokesmen, to effect wholesale devastation of the countryside or to force starvation, through crop denial, on the civilian population.

As to the use of herbicides, until 1975 the United States did not ratify the Geneva Protocol of 1925, but repeatedly declared its adherence to it in armed conflict. The United States has, however, never considered the use of herbicides and other plant-destructive agents to violate the Protocol. Now the United States will on humanitarian—not legal—grounds forego their use except in limited circumstances.

Proposition Eight

The laws of war are apparently suspended in an internal conflict.

I would agree that the methods and tactics of the Vietnamese insurgent who used the civilian population as a buffer against assaults by the established government and who ignored the rights of combatants and civilians alike were in total disregard of the laws of war. But I would not agree that internal conflict causes all parties to ignore these laws, or that the United States military did so in Vietnam as a matter of official policy. War crimes were still prosecuted, battle damage was assessed with a view to the proportionality of the military objective to civilian casualities, and those planning military training tried to include the laws of war within the combatants' general education.

The fundamental principles of humanity and military necessity and the concomitant doctrine of proportionality inspired the development and dissemination by the United States military of the rules of engagement for Vietnam. These rules had as their main purpose the alleviation of human suffering and the sparing of the civilian populace to the degree possible. It would be fallacious and dangerous to suggest to combatant personnel that because of the nature of the conflict in Vietnam the laws of war had no applicability.

In this imperfect world, in which states still resort to the use of armed force, the laws of war evolve slowly—far more slowly than the technological advances of modern arms and armies. That the slow pace of evolution leads to needless suffering is apparent in the several reports of the United Nations Secretary-General and the ICRC on the respect for human rights in armed conflict. Whatever else Vietnam has shown, it has demonstrated that the laws of war have still not succeeded, and probably never will, in eliminating the horrors of armed conflict among nations.

There is far less to quarrel with in the chapter by Mr. Jordan. This is probably explained by the fact that I, like Mr. Jordan, viewed the Vietnamese conflict from within the government. There are, however, a few areas in his discussion that I believe require some qualifications.

First of all, I would not single out the individual infantryman as the person in the "hierarchy of battle" most vulnerable to violations of the laws of war. I agree that more foot soldiers are exposed to the stress of battle than other combatants. But why is a given foot soldier any more vulnerable than the tactical aircraft commander, the side-door gunner of a helicopter, or, for that matter, the strategic bomber pilot seeking a secondary target? The air crewman, no less than the infantryman, requires the same high motivation and indoctrination in the laws of war that any other combatant needs to avoid unnecessary suffering and to attend to humane treatment of the noncombatant.

Mr. Jordan remarks that the "prevailing restriction" on the use of firepower—including aerial bombing—against villages is contained in article 25 of the Hague Regulations of 1907. That article prohibits the bombardment "by whatever means" of undefended villages, towns, dwellings, or buildings. Unfortunately, the concept of the undefended place has little significance in air operations. As undefended places, the early twentieth-century drafters of that rule conceived of towns or villages within the combat zone that were capable of being occupied by the attacking forces without further resistance from any defenders. Obviously, the devastation of such a place would be militarily wasteful as well as inhumane.

The advent of the strategic bombing raid, however, brought armed conflict into the enemy's hinterland. It raised serious questions as to the application of the rule against attacking undefended towns or villages outside the area of ground fighting. There was an effort by some, particularly after World War II, to redefine and enlarge the concept of undefended places to cover deep air strikes. For example, an early draft of a proposed (but as yet unadopted) manual on the laws of air warfare for the United States Air Force states that defended places include fortified places, places in which military forces are stationed or passing, coal mines, power plants, water reservoirs, "and generally all of the enemy's economic resources (like oil), even though they are not actually defended."[32]Since the manual was not adopted, it does not reflect official Air Force policy. It does show the post-World War II attempts to stretch pre-World War I concepts to fit modern air-combat techniques.

However, belligerents have emphatically rejected the concept of the undefended place in air operations in favor of the concept of the military objective.[33] A satisfactory definition of the "military objective," like a definition of aggression, has not yet been framed. Nevertheless, this is the term used by belligerents in alleging violations (on the part of the enemy) or establishing compliance (by their own forces) with the laws of war.[34]

Mr. Jordan's description of the field commander who has to make his decisions on less than total and absolute information is very apt. However, I am uneasy with his reference to the tactical commander's desire to "show his superiors the kind of results that mark him as promotable material." His remark leaves the impression, undoubtedly unintended, that a zealous commander who displays an aggressive spirit in a combat situation for which there is only uncertain intelligence information stands a better chance of promotion than does a cautious one. I would correct this implication. It is in committing his troops to battle that the field commander with superior judgment tempers his decisions with the principles of humanity and proportionality. It may take more courage for the key commander to reduce the level of his attack than to "go all out." It may also be more humane, more proportional to the loss of life and human suffering involved, and equally (or even more) effective militarily. It is this kind of evaluation, decision, and execution of plans under stress that sets apart the exceptional field commander who deserves promotion.

With respect to the free-fire zones, which drew such attention in the Vietnamese conflict, I would add two comments to Mr. Jordan's discussion. First, these zones are in many ways parallel to the bombing of certain occupied areas during World War II. In that war it was the practice of the Allies to give advance warning to the inhabitants of occupied France and the Low Countries that an air strike was planned in a designated area and that they should leave the area beforehand. This is similar to the notification that was given for specified strike zones in Vietnam and was designed to isolate the enemy and his military resources within a given area.

Second, the designation of such zones in Vietnam, as in the case of the advance warning in World War II, did not relieve the striking force of its obligation to select only military objectives as targets. People, places, and property that are not legitimate objectives do not become such by remaining in a zone marked off and publicized as the likely target of an air strike or ground attack. Of course, the risk of incidental damage and injury to those who stay within such zones is admittedly much greater than it is to those outside of them. But an attack on such innocent persons, rather than or in addition to one on the legitimate target, would clearly be unlawful.[35]

My final observation concerns Mr. Jordan's characterization of the phrase "imperatively demanded by the necessities of war" as setting a higher restriction on the use of force than does bare military necessity.[36] I agree that the use of the term "imperative" seems redundant if all that was intended by the drafters of the various conventions concerning the laws of war was the basic principle of military necessity. The "imperative" qualification has shown up recently in writings of the ICRC and the Secretary-General and was used as a descriptive qualification in article 4 of the Hague Convention for the Protection of Cultural Property of 1954. However, the principle of military necessity is generally admitted to be subject to the fundamental principles of humanity and proportionality. These two principles limit the application of armed violence to only that kind or degree of force *actually necessary* for the purpose of the war.[37] How can there be a higher restraint on military operations?

It seems to me that the doctrine of military necessity, properly restrained by the laws of war, needs no further qualification. To attempt to interpose various gradations of this doctrine is to invite, rather than to prevent, further dilution of the mitigating principles of humanity and proportionality.

5 Comments

L. F. E. Goldie

Introduction

In the debate regarding the concealed fighter and his enemies, Professor Falk's position and mine diverge radically because our fundamental concerns are so different. Professor Falk's basic solicitude stems from his perception of injustices in the Vietnam War and from his belief that the National Liberation Front and the North Vietnamese Army represent the juster cause and the historically more significant force. This fits into his wider perception of "world-order transition," not only as an empirical fact, but also as an example of an obligation incumbent on policy makers, international lawyers, and publicists generally to implement that order's emergence. Accordingly, he transforms Mao Tse Tung's famous tactical simile of the guerrilla as "a fish swimming in the sea" of the general population into a privilege that international law should accord to concealed fighters.

My imperative scruples, in sharp contrast with Professor Falk's, are for the received values of *temperamenta belli*. Once violence is unleashed, humanitarian rules should protect all sides in a combat situation. [1] Once again, in our day, the value of humanitarian concern is fully disregarded. Despite their protests to the contrary, most of the advocates of new privileges for secret fighters are condoning additional savagery and inhumanity in guerrilla and secret warfare. Indeed, in contrast to their protestations, they are demanding greater scope for terrorism.

Professor Falk's four "general principles of limitation" fit within this wider modern trend. Unfortunately, they merit criticism on two grounds. First, they fail to reflect specific existing rules of the laws of war. Second, they do not offer desirable norms for the future regulation and tempering of guerrilla and secret warfare. On the contrary, they point in the opposite direction from present rules. Their underlying policies must inevitably promote savagery.

Professor Falk aptly perceives that the contemporary system of states is becoming a far more complex world order that includes, and needs, complex institutional networks of supranational, transnational, and international organizations and relations. And Professor Falk correctly assesses that the emergence of such a world order, together with other factors in contemporary international relations, such as the spread of nuclear weapons, carries with it the possibility that conventional interstate warfare may become increasingly obsolete.

A cost of this emerging world order, and of the increasing obsolescence of conventional interstate warfare, may be an inevitable increase, both in frequency and in intensity, of guerrilla and secret warfare and of urban terrorism. This could, in turn, be followed by a reciprocal intensification of counterinsurgency or other military police control. The development of more complex political and legal structures does not necessarily guarantee an economic, cultural, or psychological utopia. Indeed, the more complex life becomes, the more likely it is that an increasing number of human beings will respond negatively to the claims of society—by violence and terrorism. Various political rationalizations could, no doubt, justify the terrorists' actions and add an air of conviction to their hungry drives and their discontented responses to the imperatives and displacements imposed by civilization.

It seems to me, however, that these developments do not warrant drawing broad analogies from the Vietnam situation for assessment of insurgency in other parts of the world. A critique of counterinsurgency that focuses microscopically on Vietnam may tragically distort efforts to combat the terrorist tactics of urban guerrillas and secret fighters elsewhere. Thus, what may be true about the Viet Cong may not apply to the insurgents in Uruguay, Israel, or Ulster.

General Principles of Limitation

Certainly, the laws and usages of war, or, as they are now better named, "the international humanitarian law applicable in armed conflicts," are designed to ensure that violence be limited and not indiscriminate, that the use of weapons and tactics calculated to inflict unnecessary suffering be prohibited, that distinctions be made between noncombatants and fighters, and that the wanton use of excessive or inherently cruel force be, *eo ipse*, unjustifiable. It is, moreover, correct that the principle of humanity absolutely prohibits "methods, tactics, and weapons that are inherently cruel in their effects and violate minimal notions of humanity." I agree thus far with Professor Falk.

This does not mean, however, that I find his definitions of the other "general principles of limitation" scientifically or morally acceptable. Indeed, his other "general principles of limitation" create new privileges for secret fighters and thus inevitably create greater opportunities for insurgency terrorism and so promote savagery. In addition to serving these retrograde purposes, the other principles enunciated by Professor Falk have the further deleterious quality of appearing to be in terms of the existing rules that temper savagery, but they are, in effect, contradictory to them and destroy their validity and integrity. The three other principles tempering warfare that Professor Falk restates and redefines are: the principle of necessity, the principle of discrimination, and the principle of proportionality. A discussion of them as reformulated by Professor Falk follows.

The Principle of Necessity   /   As a corollary to his principle of necessity, Professor Falk treats the illegal and terrorist activities of guerrillas and secret fighters as politically necessary. This is a second, different, and mistaken use of the doctrine of necessity. Surprisingly, however, this second use, namely the justification of otherwise illegal acts, is no novelty. Long before Professor Falk cited it in support of secret fighters' repudiation of the principle of distinction and substituted for that received principle his own coinage of the principle of discrimination, German military theorists had given this connotation of military necessity a familiar currency under the now discredited maxim "Kriegsraison geht vor Kriegsmanier."[2]

In contrast with the above connotations of necessity, the military tribunal in the *Hostages* case gave the accepted definition of the Anglo-American doctrine of military necessity, under which

a belligerent, subject to the laws of war, [is permitted] to apply any amount and kind of force to compel the submission of the enemy with the least possible expenditure of time, life and money. . . . It [the doctrine of military necessity] permits the destruction of life of armed enemies and other persons whose destruction is incidentally unavoidable by the armed conflicts of the war; . . . but it does not permit the killing of innocent inhabitants for purposes of revenge or the satisfaction of a lust to kill. . . . It does not permit the wanton devastation of a district or the wilful infliction of suffering for the sake of suffering alone.[3]

This holding should be compared with the tribunal's view in the *High Command* case that the order by the defendants for a general devastation was not necessarily a violation of the Hague Regulations, and with its position in the *Hostages* case that the Hague Regulations were relevant to some aspects of German counterinsurgent activities (notably in Yugoslavia).

On the other hand, these holdings should not be viewed as a general condonance of the plea of necessity. The limited recognition of the plea in these cases was typical of the decisions in the war crimes trials. Nor should these cases be regarded as the reinstatement of the claim of the spurious "right of self-preservation," let alone "Kriegsraison."

Neither international law nor even the domestic laws of civilized communities recognize a claim that an individual is entitled to sacrifice others to ensure his own survival. Domestic legal systems universally condemn such a sacrifice as a crime. [4] It has also been condemned as a war crime in international law following both world wars, as, for example, in the *Peleus* case. [5] In that case the officers and crew of a German submarine were charged with war crimes for having shot survivors of a torpedoed British merchant ship who were still in the water. The court rejected the defense that British air and surface patrols were in the vicinity of the attack and could learn of the whereabouts of the German submarine if the *Peleus*'s crew were permitted to survive.

Military necessity never equals the doctrine "dead men tell no tales." The decision in the *Peleus* case illustrates the civilized man's appraisal that self-preservation is not a legal right, but an instinct. If its drive prevails over the rights of others, international law, as well as domestic law, should punish those who permitted it to cause a breach of their legal duties. [6]

Finally, as the preamble to the Hague Convention No. IV expressly states:

According to the views of the High Contracting Parties, these provisions, the wording of which has been inspired by the desire to diminish the evils of war as far as military requirements permit, are intended to serve as a general rule of conduct for belligerents in their mutual relations and in their relations with the inhabitants.

This means that military necessity was taken into account in the drafting of the Hague Regulations. It cannot be resorted to as an externally operating exculpatory ground in addition to those set forth in the Regulations themselves. Far from being a ground for exculpation that validates otherwise lawless acts, military necessity is a measuring standard of the legitimate force that may validly be brought to bear in combat. Both of Professor Falk's uses of the doctrine are equally divergent from this, its true meaning.

The Principle of Discrimination /   The generation of Che Guevara believes that it is the one that discovered guerrilla warfare. [7] Reflecting this stance, Professor Falk calls for a new morality and a new regime to regulate the struggle between concealed fighters and conventional troops. In this context Professor Falk's formulation and invocation of his own newly coined principle of discrimination turn the existing principle of distinction, from which it claims descent, on its head.

The principle recognized in international law, that of distinction, calls upon all combatants who are entitled to be protected by the Hague

Regulations and Geneva Conventions, in civil and in international strife, to: (a) be commanded by a person responsible for his subordinates; (b) wear a fixed and distinctive emblem recognizable at a distance; (c) carry their arms openly; and (d) conduct their operations in accordance with the laws and customs of war. [8] In contrast with this principle of distinction, Professor Falk's principle of discrimination permits secret fighters to retain their shield as civilians while it commands conventional forces not to use weapons that are unable to discriminate between those clandestine combatants and the noncombatant population among which those irregulars conceal themselves. His proposed principle thus imposes complete vulnerability—both legal and physical—on conventional forces exposed to the secret fighters while it accords to the latter the special privilege of concealment among civilians, which is contrary to article 1 of the Hague Regulations. This legal exposure of conventional soldiers that Professor Falk advocates reinforces and supports their physically unprotected situation as they face treachery and murder by guerrilla forces.

The foregoing humanitarian protest against the lethal implications of Professor Falk's principle of discrimination can be supported both by history and by principle. The requirement that irregular and guerrilla forces distinguish themselves from the noncombatant population, and that requirement's correlative that, if they so distinguish themselves and adhere to the laws of war, they are entitled to humane and honorable treatment are neither recent nor interventionist demands. Thus, for example, in the capitulation of Quebec in 1759 there was a stipulation that the inhabitants who had borne arms should not be molested on the ground that in North America the colonists of both France and Great Britain customarily served as militia. Likewise in 1810, following Massena's order that all Spanish and Portuguese guerrillas whom the French army captured should be shot as "paysans sans uniforme" and "assassins et . . . voleurs de grand chemin," Lord Wellington (as the Duke then was) protested. In his communication he pointed out that, although the guerrillas were not in uniform, they operated as a military corps, were commanded by officers, and obeyed the laws and usages of war. He also pointed out that, early in the French revolutionary wars, troops commanded by Massena himself had not always worn uniforms and that this had not detracted from the respect they had won as a fighting unit. [9]

The provision in the Hague Regulations requiring combatants to distinguish themselves in order to be entitled to the "rights . . . of war" was written largely as a result of the activities of the *francs tireurs* in

France during 1870-71. These were irregular forces who wore no uniforms and who acted independently without any officers against the German occupiers of their country. Their distinguishing marks were a blue blouse, a badge, and a cap. The Germans refused to recognize them as belligerents, in part because blue blouses were the common dress of French working people at that time and because the caps and badges were removable. In a number of cases murders and acts of terrorism were traced to individual *francs tireurs.* The Germans took indiscriminate and brutal reprisals against the civilian population of an area in which killings of occupation troops and sabotage of their installations and support services had occurred. This was done on the ground that there was no distinction between the *francs tireurs* and the non-combatant population. The ironic result of this situation in France is that the term *franc tireur,* which was intended to apply to civilians without uniforms who rise up to defend their homeland from enemy seizure in a so-called *levée en masse*, became, in the nineteenth century, the equivalent of today's "concealed fighter," and even "terrorist."

The requirement of distinction that the Hague Regulations placed upon irregular fighters and that the Geneva Conventions also reaffirmed stemmed from a desire, growing out of the Franco-Prussian War experience, to protect the civilian population as a whole from the brutality to which it came to be exposed when combatants could not be effectively separated from noncombatants. Thus, the principle of distinction is not premised on forcing the patriot out from his cover. It is based on the desire to deny his enemy any justification for waging war on those with whom the *franc tireur* or his contemporary successor would otherwise be confounded.

This principle embodies a call for a display of courageous humanitarianism by guerrillas and secret fighters before which many of them may falter. They may be unwilling to accept the consequence of distinguishing themselves from the civilian population. Any such faltering on their part should not provide them with a basis, as Professor Falk would argue, for special privileges to kill and special legal protections against the consequences of their cowardice. They should appreciate a basic distinction that Professor Falk would ignore. Those who fight in a *levée en masse* or with distinguishable and organized guerrilla forces and who obey the laws and usages of war have been recognized as being entitled to the protection of the laws of war. This is true even though they fight in small groups and at great distances from their support—as, indeed, is the case with such conventional soldiers as paratroopers and commandos.

Professor Falk's new claims do not relate to those irregulars who have long been recognized as having rights under the Hague Regulations and Geneva Conventions. His claims are for the protection of ter-·rorist groups and secret fighters whose targets include civilians, whose shield is treachery, and whose sword is perfidy. The experience of the German occupation following the Franco-Prussian War imprinted on the minds of statesmen of that time the essential distinction between civilians who fight according to the laws of war and those who engage in isolated acts of murder and sabotage. This distinction prevents the noncombatant population from being caught in the cross fire between secret fighters' acts of terror and counterinsurgent reprisals for those acts.

Principle of Proportionality   /   In their authoritative work, Professors McDougal and Feliciano defined the principle of proportionality as follows:

"Proportionality" which, like "necessity," is customarily established as a prerequisite for characterizing coercion as lawful defense, is sometimes described in terms of a required relation between the alleged initiating coercion and the supposed responding coercion: the (quantum of) responding coercion must, in rough approximation, be reasonably related or comparable to the (quantum of) initiating coercion. . . . Proportionality in coercion constitutes a requirement that responding coercion be limited in intensity and magnitude to what is reasonably necessary promptly to secure the permissible objectives of self-defense. [10]

Proportionality in this sense reflects, on the one hand, the moral obligation to reduce devastation and violence to what is necessary for the maintenance of permissible objectives and, on the other hand, the strategists' principle of economy—the prudential maxim calling upon a commander to risk no more force (in the form of men and matériel) than is necessary to ensure success.

The McDougal-Feliciano formulation also clarifies the Anglo-American concept of military necessity by emphasizing the close limits of its contours. They present the concept not as a permissible factor in war—an exception that permits the waiver of humanitarian rules—but as a limiting and measuring standard that restricts the degree of force that may be used. They clearly set forth its character as a rule of restraint. It is thus an essential ingredient of the rule of proportionality and, further, of the basic value of *temperamenta belli.*

Professor Falk's injunction upon the commanders of conventional forces to apply his concept of proportionality may be contrasted with the McDougal-Feliciano definition. He would have modern counterinsurgent armies apply only as much force as the guerrilla enemy can reasonably sustain in defending himself. Any greater use of force against the secret fighter would be disproportionate in Professor Falk's view.

This gross distortion of the principle of proportionality has no basis in logic or law. It is reminiscent of William Pitt the Elder's criticism of the Duke of Newcastle's government's conduct of the Seven Years War (known in the United States as the French and Indian War). In a speech that led to his assumption of the government and the consequential turning of the tide of history in that contest, Pitt said: "The Government is serving up British soldiers to the French like steaks in a chop house, in easily digested morsels."

It was bad military policy for the Duke of Newcastle to meet the French forces with piecemeal commitments of British troops. And it would have been equally unwise for United States forces to follow an analogous policy of self-restraint in fighting Vietnamese guerrillas. Nothing in international law, and certainly not in the principle of proportionality, would render unlawful the refusal to engage in such self-restraint. This is not to say, of course, that "everything goes" in counterinsurgent warfare. The point is rather that there is no obligation to forego force solely because the enemy guerrilla cannot cope with it.

The Nuremberg Ethos

Professor Falk's general attack on counterinsurgent methods and tactics as reflecting repressive or imperialist policies grossly oversimplifies contemporary politics, particularly the politics of violence. In Israel, for example, or in Bangladesh, counterinsurgent tactics provide protection to the many from the attacks of the few. Furthermore, Professor Falk does not take an evenhanded moral position. Nowhere does he criticize the terrorists for their intended brutalities, their indiscriminate executions, and their wholesale bombings of populated centers that counterinsurgent activities are intended to forestall or mitigate.

Professor Falk's claims on behalf of terrorism under the slogan of "the Nuremberg ethos" are a brutal parody of the significance of the post-World War II trial of the major war criminals before the Nuremberg IMT and the subsequent war crimes trials before the Allies' military tribunals at Nuremberg. Of course, he may be taking refuge in the claim that he is coining a previously undefined term that can be given whatever currency he intends it to carry, neither more nor less. He could be saying, in effect, that it is nobody's business to argue with him over his stipulated definition of the phrase he himself has uttered.

Nuremberg, however, is no phrase maker's private coin. It carries a value given to it by the sacrifices of World War II and a generation of mankind's approbative utterance. Hence, it is already in general currency. So, a publicist who includes it in a slogan of his own minting may not give it an entirely subjective impression, because he is still using it to obtain credit for his own disapprobations.

An invocation of Nuremberg may be a claim on the reader's sensibility rather than on his sense. To support his position, Professor Falk uses Nuremberg to invoke the forceful but nonrational and subjective appeal that it has for all of us. He does not go so far as to invoke Nuremberg to enlist support for his controversial "general principles of limitation." This is fortunate since these principles, in fact, would permit conduct diametrically opposed to the values and standards of conduct for which the postwar trials at Nuremberg stand.

Before and after the signing of the London Charter in 1945 and even during the Nuremberg trials, arguments were made that the proceedings against war criminals were not, and could not be, anything other than acts of revenge dressed up in hypocrisy. The more spectacularly legalistic the trials, the more they would be suspect as a "put-up job." Indeed, the war crimes trials of Nuremberg highlight the dilemmas of both positivistic and totalitarian jurisprudence. Reflecting the former set of doubts was the good-faith opinion of many British lawyers and publicists, including Lord Hankey. They felt that a quick military trial or the mere military shooting of the Nazi leaders might provide the most effective solution. Reflecting the latter is the totalitarian evaluation that all political trials should achieve their deterrent effect through humiliation and terror.

Dr. Judith Shklar provides an insight into the characterization of the Nuremberg trials, and into the wisdom of rejecting both the positivistic and totalitarian theses. Addressing herself to the impact of the trial of the major war criminals before the Nuremberg IMT, she writes:

> The Trial fulfilled an immediate function which is both the most ancient and the most compelling purpose of all criminal justice. It replaced private, uncontrolled vengeance with a measured process of fixing guilt in each case, and taking the power to punish out of the hands of those directly injured. This alone would suffice to show its enormous social value as an expression of legalistic politics on an occasion when it was most needed. [11]

The importance of the war crimes trials at Nuremberg was that legalism, as a political value, was vindicated. This fundamental value in the administration of retributive justice calls for the rational techniques of the lawyer, namely the adduction of factual and independently probative evidence connected by reasoning to state the case. Being based on the premises of rational discourse, legal politics are opposite to the politics of confrontation. In politics of this latter mode, dialectical persuasion is replaced by the eyeball-to-eyeball reiteration of slogans. The danger of such a phrase as "the Nuremberg ethos" is that it could become a slogan denying that the Nuremberg trials were the vindication of rationality and legalism after a bloodbath of sloganeering.

If Nuremberg may be said to have an ethos, it is that of reestablishing the rule of law in Europe after the lawlessness of the Nazi regime. It reestablished the rule of law by defining issues, by specifically framing charges within those defined legal categories, and then by proving those charges by logical chains of evidence connected by reasoned analysis. Professor Falk's evocation of Nuremberg is, by contrast, a denial of the politics of legalism and of its basic values. Professor Falk seeks to replace these values with those of nonrational intercourse, which justify violence, the politics of confrontation, and brutality in insurgency. Despite his protesting, Professor Falk's values inevitably also lead to counterinsurgency. This, I suggest, is to take up a position that necessarily scorns the rational approach to value judgments; it opposes the legal process by nonrational judgment. It was graphically illustrated in George Orwell's *1984*, in which he wrote: "Some Eurasian prisoners, guilty of war crimes, were to be hanged in the Park that evening, Winston remembered. This happened about once a month, and was a popular spectacle."[12]

Is There an Attempt to Legitimate Terrorism?

Both the theory and the practice of secret fighters call for the use of terror against the noncombatant population as an essential strategy. Carlos Marighela philosophically tells us:

> The terroristic act, apart from the apparent facility with which it can be carried out, is no different from other urban guerrilla acts and actions whose success depends on the planning and determination of the revolutionary organization. It is an action the urban guerrilla must execute with the greatest cold bloodedness, calmness, and decision. . . .
> Terrorism is an arm the revolutionary can never relinquish.[13]

This is the justification that some would find for the bombing by the

Viet Cong of women and children in Vietnamese cities and villages. The "terror arm," which acts in the name of revolutionary freedom, ends up destroying all—innocent civilians along with the supposed enemy.

Still another irony underlies Professor Falk's claims of unreciprocated privileges and immunities for the secret fighter's use of the arms and tactics of terror. The secret fighter and his enemies now resort to specific weapons, tactics, and modes of appeal to the noncombatant population. Their roles, and hence their weapons and tactics, are different. But terrorism or secret warfare is as formalized a form of violence as is conventional war. Only the means have changed. The logic of war—the need to overcome the contenders' will— remains the same. Professor Falk ignores this fundamental similarity in the purpose of terrorism and counterinsurgent warfare. He would, instead, have us believe that new and different legal standards should be applied to the secret fighter's conduct in "battle." In his search to create a legal "ought" out of the factual "is" of the secret fighter's concealment, Professor Falk is seeking to legitimate terrorism as a weapon.

I question whether this claim on behalf of terrorists is constructive to their need, their role, and their mission. I doubt that their claims serve the ends Professor Falk seeks, because I believe that he is confounding two kinds of nonconventional fighters—the secret fighter and the fighting citizen in a *levée en masse*. Professor Falk appears to be demanding not only that terrorists be treated as part of a *levée en masse*, but also that they, in fact, should become part of such a movement. This would clearly involve a basic change in the secret fighter's mode of warfare. It would destroy his two best weapons, namely, his secrecy and his camouflage among the noncombatant population, without providing him with the advantages of the necessary weight of numbers that a *levée en masse* would bring him. It is as if, watching a Roman gladiatorial combat between *retiarius* and *armiger*, Professor Falk were to identify with *retiarius* and ordain that he should discard his net and take up *armiger's* shield. Bereft of the strategies that only the net could provide, *retiarius* would be a dead man, killed by his sympathizers. Bereft of his shield, *armiger* would be exposed to the trident. In this event, butchery would replace combat.

The terrorist, both psychologically and tactically, requires the camouflage of a sympathetic noncombatant population. Could he retain the charisma that alone provides him with popular support and protection to his cause if he became the darling of a massed power rather than a victim of the law? If the secret fighter were to lose his charisma, he would become as naked as the Roman *retiarius* who discards his net for the illusion of finding a safer weapon than the one that gave him his name and his calling. This is a tragic aspect of combat and of life. Despite his dreams, no man can be himself and his own opposite.

Professor Falk uses "ecocide" as an operative word in his charges against the military destruction of the Indochina landscape, soil, and vegetation in the conduct of operations. Although the precise meaning that he gives to this term escapes me, I share his environmental concern. But, given the choice of saving the lives of combatants and noncombatants or of saving even important environmental assets, one should, even with possible difficulty, choose the former. For example, while the use of Rome plows gratuitously to deny peasants their fields should be condemned, their use to deny roadside jungle cover to snipers should be seen as a means of protecting lives. To condemn the latter use would only evidence a capricious disregard for the safety of one's fellow men.

When lives are in the scales, the weighing of environmental issues is both irrelevant and inhuman. Concern for the environment should be a threshold issue. It should be weightily added to the considerations against resort to the use of force in the first place, or against choosing a theater, a field of operations, or a battleground. Those empowered to make.these ultimate decisions should be fully aware of the consequences of their actions in terms of the people they expose to violence and danger, the stress they create on their own polity, and the environmental devastation that resort to force necessarily entails. But once the decision has been made to commit lives and possibly even the future of the polity to the hazards of conflict, environmental issues should not be weighed against the safety of men in combat. To advocate otherwise would indicate either a gross lack of sensitivity to the meaning of war or a macabre frivolity in the face of other men's avoidable deaths.

6   Comments

Robert W. Komer

Professor Falk knows, of course, a good deal about the international laws of war, and I do not. But I do know something about United States performance in Vietnam. I will direct these comments mostly to the latter subject, basing them largely on my experience in attempting to build up the "other war" effort in Vietnam from the White House and later as Chief Pacification Advisor in Vietnam.

Whatever one's views on the tragic and costly United States involvement in Vietnam, it is important to sort out what actually happened from the melange of impassioned criticism, superficial media accounts, and government briefs. There is also a difference between counterproductive or incompetent policies or practices, even when these had tragic side effects, and those that could be termed deliberately criminal by Professor Falk's standards. Ignorance of the law may be no excuse, but is lack of wisdom yet a crime? On the other hand, I agree with Professor Falk that it is important to assess whether individual atrocities reflected either general practice or calculated policy. We may still be too close to Vietnam to examine such issues objectively, but I share the feeling that we should try.

In my view, Professor Falk's theses (whatever their legal merit) fail on two key grounds—evidence and intent. As a nonlawyer, I assume that these are germane to whether crimes of any kind have been committed.

Throughout Professor Falk's discussion there are statements and phrases that indicate that to him there is a commonly accepted base of both evidence and intent supporting his analysis of the legal issues. Indeed, most writing about United States "war crimes" in Vietnam seems to proceed from this assumption. I believe it is wrong. And for these writers to cite as sources some impassioned, but neither objective nor researched, accounts is hardly enough to establish their case.

The present discussion will only suggest some errors in Professor Falk's surrealistic canvas of Vietnam. I agree that the war was horrible. Indeed, it was more horrible—and unnecessary—than it should have been. We did fight a high-technology war against a low-technology enemy, causing enormous collateral damage to the fabric of Vietnamese life. But was it really as Professor Falk describes?

Ratio of Civilian to Military Casualties

Is it broadly true that "the entire civilian population became the military enemy" of the counterinsurgent? Professor Falk's only quantitative evidence for this key allegation is that the United States and the government of South Vietnam inflicted "a high ratio of civilian to military casualties (estimated at 10 to 1)."

No figures available remotely suggest such a ratio. Allegations of a "million or more civilian casualties" in the entire war are sheer guesses unsupported by any evidence. But even such a wild guess falls far short of any 10-to-1 ratio. As of the Paris Agreements in January 1973, there had been since January 1961 some 350,000 United States military casualties, 683,000 Republic of South Vietnam casualties, and possibly 20,000 casualties from other Allied forces.[1] This adds up to 1,053,000 military casualties. These should be considered together with a perhaps inflated estimate of 924,000 enemy dead alone over the same period (there must have been wounded, too).[2] Even if many claimed as enemy casualties were really civilians, there were still more military than civilian casualties—assuming the unsubstantiated figure of a million as the civilian toll.

United States as Cause of Civilian Casualties

It is also too easy to conclude that most of the civilian casualties were caused by the United States (despite our enormous advantage in firepower). The only systematic analysis even partially addressed to this problem indicates that in the years 1968 to 1970 civilian casualties from mines and mortars (favored Viet Cong and North Vietnamese weapons) far exceeded those from shelling and bombing (favored United States and South Vietnamese weapons).[3] Regrettably, there is no evidence whatsoever as to what proportion of civilian casualties was caused by each military force that took part in the Vietnam War—but I doubt that most were caused by United States forces, especially if one uses a figure like one million, which goes back to 1960.

Civilians as Targets of Counterinsurgency

One contention central to Professor Falk's thesis is that the chief target of counterinsurgent forces is the civilian population and that it was attacked in an indiscriminate way. I agree that the civilian population of

Vietnam did suffer more heavily from South Vietnamese and United States tactics than was necessary or desirable. But it is quite another thing to stretch this to the length of calling it the main thrust of policy or the dominant practice. Too many fail to realize that Vietnam from 1964 to 1971 was more than just an insurgency—it was also a quasi-conventional war fought by organized regular forces on both sides. It should also be recalled that 40 percent of Vietnam's land area is essentially unpopulated and that 80 percent of the population lives on about 20 percent of the land.

From my experience in Vietnam I would judge that between 75 and 95 percent of United States offensive combat operations in the period 1965 to January 1973 were directed against enemy main-force units in relatively or totally unpopulated jungle areas. A major exception was the 1968 Tet offensive, when the enemy attacked us; we did not attack him. Regrettably, another major exception was the coastal strip of five provinces from Quang Nam to Phu Yen, where the enemy was heavily entrenched among the population. That is where a very large part of the civilian casualties and refugee flow occurred. It was also the locale of My Lai and of the atrocities alleged by Lieutenant Colonel Herbert. But there are thirty-nine other provinces too. All these matters can and should be objectively analyzed and the facts established before sweeping criminal accusations are made.

Were There Genocidal Patterns of Thought?

Closely related to the foregoing is the issue of whether "genocidal patterns of thought" were exhibited by United States military forces or their commanders in Vietnam. Careful reading of the *Pentagon Papers* fails to reveal any such intent. I know of no such pattern of intent among my colleagues during the period I was involved, whereas there is much evidence to the contrary. Nor should "kill ratios" be seen as more than a reflection of the attrition strategy pursued by the United States and South Vietnamese military because they could not think of a better strategy. Such statistics have been used in most twentieth-century wars, and were focused on excessively in Vietnam because the military saw so few other usable indicators. But to call them evidence of genocidal tendencies is grotesque.

Use of Air Power

Professor Falk appears to contend that United States air power was mainly used indiscriminately against the civilian population. Though the difficulty of distinguishing the enemy from civilians undoubtedly led to many civilian casualties, the chief use of air power was not in populated areas but rather against remote enemy base areas and infiltration routes. An article, obviously based on a Pentagon study, points out that in January 1969, which was during the peak year of the air war, only 5 percent of the civilian population lived within a kilometer of air strikes, and that by January 1971 only .9 percent was so located. [4] Such evidence is not conclusive, but at least it is an attempt to get at the evidence. Indeed, it reflects a deliberate strategy on the part of the United States and the government of South Vietnam to push the enemy back from the populated areas to where we could fight him without so much collateral destruction.

Genocide and Ecocide

Terms like "genocide" and "ecocide" are tossed around too freely without much attempt to assess the actual magnitudes involved. How many people realize that South Vietnam's population grew at a rate of over 3 percent per annum during the 1960s—to some 18,500,000 by 1971? Does this suggest genocide? South Vietnam's rice crop for 1970-71 was the largest in its history. Does this suggest ecocide, or food denial to civilians, for that matter? Far from attempting "to destroy the value of the countryside" by a piddling and ill-conceived effort to destroy tiny food plots in the remote jungle, the United States undertook massive efforts to increase crop production. Under Public Law 480 the United States brought in perhaps thirty to fifty times as much foodstuffs for civilians, as well as for soldiers, as we ever destroyed. The extent and effects of defoliation too have often been grossly overstated, but, fortunately, are now being studied in detail.

Forced Resettlement of Civilians

The old canard about "forced-draft urbanization" is refuted by both our policy and our practice. Despite several well-publicized cases of forced relocation, in fact it was the exception rather than the norm—even in the ill-fated Strategic Hamlet Program of the period 1961-63. I doubt that more than 2 or 3 percent of the total refugee flow in any given year of United States involvement was caused by forced relocation. Even this was frequently protested by the pacification advisors. The purpose of the United States military effort was to drive the insurgent forces from the populated areas, and the purpose of pacification was to bring protection to the rural population rather than to bring the people to the protection. In any case, urbanization has been a trend in most less-developed countries; it also tends to accelerate in wartime for well-known economic reasons. It should be possible to determine how atypical Vietnam has been in this respect.

Causes for Refugees

Estimating that "in Laos, Cambodia, and South Vietnam between one-fifth and one-third of the population became refugees at some point during hostilities" is playing games with facts. At one time or another during the seven years 1964-70, some five million people in South Vietnam either became refugees or suffered personal injury or property damage, according to the best available figures provided by Ambassador William Colby to the Senate Subcommittee to Investigate Problems Connected with Refugees and Escapees.[5] But horrendous as this cumulative total is, it should not be misstated as meaning that there are five million refugees today, or that there were anything like that number in any given year. One million were people whose homes were destroyed or damaged in the enemy Tet and May 1968 attacks on the cities. Some 1.6 million were casualty or damage claimants. There was also a great net reduction in refugees in the last years of the war.

Was Vietnam Just an Insurgency?

This issue is important to Professor Falk's argument. Certainly by 1964 there was superimposed upon the Viet Cong insurgency a quasi-conventional war fought by large, organized regular-army formations on both sides. Some would call it a civil war, since both North and South are Vietnamese, but this seems to beg the question. I would submit that many of the tragic side effects occurred because the United States and South Vietnamese military regarded themselves as fighting a full-scale war and helping to resist an invasion, rather than dealing with an insurgency. There is ample evidence, though only a small amount of it is cited here, that most of their military effort, including air strikes and artillery fire, was devoted to the main-force war—not to what is termed "counterinsurgency." Also, by 1968 there were many more North Vietnamese soldiers in the enemy main-force order of battle than there were Viet Cong troops. The proportion of North Vietnamese continued to grow. So the crucial issue of what kind of conflict Vietnam was cannot be resolved simply by pinning labels of convenience on it.

Direction of Vietnam War Policy

Who ran the war? Professor Falk argues explicitly that the direction of the "counterinsurgent" effort was "external," that "military policy making remained centered in Washington.

The theory that the government of South Vietnam and its military forces were mere "United States puppets" during the Vietnam War (as Hanoi kept saying) is hard to swallow for anyone who dealt with them. As any newspaper reader knows, the South Vietnamese government, under both President Diem and his successors, hardly operated under United States direction—either politically or militarily. Moreover, though it does not excuse any excesses the United States may have committed, my impression is that Vietnamese governments, both North and South, and their military forces were far less concerned over civilian casualties and damage than were the Americans (granted, however, that United States technology was more lethal).

Pacification

Though my viewpoint may be unduly parochial, I am also sorely troubled by the cavalier way in which pacification and "the other war" are so often lumped indiscriminately with the "big unit" conflict. We made many mistakes, and our effort was belated and inadequate. But the evidence is overwhelming that the South Vietnamese pacification effort that the United States supported was basically constructive in both intent and execution. As I have described elsewhere, this multi-faceted effort emphasized arming the people to protect themselves, restoring village autonomy, rural development through self-help, economic revival, refugee care, land reform, and the like. Could even Professor Falk see genocidal tendencies in the free distribution of 2,500,000 acres under the 1971 Vietnamese Land to the Tiller Law?

Ignoring all these positive aspects of pacification, the critics tend to focus only on the so-called Phoenix Program. It was not "administered" by the United States. Like all other facets of pacification, it was wholly administered by the government of South Vietnam. The United States advisory contribution was almost exclusively focused on collation and intelligence procedures. The United States financial contribution to the Phoenix Program was tiny—less than one-tenth of one percent of United States pacification-support expenditures alone. It was not a program of "capture and assassination of civilian suspects." It was a wartime attempt to put out of action the politico-administrative-military cadres who ran the enemy side of the war. Far more of these cadres rallied or were captured and imprisoned than were killed. And most of those killed were casualties of military operations in no sense targeted on individuals; the dead were only later identified as Viet Cong cadre. Excesses were committed, but the record will show that the chief critics of the Phoenix Program were the United States advisors themselves. This subject also merits detailed scrutiny of the evidence before harsh accusations are accepted.

In conclusion, if one accepts Professor Falk's allegations as tantamount to evidence, then he might have a case. But there is no proportionality between his allegations and the evidence he adduces to back them up. Here I suspect Professor Falk is himself a victim of the critical reporting on the war, so much of which consistently played up those themes that his criticism echoes without any sober assessment of how widespread such practices were in fact.

Nor, though I recognize that some may regard me as a tainted witness on this score, am I aware of any evidence that the United States deliberately made war on the Vietnamese people as a matter of calculated policy. Indeed, Professor Falk himself advances no credible evidence on this score. Those who advance such arguments have an obligation to do their homework better.

There is no gainsaying that the United States and the government of South Vietnam, as well as the Viet Cong and North Vietnam, fought a particularly brutal kind of war, largely inherent in both sides' style of warfare. Partly as a result, civilian death and damage did reach tragic proportions. And insofar as the United States and South Vietnam were concerned, it was not even a very effective counterinsurgent response. While costly in human and material terms, it was often counterproductive in its impact. But Vietnam was not by any means so different from other wars as Professor Falk seems to suggest. Comparative analysis of Vietnam's tragic civilian costs with those of other conflicts would illustrate this point.

7   In Reply

Richard A. Falk

Critics of my discussion in chapter 1 of this book raise a wide range of factual and doctrinal issues. Most of these cannot be considered in this brief response. Instead, I will deal with some principal lines of objection that go to the heart of the controversy about the role of international law in situations such as that created by the Vietnam War. Let me first summarize my critics' objections.

Professor Baxter and, to some extent, Professors Goldie and De-Saussure maintain that the four principles of restraint upon which I rely to assess the legal status of counterinsurgent methods and weaponry do not form part of customary international law. Hence they consider those principles to be, at most, personal proposals as to what the law should be in the future.

According to Professor Goldie, and to some extent Professor Baxter, such principles, if viewed as proposals, are undesirable because they tend to vindicate recourse to terror by insurgent forces and, in the main, to use Professor Goldie's language, "promote savagery."[1]

Ambassador Komer and others contend that a balanced assessment of the evidence suggests, contrary to my contentions, that policy makers planning the American involvement in Vietnam were generally sensitive to the restraints enumerated in these four principles.

Mr. Komer further argues that, in any event, no fair-minded consideration of the evidence, including the *Pentagon Papers,* demonstrates the sort of willful intent on the part of American policy makers that is a necessary basis for responsible charges that American leaders are hypothetically indictable for war crimes.

Professors Goldie and DeSaussure are of the mind that my analysis of counterinsurgent warfare in chapter 1 is overly conditioned by the special circumstance of the Vietnam experience and that it provides neither authoritative nor beneficial guidelines for internal armed conflict in general.

The Legal Status of the Four Principles

It is my basic contention that the four principles of necessity, discrimination, proportionality, and humanity provide authoritative guidelines for the identification of what is legal and what is not in the context of the Vietnam War. To some extent, these guidelines are embodied in the treaty law, especially in the Hague Regulations of 1907, and these provisions can be properly invoked. In the main, however, modern counterinsurgent warfare, fought in a remote tropical terrain, is quite unlike any form of belligerency that was in the minds of the Hague rule makers. But what was in their minds, and should be in ours, were basic limitations on what is permissible in the name of war or, in its more apt German expression, in the name of "Kriegsraison." These limitations were legacies of an evolving moral tradition with roots in ancient civilization, in Christian thought, and in the chivalric codes of the Middle Ages. Such limitations were part of the received legal (and moral) tradition that underlay deliberations of government representatives who at various times gathered to provide more specific legal guidelines in treaty form. These limitations also enjoy the status of *jus cogens* and exist beyond the realm of intergovernmental consent and independently of their embodiment in treaties. [2]

This contention is not without firm foundation in positive law materials. Indeed, it is dramatically stated in the famous preamble to the Fourth Hague Convention of 1907, which included the Hague Regulations as an annex:

> According to the views of the High Contracting Parties, these provisions, the wording of which has been inspired by the desire to diminish the evils of war, as far as military requirements permit, are intended to serve as a general rule of conduct for the belligerents in their mutual relations and in their relations with inhabitants.
> It has not, however, been found possible at present to concert Regulations covering all the circumstances which arise in practice;
> On the other hand, the High Contracting Parties clearly do not intend that unforeseen cases should, in the absence of a written undertaking, be left to the arbitrary judgment of military commanders.
> Until a more complete code of the laws of war has been issued, the High Contracting Parties deem it expedient to declare that, in cases not included in the Regulations adopted by them, *the inhabitants and the belligerents remain under the protection and the rule of the principles of the law of nations, as they result from the usages established among civilized peoples, from the laws of humanity, and from the dictates of the public conscience.* [3]

The four principles represent my attempt to give content to the italicized language in the so-called Martens clause just quoted. [4] Another writer might formulate these principles more adequately, but as matters now stand, I would put forth my formulations as useful guidelines for the identification of what is and what is not permissible in a counterinsurgent war.

In this regard, Professor Baxter's explications of treaty law are not responsive to my basic claim. I maintain that the most significant legal guidelines, and those with greatest operational relevance to armed internal conflict, derive from the content of customary international law, especially from that portion of customary international law that poses such minimal or underlying requirements of decency as to be embodied in *jus cogens*. For these reasons, I believe that Professor Baxter, despite his expert craftsmanship, impoverishes the law of war by relying excessively upon its embodiments in treaties. This overreliance is especially unfortunate in a Vietnam-type context in which, as he implicitly suggests, treaty law does not generally prohibit barbaric modes of warfare.

A farther-reaching contention underlying my appraisal of customary international law is that in this realm of conduct, governments are not competent to grant or withhold their consent to certain limitations on their discretion to use instruments of violence. The notion of *jus cogens* is useful for emphasizing, in juridical terms, that the basic content of the laws of war lies beyond the reach of positivistic jurisprudence and is truly nonnegotiable. That is, what is fundamental to the laws of war lies beyond the competence of governmental representatives to repudiate or revise. But it is not, of course, beyond their competence to embody these principles of law in some detailed and agreed-upon fashion. [5]

I would stress that this jurisprudential position is both a challenge to the position of other international lawyers and fundamental to my interpretation of the laws of war. Indeed, it is my position that if governments were to assemble at Geneva in 1976 and formulate a new set of guidelines for the laws of war that failed to embody (or actually contravened) the four principles, then their efforts, even if embodied in a treaty, would probably be void. [6] The four principles would continue to be authoritative, legally binding guidelines and their willful violation by high officials would still constitute an indictable offense against the law of nations.

I recognize that serious practical problems arise from these views. How can a beleaguered government be expected to forego tactics and weaponry that may be essential to its survival? Would not adherence to such principles by the incumbent side in civil-war situations tip the balance of forces decisively in favor of the insurgent? Should not applicability of these principles to a given conflict be conditional upon their acceptance by the insurgent side? Have not all civil-war situations involved comparable methods of counterinsurgent warfare to the extent that the insurgents were intermingled with the population? These difficulties are substantial and may place an unbearable strain on legal standards in certain settings. In view of these strains and the absence of sanctions to enforce the laws of war as I interpret them, perhaps it is necessary to admit that in certain civil-war settings there will be partial or total "no law" zones. This possibility is likely to exist at least until a legal regime satisfactory to both sets of belligerent interests can be created. But by acknowledging that this may occur, I do not, of course, mean to welcome or condone what I regard as lawless conduct in warfare.

In the interim, however, to the extent that legal criteria are relied upon, it seems reasonable to appraise the legality of government action by reference to the four principles formulated in chapter 1. If this view of international law inhibits governments from undertaking foreign counterinsurgent roles, then this seems like a valuable by-product. And if such guidelines draw into question the basic military and absolutist image of internal security, then this too seems desirable. Let us agree, finally, that agonizing choices will persist, and that we may even be prepared to consider a doctrine of civil disobedience put forward by governments confronted with certain forms of persistent terrorism. But let us also remember the wisdom of those who drafted the Magna Carta and understood that the greatest civilizing steps of human progress have involved shackling governmental authority rather than shackling the enemies of governments.

The Policy Implications of the Four Principles

To some extent, I have anticipated this set of issues in the preceding section by discussing the possible pressure to violate the four principles of limitation attributed to customary international law. But the main thrust of Professor Goldie's argument is more fundamental. He maintains that erecting legal inhibitions on the counterinsurgent side legitimizes the mission of the secret fighter and, as a result, encourages insurgents to resort to the most barbaric forms of political behavior. What is one to say of Arab liberation strategies of the Black September variety? Who would not grieve for the Israeli athletes killed in 1972 at the Olympic Village in Munich? Or for the random victims of bombings and acts of disruptive terror elsewhere?

It is not even possible to argue that such tactics never work. Palestinian liberation aims are probably better understood and more seriously entertained today than they would have been had there been no terrorist activity. It is also hardly reasonable to suppose that a target society should be rendered helpless in the face of terroristic assaults. But should the leaders of that target society be entitled to torture suspects for information or to inflict collective reprisals on villages that display sympathy for the insurgent cause? The answer to this question discloses a fundamental feature of my position—namely, that governments are by law prohibited under any circumstances from taking certain kinds of actions against insurgency. These prohibitions are absolute.

Such a position expresses, in summary form, six conclusions about the practical and moral sides of armed internal conflict: counterinsurgent capabilities to acquire arms and inflict violence are very great; these capabilities can be deployed in conformity with the four principles; these four principles also apply to insurgent military operations; adherence to these principles would not promote savagery by either the insurgent or the counterinsurgent, but would tend to mitigate it; violations of these principles by either side do not legally or morally vindicate violation by the other side; and, finally, the burden of responsibility for civilian casualties and property destruction in Vietnam and elsewhere, especially in the Third World, lies heavily with the counterinsurgent side because of its reliance on high-technology, capital-intensive superiority in firepower and its tenuous links to the domestic civilian population.

Correctly understood, then, the four principles provide authoritative legal guidelines for both sides in an internal war. As with any other general principle of law, there would be room for reasonable disagreement about lines of applicability—for example, would selective violence against certain government-appointed officials, such as village chiefs, prison officials, and tax collectors, represent legally permissible behavior by insurgent forces? On the other hand, I see no room for disagreement over the clear violation of the four principles by such insurgent conduct as firing rockets into the civilian neighborhoods of cities or machine guns into crowded airports. These actions would represent an illegal type of insurgent strategy entailing individual criminal responsibility for their perpetrators and planners.

We need a world conference of governments and other interested parties (including liberation and humanitarian groups) to reach a new positive-law consensus on conditions of mutuality for internal armed conflict. In the meantime, the four principles derived from customary international law set forth binding inhibitions on both sides that are not suspended in the event that one side allegedly violates them. Obviously, a rule of reason applies here, as elsewhere, in the laws of war, and exceptions permitting retortion could be imagined, but only for extraordinary circumstances.

Finally, it is my belief that the National Liberation Front in South Vietnam by and large conducted its belligerent operations in conformity with reasonable interpretations of the four principles, and that their opponents did not. Such a belief is obviously controversial and represents a complex process of appraisal, but one that seems to be supported by those whom I regard as the more impartial observers of the war. [7] It seems proper to place most of the blame for the savagery of the Vietnam War (and that in Laos and Cambodia) upon the tactics and weaponry of the counterinsurgents. These brutal methods of counterinsurgency were relied upon as a substitute for popular backing from the citizenry. [8] For all these reasons, Professor Goldie, in my view, shoots his learned arrows of indignation in the wrong direction, thereby, contrary to his intention, making law serve the brute rather than protect the innocent victim.

Weighing the Evidence, Assessing the Intent

Anyone who attempts to appraise the legal status of the various controversial patterns of warfare relied upon by the United States in Vietnam is up against some formidable obstacles. The main architects of the policies continue to occupy positions of public trust and eminence. They participate in the ongoing national debate as interested parties, invoking their participation in order to claim superior access to the facts. At the same time, these men often resist any scrutiny of the possibly self-serving character of their interpretations of these facts. Furthermore, the failure of the United States government to repudiate the American role in the Vietnam War increases the difficulty of getting relevant evidence into the public domain.

    For these reasons, there is no consensus as to what constitutes reliable, much less authoritative, evidence and interpretation. Participants in the debate distrust the sources relied upon by their antagonists and feel confronted by a polemic rather than by reasoned argument. These concerns underlie my response to Mr. Komer's critique of my contribution and provide an essential background for the comments that I will make.* Suffice it to say that I believe it relevant to an appraisal of Mr. Komer's credibility as an interpreter of American war policies to consider the possible biasing effects of his role as an official concerned with the successful prosecution of the war, especially during the period 1967-68, when he served as American pacification chief in Vietnam. [9]

    In my judgment Mr. Komer's comments consist mainly of unsup-

---

*The following reply to Mr. Komer is a revision of the version originally submitted to the editor for publication. Because of objections by Mr. Komer and the editor of this book to the original version, I have revised the original reply even though I do not agree with those objections.

ported, and I believe misleading, if not mistaken, assertions that derive most of their authority from his personal experience and knowledge. Mr. Komer makes little effort to examine or refute contrary evidence and interpretations contained in the publicly available literature, including official documentation and interpretations present in the *Pentagon Papers.* [10]

Mr. Komer makes three interlinked criticisms of chapter 1 in relation to the war crimes issue. He argues that:

— I have exaggerated the scope and nature of the atrocities committed by our side in the course of the war, and such exaggerations are important because they help create a false impression that United States conduct was particularly deserving of legal and moral condemnation.

— My interpretation of the counterinsurgent strategy of the United States and of the government of South Vietnam wrongly attributes a deliberate intention on the part of American policy makers to wage war against the civilian population of Vietnam.

— My presentation of the American role in Vietnam is unbalanced, as it fails to take into account efforts to improve the lot of Vietnamese peasants and civilians through technical assistance, land reform, and the like.

Mr. Komer contends that civilian casualties among the Vietnamese were smaller than I allege. He says that the tactics were generally devised to avoid, rather than cause, damage and disruption of civilian patterns of existence. Here we run smack into the center of the evidentiary question. I would not maintain that any set of numbers is authoritative, or even nearly so, at this point. But there is ample evidence that the magnitude and dimensions of the American war policies are as I described them in chapter 1. This position is in line with the general contours of agreement on civilian impact and counterinsurgent strategy made by such observers as Don Luce, Fred Branfman, Jonathan Schell, Frances Fitzgerald, David Halberstam, and those who reported to the Senate Subcommittee to Investigate Problems Connected with Refugees and Escapees (Senate Subcommittee on Refugees), of which Sen. Edward Kennedy is chairman. Furthermore, I regard the Phoenix Program, search-and-destroy missions, free-fire zones, and crop-destruction programs as illegal combat operations that inflicted inhuman damage upon the Vietnamese civilian population.

Perhaps Mr. Komer is correct when he suggests that American policy makers were so preoccupied by the effort to devise a winning strategy in an unprecedented war situation that presented them with many frustrations that they often overlooked other considerations. At the same time, such a view is beset by difficulties. Why did these policy makers persist in policies that were so clearly abusive of the Vietnamese civilian population? Why does the United States government continue to this day to provide support and guidance for the South Vietnamese government's prison system when it is known that the torture of political prisoners incarcerated in them is widespread? Why did the United States bomb so brutally despite the information available on its limited military effect? Why did the war makers persist in the use of napalm and antipersonnel weaponry against civilians when so many accounts of their effects were known? And why were no official surveys ever made of the civilian damage being caused by the military policies? No official has yet denied, for instance, Daniel Ellsberg's frequent claim that his recommendations at the highest levels of command and government to study civilian war damage were spurned and that the war makers had what he has called, in a reversal of security classification jargon, "a need not to know."

In his statistical summaries presented to the Senate Subcommittee on Refugees, Wells Klein offered a careful effort to appraise the impact of the war on the civilian population. As Mr. Klein put it in his testimony before the subcommittee:

Surely the most enduring legacy of the Vietnam War will be its cumulative impact on the lives and social structure of the people of South Vietnam. Over half of South Vietnam's estimated population of 18 million people have been forced to move as refugees, often many times over, since the war escalated in late 1964 and early 1965. As Table I indicates, the cumulative total of refugees since 1964-65 now stands at 10,369,-700. [11]

To this total one must add 1,390,000 civilian casualties, including an estimated 425,000 deaths (not to mention the civilians included under military casualties). These casualty estimates result from conservative methods of assessment.

To compare the American and the South Vietnamese government's contribution to these totals with that of the NLF and the North Vietnamese government, one can consult the exhaustive presentation of material by Noam Chomsky and Edward S. Herman in their monograph *Counterrevolutionary Violence: Bloodbaths in Fact and Propaganda*. Professors Chomsky's and Herman's account, which is filled with detailed information of United States and the South Vietnamese government's counterinsurgent and battlefield practices, should be contrasted with Mr. Komer's bland reassurances about "pacification" and discriminate warfare.

Mr. Komer makes the specific assertion that the increase in the South Vietnamese population during the war virtually by itself refutes the charge of genocide. But genocide is a technical concept that is embodied in a widely ratified treaty and is defined more broadly than an attempt to kill off a given population. The definition contained in article 2 of the Genocide Convention is clear about this: [12]

In the present Convention, genocide means any of the following acts committed with intent to destroy, in whole or in part, a national, ethnical, racial or religious group, as such:
  (a) Killing members of the group;
  (b) Causing serious bodily or mental harm to members of the group;
  (c) Deliberately inflicting on the group conditions of life calculated to bring about its physical destruction in whole or in part;
  (d) Imposing measures intended to prevent births within the group;
  (e) Forcibly transferring children of the group to another group.

The point is that the magnitude and intentionality of the harm inflicted on the Vietnamese by the American war policies make it clearly plausible to consider charges of genocide in relation to parts b and c of the definition.

On the other issues, I will have to refer readers back to the arguments and citations in chapter 1. There are some fundamental questions left over—Was the war directed by the American (rather than Vietnamese) policy makers? Do the patterns of high-technology counterinsurgency provide sufficient evidence of a deliberate intention on the part of policy makers to support an inference of indiscriminate warfare? Would such an inference provide the basis for indictment of responsible individuals if a Nuremberg-type procedure were available in the post-Vietnam context? I am convinced that an objective assessment of these questions would produce affirmative responses, but the supporting arguments cannot be presented here. [13]

Reasonable Basis for Alleging Criminal Responsibility

In his comments, Mr. Komer acknowledges that the American role in Vietnam had "tragic side effects," was "brutal," and "more horrible . . . than it should have been." But he distinguishes sharply between "counterproductive or incompetent policies or practices" and "those that could be termed deliberately criminal." He sums up his position on these issues with this question—"Ignorance of the law may be no excuse, but is lack of wisdom yet a crime?"

I find such a response to involve a gigantic begging of the question. Food-denial programs, free-fire zones, massive use of antipersonnel weaponry, forcible removal of civilians, destruction of villages, B-52 pattern bombing of populated areas, and the Phoenix Program of civilian assassinations were all deliberate programs carried out over time under the direction of the top United States military and civilian leaders. Whatever else, these policies were not accidental deviations from mainstream combat practices. Whether they were imcompetent in execution or counterproductive in effect is completely beside the legal point. Whether the policy makers were willfully violating legal norms with which they were not familiar is also beside the point if they should have known of their existence. Finally, the sincerity of the war makers as to their righteous purposes is no more germane to the question of their legal responsibility than was the sincerity of Egil Krogh's belief that in ordering the burglary of Ellsberg's psychiatrist he was promoting national security (a point, to his credit, Krogh has now conceded). [14]

We should take particular note of the moral ease with which decent and sincere men can do horrible things in a distant war fought against a foreign race. One purpose of an international criminal law is to convert hindsight into foresight. Many of us on the side lines had no difficulty perceiving its horror, by any normative standards, while it was transpiring. And to put the Vietnamese fighting for the political destiny of their country on the same moral and legal plane as Americans who came as outsiders from thousands of miles away is to persist in missing the main point about why the United States efforts were not only tragic and counterproductive, but particularly evil and illegal, a point not lost on most of the rest of the world.

Finally, all I would argue is that American policy makers are indictable if Nuremberg tests of criminal responsibility are used. I would, of course, not prejudge their defense or deny their presumption of innocence. Since such indictments and trials will not come to pass, we shall never have to face the question as to whether a prosecutorial approach would have been beneficial. And there will be no test of whether the Nuremberg experiment would be constructive if applied to American war makers, as most of our population had thought it was when applied to German and Japanese war makers after World War II.

Vietnam As a Special Case?

Some critics of my analysis in chapter 1 argued that general legal con-
clusions were being drawn from exceptional circumstances. Would one
favor inhibiting the counterinsurgent efforts of Israel and Northern
Ireland in the same way as one favored inhibiting the United States in
Vietnam or as one would favor such restraints throughout the Third
World?

I believe that the four principles of limitation are of general application and brook no exception as to time or place. It is true that such a
position puts me in fundamental legal, moral, and political opposition
with Professor DeSaussure, who says that "a government whose very existence is endangered by armed attack from within or without must have
the right to the full use of its superior forces and capability to defend itself."[15] Such a view of statist logic, admittedly very prevalent, is utterly
nihilistic of any form of normative restraint. While it does not advocate
illegal conduct, it provides a basis for those with less respect for legal restraints than Professor DeSaussure has to sweep them aside with a
peremptory governmental claim of necessity, an indulgence that certainly would never be accorded to enemies of governments.

In the wrong hands, the argument of necessity leads right to the
torture chamber.[16] Who could deny that torture is an effective device
for a ruler who seeks information about enemies or hopes to terrorize
actual and potential opposition? And who could deny that an unpopular government faced by enemies from within (or without) might possess
no alternative means to assure its survival? But the point of legal restraint is not to side with the punches thrown by nervous or pernicious
governments. Rather it is to formulate in periods of calm a set of normative restraints that are binding under specified circumstances and cannot be discarded for the sake of governmental convenience, or even
necessity.

And this is not because, as Professor DeSaussure puts it, I would
"reduce internal armed conflict to a game of sport in which the sides
must be equal in size and capability."[17] On the contrary, internal armed
conflict is such grim business and governments are so deft at excusing or
hiding their own barbarities that it is essential to place certain rules of
restraint on both sides and to find a way to promote their implementation. A detailed paper could have been—and should be—written on
the application of the four principles to the insurgent side in civil strife.
But that is another topic that this book, because it focuses principally on

American legal responsibility for controversial war policies in Vietnam, quite properly omits.

In conclusion, three elements of my position should be emphasized: First, the four principles apply in all situations of counterinsurgency; second, those principles are also binding upon the insurgent side; and, finally, violations on one side do not vindicate those on the other side.

As a matter of description and prescription, I interpret this fundamental content of the international law of war as absolute and immutable. It embodies that elementary humanism that serves to differentiate organized social intercourse, even if it degenerates into warfare, from bestiality and barbarism.

8   In Reply

Robert W. Komer

It is, of course, clear to any reader who has gotten this far that Professor Falk's rebuttal in chapter 7 does not really respond to my dozen or so major substantive comments in chapter 6. Instead he again evades the issues of evidence and intent in favor of an attempt to impeach the witness.

For example, Professor Falk has questioned my "credibility as an interpreter of American war policies." Of course, I had already pointed out (see pp. 99-100) that whatever I wrote would inevitably be regarded by some as self-serving. But the reader is entitled to know that I was not, as Professor Falk implies, a "main architect" of the policies he deplores, that I do not still occupy a position "of public trust and eminence," and that I do not "resist any scrutiny of the possible self-serving character" of my views.* On the contrary, my consistent record is one that welcomes free discussion, frank disclosure, and accessibility (as the media can attest), both when I was involved with Vietnam (1966-68) and since that time.

Nor can Professor Falk wave aside my critique by alleging that it derives most of its authority from my "personal experience and knowledge." Naturally, this knowledge is based on actual operational documents, reporting, and analysis, particularly that of a comprehensive network of civilian and military advisers in every part of South Vietnam. When Professor Falk finds that the resulting official figures serve his purpose, he uses them himself; but when they do not, he naturally finds them suspect.

Moreover, why shouldn't I have some knowledge of evidence and intent? After all, I was there—in a senior advisory capacity to the pacification effort by the government of South Vietnam. And the overwhelming weight of evidence is that this program was designed to help the population of South Vietnam, not to conduct war against it, as Professor Falk alleges. Even so, all I ask is that such issues be examined on their merits and not in what I regard as thinly veiled ad hominem attacks. [1]

*Suffice it to say that I am more than willing, as my contributions to this book demonstrate, to discuss *on the merits* my conduct during and my views concerning the Vietnam War.

If my critique of Professor Falk's chapter made "little effort to examine or refute contrary evidence and interpretations contained in the publicly available literature," it was because I found very little in the literature he cited that could properly be called evidence to sustain his interpretations. For example, my own careful reading of the entire *Pentagon Papers* reveals no support in them for his main contentions. If there were, I am sure he would cite it copiously.

In sum, whether or not I am a biased witness, Professor Falk has still advanced no credible evidence that the United States deliberately made war on the Vietnamese people as a matter of intentional policy. And he has sedulously ignored all the evidence to the contrary, including that stemming from United States pacification support and economic assistance. For example, the evidence shows that United States bombing and ground operations were overwhelmingly concentrated on seeking out organized Viet Cong and North Vietnamese forces in their remote base areas, not in populated areas (of course, major exceptions occurred during Tet 1968 or Easter 1972, when the other side attacked).

Nor am I aware of any credible evidence of "B-52 pattern bombing of populated areas" in South Vietnam (every effort was made to avoid this) or of "massive" use of napalm and antipersonnel weaponry against civilians. Lastly, to call the government of South Vietnam's Phung Hoang or Phoenix effort to dismantle the other side's politico-military control apparatus a "[p]rogram of civilian assassinations" is to parrot a gross misconception arising almost entirely from the inclusion of battlefield identifications in the figures on Viet Cong cadres killed. [2] There has been too much impassioned mislabeling of this sort, without credible analysis or evidence to back it up. This was the real point of my commentary on Professor Falk's paper, and it applies as well to many other critics whom he cites.

Part One

METHODS AND MEANS OF WARFARE

Air Warfare– Christmas 1972

9   *Hamilton DeSaussure and Robert Glasser*

*. . . North Vietnam . . . had no real warmaking industrial base
and hence none which could be destroyed by bombing. . . .*
*. . . There is no basis to believe that any bombing campaign, short
of one that had population as its target, would itself force Ho Chi Minh's
regime into submission.*

ROBERT S. MC NAMARA
Secretary of Defense
Washington, D.C.
25 August 1967[1]

Prior to World War I, nations conducted warfare almost exclusively on
land and sea. In the short time since that war, the conduct of warfare in
a third dimension—the air—has assumed tremendous proportions. Because air warfare will continue to increase in intensity and importance
in conflicts, its regulation is paramount. Although one cannot predict
the degree of its intensity in future conflicts, one can look back to the
dramatic consequences of the use of air power in the Vietnam War.

The eleven-day air campaign conducted by the United States in the
Hanoi-Haiphong area of North Vietnam in December 1972 culminated
the use of United States strategic air power in that conflict. That experience demonstrated the need to impose specific restraints on any
future application of this country's air power. Such restraints can be
neither self-imposed nor derived by simple analogy from the laws of
land-and-sea warfare.

According to Gen. John C. Meyer, Commander in Chief of the
Strategic Air Command, United States Air Force, the so-called Christmas bombings over Hanoi and its environs began on 18 December 1972
and terminated on 30 December 1972.[2] French and Swedish press reports of the initial bombing said that the B-52s, some flying at low
altitudes, launched their first attack in nine waves throughout the night
of December 18-19.[3] The assigned mission of the Christmas bombings
was the deliberate destruction of military targets in North Vietnam.[4] In
the eleven-day period, in over seven hundred sorties, B-52 bombers
dropped their arsenal of devastation over the political and industrial
heart of North Vietnam—Hanoi and the Red River Delta.[5]

The roots of the Christmas bombings go back to an earlier stage in the Vietnam War. The United States Air Force began its declared bombing of North Vietnam in February 1965. [6] Adm. Ulysses S. Grant Sharp, Commander in Chief of Pacific Forces, later outlined in his year-end report for 1967 three objectives that the air campaign was seeking to achieve: disruption of the flow of external assistance into North Vietnam, curtailment of the flow of supplies from North Vietnam into Laos and South Vietnam, and destruction "in depth" of North Vietnamese resources that contributed to the support of the war. [7]

Early in the air campaign the Joint Chiefs of Staff appeared to favor an immediate and overwhelming use of large-scale strategic bombing to eliminate North Vietnam's infiltration of South Vietnam. [8] However, this policy was not adopted because of considerable apprehension that it might trigger large-scale Chinese intervention. It was also feared that such a policy, if declared publicly, would arouse increasing domestic and international indignation against the United States government. In all likelihood this anticipated protest would have been exacerbated by the use of the overwhelmingly superior air power of the United States upon a small, underdeveloped nation like North Vietnam.

The policy finally adopted by Washington was the gradual application of United States air power to selected targets in North Vietnam. The Secretary of Defense and the White House had to approve all designated targets in the North for United States aircraft. [9] Initially, these targets were selected to prevent the flow of personnel and matériel into the South. Transportation routes and storage areas for resupply were the areas principally targeted. [10] By the beginning of the summer of 1966, the main air objectives became the North Vietnamese storage facilities, principally those for oil. [11] By the end of that summer, 70 percent of the oil storage capacity of North Vietnam had been destroyed. [12]

Early in the fall of 1966, Admiral Sharp was optimistic about the situation. He believed that the destruction of these facilities would lead to a negotiated truce settlement with the North Vietnamese. The Admiral believed this would truly extinguish any insurgency movement in the South. [13] Unfortunately, time has proven his optimism to have been ill founded.

During much of the bombing of the North, bomber crews received instructions to avoid populated areas. In order to maximize high-precision delivery of their bomb loads, they were told to use visual identification. As the bombing campaigns progressed, more sophisticated and quite accurate means were introduced into the B-52 bombing-guidance system, not the least of which included television identification mechanisms. These were intended to permit pinpointing of military supply targets.

The destruction of 70 percent of the oil storage facilities of North Vietnam failed to have either of the desired effects predicted by Admiral Sharp, and so additional targets were designated, even though Gen. Earl Wheeler, then Chairman of the Joint Chiefs of Staff, said prior to this expansion that the "bombing campaign is reaching the point where we will have struck all worthwhile fixed targets except the ports." [14] In the period after 8 April 1967, President Johnson approved the bombing in the Hanoi-Haiphong vicinity of a power transformer, a cement plant, and an airfield, along with additional ammunition-and-oil storage facilities. [15] Secretary of Defense Robert McNamara reported in May 1967, following destruction of these targets, that "excluding the port areas, no major military targets remain to be struck in the North." [16] He added that "[a]ll that remains are minor targets, restrikes of certain major targets, and armed reconnaissance of the lines of communication . . . —and under new principles, mining the harbors, bombing dikes and locks, and invading North Vietnam with land armies."

At the same time, the Secretary of Defense noted that there was increasing United States and worldwide concern over the picture of massive air power being used by the "world's greatest superpower . . . to pound a tiny backward nation into submission on an issue whose merits are hotly disputed." [17] Secretary McNamara recommended that bombing should revert to its initial objectives and concentrate on interdiction of trails in the North through which North Vietnamese men and supplies passed on their way to Viet Cong forces in the South.

In April 1968 President Johnson announced his intention not to seek reelection and ordered a bombing halt over part of North Vietnam. One of the obvious reasons for this partial suspension of air attacks would seem to be that, as General Wheeler's statement and Secretary McNamara's report indicate, there remained few significant military targets susceptible to destruction by air operations over North Vietnam.

The air campaign over the North was officially halted in November 1968. [18] However, raids continued under the official guise of "protective reaction," or anticipatory defense, in military jargon. As broadly construed by the then Commander of the Seventh Air Force, Gen. John D. Lavelle, this strategy permitted attacks against missile and antiaircraft installations or against enemy troops whenever a United States aircraft was fired upon. Further attacks were authorized when North Vietnamese electronic fixes tracked American aircraft. Such fixes had been employed long before this policy was adopted, and their use continued despite it. [19] As a result, there was a necessity for continuous protective-reaction attacks, which were carried out by lighter aircraft (medium fighter bombers) rather than heavy bombers (B-52s). More-over, there was no interruption in bombing to interdict the flow of troops and supplies to the South even under the protective-reaction policy. [20]

According to information gathered by the Center for International Studies at Cornell University, "the bombing [prior to the 1968 suspension] had not discernibly weakened the determination of the North Vietnamese leaders to continue to direct and support the insurgency in the South."[21] But the principal purpose of the bombing had been the elimination of support of the insurgency in the South. From a military standpoint, the bombings had apparently failed to achieve their objective. In these circumstances, their suspension seemed advisable, for their continuation could only have been in pursuit of a new policy—namely, bombing predominantly and specifically for the purpose of weakening the political determination, rather than the military strength, of the North Vietnamese.

North Vietnam as a Bombing Target

A brief review of the character of the North Vietnamese heartland is necessary to appreciate fully the importance of the United States policy of conducting air attacks there for essentially political objectives. Hanoi, the capital of North Vietnam, lies in the Tonkin area of North Vietnam, at the apex of the Red River Delta. Over nine million people live on the Red River Delta, where population density exceeds fifteen hundred persons per square mile. In the Delta, over fifteen hundred miles of dikes prevent flood damage and improve irrigation. The people of the Delta region live in closely spaced small villages, on levees (man-made embankments), or on old sand dunes. This life style is partly for protection from floods and partly for security from the dangers inherent in nearly thirty-five years of intermittent fighting with the Japanese, the French, and, finally, the Americans.

The two major cities of the Delta region are the capital, Hanoi, and the harbor city, Haiphong. Hanoi protects its 700,000 residents with giant dikes, for during the summer period the Red River may rise over twenty-five feet above the city. [22] Throughout the French occupation, Hanoi was divided into three main sections. In the administrative section were located may of the governmental, educational, and social institutions. A second section embraced the thickly populated tenement district. The third section was largely residential. Hanoi is the most important industrial and communication center in North Vietnam.

Estimates indicate that one-third of North Vietnamese industry operated in the Hanoi area prior to the major relocations caused by United States attacks from 1965 to 1968 and again in 1972. There is little doubt that the air campaign over North Vietnam between 1965 and 1968 caused significant numbers, estimated at several hundred thousand, of students, technicians, and government personnel to evacuate Hanoi. [23] But even with this evacuation, Hanoi remained an important political, industrial, and cultural center for the North Vietnamese people.

Objectives of Aerial Attacks

To return specifically to the policies behind aerial attacks, there are essentially five types of objects against which air bombardment might be employed in armed conflict. [24] First, there are those objects that comprise the enemy's direct and immediate military strength: its armed forces, its military equipment and facilities, and its military supply and storage areas. Second are those objects labeled as the "quasi-combatant workforce and resources." These include transportation facilities (carrying both civilian and military supplies and personnel), lines of communication, industrial plants serving the enemy's civilian and military needs, together with any natural resources capable of refurbishing soldiers as well as civilians.

Third, there are objects of purely economic character that support the military strength of the enemy only indirectly. These objects are factories producing the necessities solely for civilian life, such as food-processing plants, civilian transportation and communication systems, and urban utilities not connected with the war effort but generally supporting the civilian population. Fourth are the psychological objectives, which are, broadly speaking, those whose destruction would primarily weaken the will, rather than reduce the military strength, of the enemy. "Terror bombing," or "morale bombing," which is intended to have a coercive political effect on the adversary, would be within this category.

The fifth type of object that might be bombed is a target chosen to carry out reprisals against the enemy. Under international law, reprisal is permissible against otherwise unauthorized objects if the enemy has previously engaged in unlawful military activities. Clearly, reprisal raids could have opened the door to consistent and unjustifiable attack upon civilian objects in North Vietnam.[25] It is admirable that the United States Air Force never sought to justify on this tenuous and debatable ground the use of an estimated seven million tons of bombs over Indochina.[26] This was over three times the total tonnage dropped during World War II and ten times that dropped during the Korean War.[27]

International Legal Restraints on Air Warfare

Dr. J. M. Spaight, one of the foremost legal experts on the rules of air warfare, concludes that international law defines limits within which air power may be legitimately used for exerting psychological pressure upon an enemy.[28] Dr. Spaight states that there is, at present, no law or custom authorizing bombardment for a specifically moral or political purpose and emphasizes that its use for this end has been repeatedly condemned. He acknowledges that bombing of military objectives inevitably harms noncombatants incidentally and thereby necessarily affects morale. "But," he explains, "deliberately to reckon with that moral effect, to take care that one's aircraft so attack military targets, or attack only military targets so situated that psychological pressure is also exerted, and, in fact, to misapply the doctrine of the military objective to a purpose never contemplated in the rules, would unquestionably be a breach of international law."[29]

Several international jurists would qualify this view of international law to permit the inclusion of the quasi-combatant work force as a permissible target.[30] Professor Julius Stone explains that acceptance of this position permits reconciliation of the international legal regime for air warfare with the hard fact that belligerents generally regard the morale of the enemy's quasi-combatant work force as a distinct military objective. At the same time, this approach serves to distinguish bombing of the quasi-combatant work force from more generalized morale bombing against other civilians who are, in law, immune from such attacks.

This theory, however, is regrettably not applicable to guerrilla warfare. It is well recognized that in guerrilla warfare the combatant and the civilian become indistinguishable. Thus, the addition of another category of lawful object, the quasi-combatant, only further confuses the distinction between legitimate and unlawful targets.

Morale Bombing during World War II

Indeed, the theory becomes difficult to apply even in conventional warfare. During World War II, there were great problems in maintaining any distinction between the enemy's quasi-combatant work force and the "genuine civilians." In the case of the area attacks over Germany and Tokyo, it became impossible to differentiate. Morale bombing (or terror bombing, depending upon whether you were in the air or on the ground) brought profound changes to strategic bombing. It generated deep concern on the part of humanitarian forces, such as the International Committee of the Red Cross.[31] Nearly one-quarter of the total bomb tonnage dropped in the European theater (over six hundred thousand tons) was devoted to urban area raids and was intended to spread destruction over a given sector rather than to strike precise military installations, facilities, or troops.[32] Many of the bombings were made at night and were intended primarily to destroy morale, particularly that of industrial workers.[33] The same was true in the Pacific theater. Urban-area incendiary attacks carried out over Japanese cities had for their "predominant purpose . . . to secure the heaviest possible moral and shock effect by widespread attack upon the Japanese population."[34]

   During World War II, the supposed reliance on precision bombing of military targets was, at best, ignored in the bombing raids that occurred over Dresden on 14 and 15 February 1945 and over Tokyo in March 1945. In both cases the objective seems to have been the total destruction of the cities themselves. However, surprising as it may seem in retrospect, "[m]ilitary experts today admit that the results of Allied bombing raids on Germany fell very much short of expectations, that they did not become effective until they concentrated on sources of energy and transport, and that the brutality of that form of warfare, far from shattering the enemy's morale, may have even encouraged a spirit of resistance which prolonged the war."[35]

   As World War II escalated in intensity and involvement, the scope of permissible military objectives clearly broadened in the absence of any internationally accepted limitation on lawful targets. According to historians of the United States Air Force, the "night raids [on Dresden] by the R.A.F. Bomber Command were intended to devastate the city area itself . . . and disrupt normal civilian life upon which the largest communications activities and the manufacturing enterprises of the city depended."[36] This review of the two-day Dresden air attacks and the later United States Strategic Bombing Survey indicated that "area raids" of German cities had four principal characteristics: "they were made generally at night; they were directed against large cities; they were designed to spread destruction over a large area rather than to knock out any specific factory or installation; and they were intended primarily to destroy morale, particularly that of industrial workers."[37] Whether the morale of industrial workers or any other group was affected by these attacks is difficult to calculate. But, as a result of the Dresden raids, it is reasonably estimated that twenty-five thousand people were killed and thirty-eight thousand injured.[38]

British and American views of aerial bombardment during World War II sharply diverged, and these differences are significant in considering the Christmas bombings in Vietnam. In World War II, the British concentrated upon "mass air attacks of industrial areas at night to break down morale"; the United States, however, believed (at least in the European theater) in the systematic destruction of selected vital elements of the German military and industrial machine through precision bombing in daylight.[39] "All proposals frankly aimed at breaking the morale of the German people met the consistent opposition of General Spaatz, Commander of the Eighth Air Force, who repeatedly raised the moral issue involved."[40] In addition, General Spaatz was strongly supported by Army Air Force headquarters in Washington on the ground that such operations were contrary to Air Force policy and national ideals.[41]

There are undoubtedly multiple distinctions between World War II, an armed conflict involving most of the great industrialized nations locked in unconditional war, and the type of limited conflict in which the United States engaged in Vietnam. However, the nature of bombing designed to affect the enemy's morale directly is certainly comparable in both situations. Morale bombing does, of course, encompass a spectrum of objectives. These range from seeking total submission of the enemy by destroying his will to continue the struggle to more limited goals, such as coercing the enemy to begin or resume truce negotiations. It is well known that during World War II, General Spaatz disapproved of many projects to break German morale by the use of heavy strategic bombing over densely populated urban areas. General Eisenhower and the Army Air Force concurred. Yet it would appear that this is precisely what was planned for the United States Air Force in the Christmas bombings of December 1972.

The decision to launch the Christmas bombings can be compared to the British Cabinet's decision during World War II to authorize a bombing policy that included attack on the enemy morale and that was later justified by the prior unrestricted air attacks of the German Luftwaffe over London, Coventry, and Warsaw. [42] The United States never adopted this British policy in the European theater. Yet, in the Pacific in 1945 the United States conducted air operations comparable to those of the British with B-29 raids over Japan and ultimately with the Hiroshima and Nagasaki atom-bomb attacks. The position of the United States before Christmas 1972 is best capsulized by the Air Force Judge Advocate General's Office in a memorandum to the Director of Plans that set forth as the applicable legal principles for air warfare the well-accepted view that "all air attacks against the enemy must be against military objectives" and that "since the [advent of] hostilities waged from the air, and under the pressure of military necessity, the scope of the legitimate military objectives has been unchanged. It now [sic] includes the entire military, economic and industrial strength of the enemy." [43] Morale is not included in the memorandum as among the lawful military targets.

Air Attacks during the Korean War

The situation in Vietnam toward the end of 1972 was somewhat analogous to the conditions prevailing in Korea in the spring of 1953. When the armistice negotiations began at Panmunjom in April 1953, Gen. Otto P. Weyland, Chief Truce Negotiator, was willing to approve irrigation-dam attacks to release floodwaters that would interdict the enemy's lines of communication and speed up truce negotiations. [44] Eventually, when the Panmunjom truce talks stalled, air attacks were used to breach the North Korean irrigation system. [45] It has been well documented that United States strikes in May 1953 on certain Korean dams caused the flooding of the main road and mail communication systems north of the hospital in Panmunjom. [46] Further, the threat that the remaining North Korean dams might be hit and cause even more flooding may have influenced the North Korean position and expedited the signing of an armistice on 27 July 1953. This bombing to force negotiations represented a reversal of the expressed United States policy in North Korea of carefully limiting the permissible targets of attack to only military objectives. Since United States forces in North Vietnam never deliberately bombed the Vietnamese dikes, the Air Force strategy in Korea would also seem to be different from subsequent Air Force policy.

During the Korean conflict, as well as throughout World War II, the United States followed a practice of warning the civilian populations of cities in advance of air attacks. [47] This policy was maintained for much of the Korean War even though there is no legal requirement to give prior warning of air strikes. In fact, such advance notice frequently posed great danger to the attacking air force. In most instances, thousands of leaflets were dropped by low-flying aircraft over the cities to be attacked. Where surprise was essential, such warnings were given only in a general way, without naming the time or the specific identity of the particular objective. Yet, if the urban bombing was in reality aimed solely at military targets being attacked for distinct military advantages, a good case can be made that the United States should have announced in the prior warnings that the attacks were intended not to alarm or surprise the civilian population, but only to weaken the enemy's military strength.

Evolution of United States Policy concerning Air Attacks in Vietnam

The rules of engagement of the Military Assistance Command, Vietnam (MACV), governing ground operations in South Vietnam between 1965 and 1969, contained many safeguards intended to protect against civilian casualties. These safeguards included the use of specified strike zones and forward air controllers along with the requirement of prior approval of potential targets by South Vietnamese civilian and military authorities. In the South, prior to commencing air attacks on urban areas, even when fire was received from the area, these rules instructed that leaflets, loudspeakers, and other appropriate means should be used to warn the civilian population. [48]

The action taken by the United States Air Force during the period 1965 to 1969 to limit civilian casualties was especially admirable in view of the exigencies of the situation and the nature of guerrilla warfare. The situation remained such that the enemy was able to take effective countermeasures that resulted in the maintenance of, and even an increase in, the flow of supplies to the South. [49] Long before December 1972 the North Vietnamese had adapted their military operations and resupplying of the South so that they could continue to operate without the physical or matériel facilities of Hanoi itself. In early 1969 the new Nixon Administration was told by responsible United States agencies that "[i]t is clear that the bombing campaign, as conducted, did not live up to the expectations of many of its proponents. . . . There is little reason to believe that new bombing will accomplish what previous bombings failed to do, unless it is conducted with much greater intensity and readiness to defy criticism and risk of escalation." [50]

On 22 October 1972, after disclosure that Dr. Kissinger and Le Duc Tho had worked out a draft cease-fire agreement, the President halted all mining of North Vietnamese ports and bombing north of the twentieth parallel. [51] Following this action and prior to the Christmas bombings, President Nixon began to consider a new military initiative to force the North Vietnamese into reaching an early cease-fire agree-ment—namely, a sudden replacement by air of mines in Haiphong Harbor and a resumption of some bombing of military targets north of the twentieth parallel. Clearly this action would be designed not to gain any military advantage over the enemy, but rather solely to place polit-ical pressure on North Vietnam.

When negotiations over the cease-fire agreement were hopelessly stalled by 16 December 1972, the Christmas bombings were approved as the most expeditious means to force the hands of the North Viet-namese authorities. But how could the United States have expected to coerce the North Vietnamese by these air attacks on Hanoi? After all, the North Vietnamese armed forces, through such means as evacuation, redistribution of supplies, rerouting of essential military lines of com-munication, relocation of military headquarters, and "digging under," could unquestionably withstand and survive any military advantages achieved by such bombing. The answer would seem to be that if life was made so miserable and wretched for the remaining large population of Hanoi, public pressure would be brought on the North Vietnamese au-thorities to resume serious truce negotiations.

By almost all accounts, every major military target and installation that could directly weaken the enemy forces in the South had been destroyed well before December 1972. [52] It is true that any object is a potential military target. Use can readily convert a nonmilitary target into a military one. For example, in World War II the Germans used the Abbey of Montecassino as a fortified stronghold in Southern Italy. Whether a target is the lawful object of an attack turns upon the appli-cation of the rule of proportionality, military necessity, weapons capa-bilities, and the military advantage to be gained. The question that arises with respect to the Christmas bombings is this: Were the attacks conducted by the United States during an eleven-day campaign for the purpose of obtaining a distinct military advantage for South Vietnam and the United States so that they were permissible under the laws of war, or were they designed solely to force North Vietnam to reach a quick political settlement and, thus, not sanctioned in our view by in-ternational law?

The answer turns on what definition is accepted for "legitimate military objective" and on exactly what the doctrine of military necessity justifies in connection with air attacks. In determining whether a particular object is legitimate and whether an attack is necessary from a military perspective, one must weigh the military importance of destroying the target against the civilian losses that an attack will cause. The commander making this judgment is required to use his "best efforts" to reach a sound decision. But he is not to be held criminally liable if, in hindsight, his action was justified, based on what he should have known, but the civilian losses turned out to be greater than could have been anticipated.

Assessing the Purpose of the Christmas Bombings

Gen. John C. Meyer, in an address in March 1973, stated that the principal objective of United States operations during the Christmas bombings was "the deliberate destruction of military targets in North Vietnam." He said: "That was our assigned mission." [53] But what exactly were these military targets? According to General Meyer, they were railways and railway cars, two major oil-products plants, large warehouses and oil storage areas, MIG fighter bases, resupply facilities, and surface-to-air missile (SAM) sites. This statement contrasted with National Security Council Memorandum No. 1, prepared in 1969 for Dr. Kissinger, in which it was reported that Hanoi was able to cope with the problems created by the bombing of North Vietnam "so that the air war did not seriously affect the flow of men and supplies to the South." Further, "the North Vietnamese surprised many . . . by holding the North together and simultaneously sending ever-increasing amounts of supplies and personnel into the South during 3½ years of bombing." [54]

Althouth General Meyer referred to military targets as "the principal objective of the air operations" during the Christmas bombings, he conceded that the real objective was to get the North Vietnamese back to the truce negotiations. [55] General Meyer quoted Dr. Kissinger as saying that in mid-December 1972 there had been a deadlock in the negotiations with North Vietnam. When negotiations resumed on 8 January 1973, the record shows, and General Meyer emphasized, that there was a rapid movement toward settlement.

This raises the issue of whether the lawfulness of a specific air attack is to be judged by its predominant, as distinguished from its ostensible, purpose. Certainly all military strength is nurtured and concentrated to win the conflict, that is, to bring a victory. But we believe the principle is well settled that military power is to be applied to gain military advantages, not to serve immediate and short-range political ends. The use of military power for immediate political gains only obscures the laws of war. Can bombing be considered lawful because the attacking party has declared that the bombed enemy areas contain "military" targets when such targets are, in fact, not distinctly and primarily essential to the enemy's military strength? We think that it cannot.

General Meyer related that from 18 December until 30 December there were 729 B-52 sorties over the Hanoi-Haiphong area. This indicates that probably half of the two hundred B-52s committed by the United States to the entire Indochina conflict participated in the air raids during this period. [56] Each B-52 carried more than twenty tons of bombs. These planes drop their bombs in a rectangular carpet roughly a half mile wide and a mile and a half long. [57] Everything within that area is substantially impacted, if not destroyed. In addition, each bomb blast affects an even larger area. Windows are blown out, flimsy housing is knocked down, and the civilian population is disrupted over perhaps twice as large an area. [58]

The B-52 air raids during the Christmas bombings were conducted in flights of three planes so that an enhanced rectangular pattern of destruction inevitably resulted within Hanoi and its environs. [59] B-52s are comparatively larger, slower flying, and less maneuverable than fighter bombers. For this reason, B-52s were not used during the sustained 1967-68 bombing campaign over North Vietnam. [60] Their accuracy in providing tactical support in the South was greatly increased by the use of forward air controllers and ground-station cross-references so that more precise bombing could be carried out. But these aids to precision were not available in the North. In addition, hostile fire in the North was greatly increased by an extensive network of SAM and antiaircraft sites. This prompted United States commanders to concede that the probability of accidental bombing of the civilian population was greater in the North than it had been when B-52s were used in the South.

Even if only military targets were programmed for destruction in the Hanoi-Haiphong region, the population density of the areas surrounding the military targets made hospitals, universities, dikes, and urban areas predictable and inevitable objects of incidental bombing damage. In fact, such facilities and emplacements were hit within the environs of Hanoi. This, it would seem, should have been readily foreseeable. B-52s flying 729 sorties through defenses provided by at least two hundred SAM sites would invariably bring about great civilian casualties and destruction. These missile sites are reported to have fired more than one hundred SAM-2 missiles daily against United States aircraft. [61]

How much civilian damage was occasioned by the Christmas bombings can only be determined by an independent survey such as the one conducted by the United States Strategic Bombing Survey Team that assessed the effects of the Allied bombing operations in World War II. The North Vietnamese authorities, as well as some neutral sources, stated that as much as one-third of Hanoi's hospital facilities were destroyed, including a large part of a centrally located one-thousand-bed hospital. [62] The North Vietnamese Minister of Health stated that one principal hospital suffered serious damage, some hospital staff were killed, and operating rooms and medical supplies were destroyed. [63]

Some United States Air Force officers admitted unofficially that "we have hit a few targets we did not mean to hit like the Gia Lam Airport in Hanoi." [64] One officer reported seeing photographs of the damage and remarked that there had apparently been very significant civilian damage. [65] This admission—that bombing of military targets in Vietnam spilled over to cause accidental damage to the civilian population—had already been well documented in submissions assembled by Senator Kennedy's Subcommittee on Refugees. By 1969 it was estimated that approximately fifty-two thousand civilians had been killed in North Vietnam by United States air strikes. [66] Navy carrier pilots conceded that, although "off limits" objects included dikes, hospitals, churches, clusters of homes, and POW camps, "there can be mistakes, especially in a hot environment—when there is heavy antiaircraft fire." [67]

Has there ever been a more intensive "hot environment" than the one that was witnessed from 18 through 30 December 1972 over Hanoi? In concentrated air attack, unlike naval and land bombardment, it is possible to single out a sensitive and populous area well behind the region of active surface combat. And a concentrated attack affects the life of every individual in the selected zone, every minute of the day. During the intensive Christmas bombings, Hanoi was "said to be about 50 percent evacuated, although there [were] still plenty of men, women, and children there. [We] were very surprised at the number of children still in the city." [68]

Several Americans who visited Hanoi in early January 1973 described the bombing damage as overwhelming. They reported seeing several blocks that had been destroyed, a hospital and elementary school that were extensively damaged, and at least several areas of closely packed houses that were razed. [69] Indeed, the attacks were so devastating that two United States pilots refused to continue bombing during the eleven-day attack. [70] A Swedish member of a group invited to inspect the damage occasioned by the bombing reported that at least one-fifth of Hanoi was destroyed, although this remains unverified. [71]

While the damage to civilian life and property caused by the air attacks during those eleven days must await a more objective tally, it would appear reasonable to conclude that it was extensive. The bombings may have been aimed, as General Meyer stated, at "military targets." Nonetheless, their principal objective clearly seems to have been not to reduce the enemy's military strength but rather to weaken his political determination to continue stalling in the cease-fire talks. According to General Meyer, "we probably won't have a complete readout of the damage level achieved on those military targets but we know we hit them where it hurt in military and consequently political terms." [72] This leaves unanswered the question of whether the attacks sought principally to weaken North Vietnamese political power under the guise of using United States air power to seek distinct military advantages.

In effect, in the Christmas bombings the United States departed from the stated Air Force policy against morale bombing as that policy evolved in World War II and the Korean War. No official, advance warning is recorded as having been given before the 1972 bombings. Such notice might have saved some civilian lives and property by permitting civilians to take more precautions against the unintended effects of the air raids. In addition, precision bombing could not be employed in the night raids over a high-density area protected by antiaircraft and SAM defensive sites. Hanoi was one of the most heavily defended cities in the history of air warfare and by far the most heavily defended in a limited conflict.

It might be said that bombing in less defended and more identifiable areas during daytime raids is indiscriminate. But given the low visibility during a night raid and the presence of strong antiaircraft and SAM defenses, the same attacks might not be considered indiscriminate if carried out at night. This does not explain, however, the real issues relating to the legality of the Christmas bombings. They are not whether the loss to civilian life and property was indiscriminate, or disproportionate to the military objectives; neither are they whether area or pattern bombing over dense civilian areas can be justified in limited warfare. The real issues presented are these: first, can air attacks ever be justified when the predominant purpose of the raid is political and when political, not military, advantages are the immediate end sought by the specific attacks; and, second, are air attacks unlawful per se

when the predominant purpose of the attacks is to weaken the morale
and will of the people, although it is stated to be the destruction of military objectives?

Determining Lawful Objectives of Air Attacks

By December 1972 the destruction of any military objectives in Hanoi
could have only marginal effects on the enemy's actual military
strength. All prior air attacks had failed to stem the steady stream of men
and supplies flowing south.[73] What little was left in North Vietnam of
the oil storage capacity, or of the railheads and transportation facilities,
or even of the industries to support the armed factions in the South could
not justify such a heavy air attack on Hanoi. This view is confirmed by
President Nixon's statement at his 27 July 1972 press conference:

> . . . our military commanders . . . while they do give me their
> judgment as to what will affect the military outcome in Vietnam, . . .
> have never recommended, for example, bombing Hanoi. . . .
>   Our military doesn't want to do that. They believe it would be
> counterproductive, and secondly, they believe it is not necessary. It
> might shorten the war, but it would leave a legacy of hatred throughout
> that part of the world from which we might never recover. So our mili-
> tary have not advocated bombing the dikes; they have not advocated
> bombing civilian centers. They are doing the best in carrying out the
> policy we want of hitting military targets only.[74]

Domestic and foreign critics of United States actions in the Christmas
bombing alleged, in essence, that no matter who was to blame for the
breakdown in talks, this massive, indiscriminate use of the overwhelming aerial might of the United States to try to impose an American
solution on Vietnam's political problems was terrorism on an unprecedented scale.[75] Unfortunately, the United States government was not
very articulate or public in responding to such allegations. All too often
it merely relied on the frequently repeated theme that the United States
Air Force has always limited its bombing to military objectives and will
continue to do so. The tragedy of this response is that, by refusing to justify its actions with details, the Administration sacrificed what President Kennedy called "the most valuable asset that any nation possesses
. . . the loyalty and trust of its population."[76] It is virtually impossible to
empathize with those political leaders who caused these consequences
for the United States in view of their tolerance of nearly meaningless official statements by American military authorities that "although civilian casualties did occur, they did not result from any lack of a clearly
stated and constituted command policy."[77]

It seems amazing that after forty years of intermittent use of air power in armed conflict on an ever-increasing scale of destruction, only one official international attempt was made to codify rules for aerial bombing, by the International Commission of Jurists at The Hague in 1923. [78] The Hague Convention No. IX of 1907 relating to maritime war, rather than the more familiar 1907 Hague Regulations concerning land warfare, was the guide for those jurists. [79] The analogy to sea warfare seemed clearer, for the pilot can bomb, but he does not seek to occupy the enemy's territory. Any actual invasion is left to ground troops. Thus, it seems natural that the jurists would list military objectives in 1923 by drawing from the traditional rules of maritime assault.

Under the 1923 draft rules, proper bombing objectives from the air included "factories constituting important and well-known centres engaged in the manufacture of arms, ammunition or distinctively military supplies; [and] lines of communication or transportation used for military purposes." It should be especially noted for our purposes that the draft air warfare rules expressly stated that "[a]erial bombardment is legitimate only when directed at a military objective, that is to say, an object of which the destruction or injury would constitute a *distinct military advantage* to the belligerent." [80] Bombing for the purpose of "terrorizing the civilian population" was specifically prohibited by the 1923 draft rules.

These same principles were again enunciated in the 1930s. First, in 1932 the General Commission of the Disarmament Conference adopted a resolution that "air attack against the civilian population shall be absolutely prohibited." [81] In 1938 the nineteenth assembly of the League of Nations specified in a resolution that (1) intentional bombing of the civilian population is illegal; (2) targets attacked from the air must be legitimate and identifiable military objectives; and (3) in bombing such targets, reasonable care must be taken to avoid accidental bombardment of the nearby civilian population. [82] But it is evident that respect for these principles can only be assured if some provision is made for impartial and neutral determination by an entity independent of the parties at war.

The 1923 draft rules did not anticipate the area bombing of World War II, in which whole industrial complexes and, indeed, entire cities became the target. Despite that experience, nations have not openly sought to abandon the principle that there must be some relation between the object attacked and its military value to the enemy. On the other hand, the major air powers have shown no eagerness to promulgate unilaterally their understanding of the general laws governing air warfare.

In a letter to Secretary of Defense Melvin Laird dated 3 May 1972, Sen. Edward Kennedy wrote: "There are currently in existence manuals on rules of land warfare and on rules of naval warfare. What is the status of proposals on a similar manual relating to the rules of air warfare?"[83] The facts are that the Air Force Judge Advocate General's Office has been working on a draft manual on the rules of air warfare since 1956 without successfully bringing its work to fruition. Among the reasons for this situation is that there are strong currents within the Air Force that are against explicitly delineating such rules out of fear of the possible repercussions to the United States. In addition, it is our understanding that throughout the Vietnam War the Air Force had virtually no training program to inform or instruct Air Force personnel on the laws of war as they apply to aerial operations.

No responsible person can honestly believe that the Air Force, or its pilots, would deliberately inflict needless suffering upon innocent civilians. But moral ambiguity becomes possible when the rules are imprecise, unpublished, and not properly taught. And even if the rules were published, their utility would be questionable if, for example, they leave open whether particular air attacks are legitimate by referring to "military objectives" or "military targets" without further definition. By this approach of ambiguity the Air Force might strengthen its ability to respond to future protests that it is violating its own rules of air warfare. Yet, by not establishing boundaries on such key terms as "military objectives" for air attacks, it may be argued that any bombing, deliberate or accidental, of a military target that is not universally accepted as such is a violation of international law. That result would certainly not be in the interests of the Air Force. Thus, failure to be specific in any future Air Force rules for air warfare could produce precisely the opposite result from the objective of those seeking to avoid precise rules.

The lack of rules expressly governing air warfare was stressed by the Swedish delegate, Hans Blix, in an address to the U.N. Third Committee in 1970. Mr. Blix emphasized that aerial warfare has never been subject to systematic regulation, but has only been regulated by a limited number of rules that are applied by analogy or custom.[84] In light of the present aerial military strength of the major powers, it would benefit the ICRC and the major powers to make a serious attempt to rectify this dangerous situation.

Since no belligerent has ever announced its bombing of nonmilitary targets, the present United States position on the rules of air warfare should be of concern to laymen and international lawyers alike. The term "military object" has defied numerous attempts to clearly define it. It seems to expand and contract with the intensity of the conflict and the overall political objectives of the warring parties. More than thirty years ago, as World War II escalated in intensity and involvement, the parameters of military object clearly broadened in the absence of some limitation on the extension of its definition. For example, the Army Air Forces contended that they aimed at military targets in Dresden on the fateful nights of 14 and 15 February 1945. But a study of the attacks found that "the night raid by the R.A.F. Bomber Command was intended to devastate the city area itself . . . and disrupt normal civilian life upon which the larger communications activities and the manufacturing enterprises of the city depended." [85]

Legality of the Christmas 1972 Bombings

The Christmas bombings represent an interesting parallel. That bombing was implicitly legitimate as long as it was directed only at military targets. Yet, in the case of the Hanoi raid, as with Dresden, military authorities refused to recognize that even attack on military targets may be unjustified when the military advantage to be gained is not significant and political motives for the attack predominate.

This, of course, brings this analysis full circle back to the question raised at the outset regarding the meaning of "military target." If one grants that only facilities clearly connected with military operations should be targeted, are attacks on such facilities nevertheless permissible when the fear and damage to be caused exceed the military advantage of the destruction? Specifically, were the Christmas bombings designed to achieve a distinct military advantage for the South Vietnamese and the United States, or were they more in the nature of morale or even terror bombings, which are regarded by most authorities as unlawful?

Dr. Spaight recalls J. A. Farrer's statement in 1885 that if the final justification for the use of air power is to shorten the war, "the ground begins to slip from under us" [86] in seeking to prohibit other clearly inhumane means of warfare, e.g., using "clothes infected with smallpox" against the enemy. Dr. Spaight asserts "that judgment has not lost its validity." But it is by this very rationale of shortening the war that the atomic raids on Hiroshima and Nagasaki toward the end of World War II were justified, as were the air raids on Dresden and Tokyo.

If bombing for political ends, such as morale bombing, were lawful, nations using air warfare would be completely free to exercise subjective judgment about which targets should be hit. The distinct advantage of such bombing is not military, but political. Its real purpose is not the destruction of a particular bridge, airfield, or military supply depot, but rather coercion of the enemy leaders by the application of pressure on the civilian population. It should be recalled here that in his press conference of 24 January 1973, Dr. Kissinger, when asked if the bombing of the North was the key to achieving agreement, answered: "there was a deadlock . . . in the middle of December . . . there was a rapid movement when negotiations resumed . . . on the technical level on January 3, and on the substantive level on January 8. These facts must be analyzed by each person for himself."[87]

Some statements made publicly about the Christmas bombings concentrate on the general and vague terminology of military targeting. But the highest authorities seemed to admit publicly that the purpose of the raids was to bring the enemy back to the conference table and to force him to accept a just and reasonable settlement. Lieutenant General McBride, Commander of the Air Training Command, recently said that the North Vietnamese bombings were a "key factor" in bringing Hanoi to terms regarding the settlement.[88] Pilotless reconnaissance planes had been photographing Hanoi for months prior to December 1972. The scarcity of distinctly military objects in Hanoi, that is, objects the destruction of which would weaken the military strength of the North Vietnamese armed forces, was undoubtedly recognized by United States authorities. The degree to which the North Vietnamese military effort could have been expected to suffer by such attacks seems insignificant.[89]

Professor Telford Taylor of Columbia, a visitor to Hanoi during the 1972 bombings, questions the legality of the Christmas bombings on a different basis.[90] His condemnation of them is based on the principle of proportionality—i.e., the reasonable relationship between the military objective and the damage and suffering that its attainment will inflict. The difference between Professor Taylor's thesis and the one put forward here is fundamentally whether the emphasis is on accidental or on intentional injury to the civilian population. Professor Taylor believes that the military objectives in the North "even as described by the Pentagon" were apparently insignificant when compared to the destruction that would predictably be inflicted on the civilian population by United States B-52s. He concludes that the military advantages to be gained by the bombing were not, as the principle requires, proportionate to the massive civilian injuries and damage that the raids were likely to cause and, in fact, did cause.[91] On the other hand, the view taken here is that even if the predictable military gains were proportionate to the civilian toll and even if they were against "military objects" (broadly defined), any destruction that is not primarily and predominantly designed to weaken the enemy militarily is unlawful. When its foremost purpose is to coerce an immediate political settlement, it is illegal per se, even though military objects are targeted.

Approximately 125 nations convened at Geneva in 1974 to consider revision of the international humanitarian law of armed conflicts and have determined to reconvene in 1975. In our view these nations should consider a simple, but important, clarification of article 47 of the document before them, the Draft Additional Protocol I to the Geneva Conventions of August 12, 1949, and Relating to the Protection of Victims of International Armed Conflicts. The present Draft Protocol is the work of a committee of experts summoned by the ICRC to improve humanitarian laws of armed conflict, and it has been revised by the ICRC itself.[92] At present, article 47 provides the following:

General protection of civilian objects
1. Attacks shall be strictly limited to military objectives, namely, to those objectives which are, by their nature, purpose or use, recognized to be of military interest and whose total or partial destruction, in the circumstances ruling at the time, offers a distinct and substantial military advantage.
2. Consequently, objects designed for civilian use, such as houses, dwellings, installations and means of transport, and all objects which are not military objectives, shall not be made the object of attack, except if they are used mainly in support of the military effort.

In an attempt to reduce the degree of suffering of innocent victims of war and to maximize the protection available to civilians during hostilities, a clarification should be inserted in article 47. This amendment would make clear that military objectives should be further limited to include only those whose destruction is sought to achieve a distinct military advantage and to exclude those whose designation as a target is for an immediate and predominantly political purpose. A simple addition, possibly as paragraph 3 of article 47, would alleviate this fundamental concern so graphically illustrated during Christmas 1972. Accordingly, we recommend that article 47 be amended to provide the following in a third paragraph:

3. Further, attacks for immediate and predominantly political purposes are unlawful.

10 Comments

Townsend Hoopes

I have no difficulty in accepting Professor DeSaussure and Robert Glasser's basic contention with respect to the 1972 Christmas bombings. It is that, since high United States authorities, including the Secretary of Defense, concluded as early as mid-1967 that "no major military targets remain to be struck" in North Vietnam, one is justified in treating with skepticism the 1973 contention by the Commander of the Strategic Air Command that the main purpose of the Christmas bombings was "the deliberate destruction of military targets in North Vietnam."

The evidence is overwhelming that the purpose of these air attacks was political. They sought to break the impasse in the cease-fire negotiations by resorting to heavy carpet bombing of the most densely populated and politically important part of North Vietnam—namely, Hanoi and its environs. This area contained all the major government buildings, hospitals, universities, and urban communities in that country. The aim of the bombing was not to strike military targets that could have any appreciable effect on the battlefield situation. It was to conduct terror-morale bombing—in DeSaussure and Glasser's words, to make "life . . . so miserable and wretched for the remaining large population of Hanoi" that "public pressure would be brought on the North Vietnamese authorities to resume serious truce negotiations."

Statements to the contrary—insisting that the raids involved only military targets and military purposes—were designed to protect the White House and the Air Force against widespread expressions of moral outrage and charges that international law had been violated. In fairness, of course, it should be understood that the Air Force was merely the agent of a policy made by, and aimed at realizing the political purposes of, President Nixon and Dr. Henry Kissinger.

I find it more difficult, however, to accept the broad legal and philosophical conclusion that Professor DeSaussure and Mr. Glasser draw from this situation—i.e., their categorical assertion that any application of air power aimed not at gaining a self-evident military advantage, but at serving short-range political purposes, is a universally recognized violation of international law. "The principle is well settled," they say. One wonders whether the matter is really settled at all in any meaningful sense.

The history of air warfare since 1940, if it does not constitute the whole story of terror-morale bombing (either blatantly proclaimed or thinly disguised), is at least replete with examples of that practice. Hitler started it over Rotterdam, Warsaw, and London. The British followed suit, motivated by a spirit of reprisal, a lack of the technical means for precision bombing, and a desire to minimize their bomber losses by making night attacks. The United States Eighth Air Force under General Spaatz attempted, initially, a more finely tuned effort. But as the bombers grew in numbers, as the antiaircraft defenses became more accurate, as General Spaatz gave way to Gen. Curtis Lemay, the American bombing became ever more massive, imprecise, and indiscriminately destructive.

American bombers played a large role in the wholesale destruction of Dresden. Few have sought to present the fire bombing of Tokyo as anything other than a campaign to destroy civilian morale in Japan and thus force the Imperial Government to surrender. In fact, when that tactic proved inconclusive, new and wholly unambiguous terror weapons were used to obliterate Hiroshima and Nagasaki. Washington's aim was to bring the war to swift conclusion by creating such intense Japanese fear of America's spectacular new weaponry that there would be no need for the bloody trial of a land invasion.

There is no disputing that the objective of American strategic bombing in World War II was broadly political or that it was directed beyond narrowly defined military targets or objectives. Yet in that context of a genuinely global war that had already claimed the lives of countless millions, this United States course of action was neither irrational nor nakedly immoral. Indeed, it can be defended as one of the more humane options available at the time except as compared, in the Pacific theater, to a strategy relying on a combination of air-naval blockade, conventional air attack, and patience to bring the insular Japanese war machine to a grinding halt. (As they closed in on the doomed Japanese in mid-1945, the United States government and the American people were not notably patient.)

So it is not clear to me how Professor DeSaussure and Mr. Glasser arrive at their conclusion that all bombing for political purposes is universally recognized as a violation of international law and that this principle is "settled." For if one examines the actual practice of the major military powers over the past thirty years, it is apparent that the 1972 Christmas bombings of Hanoi are merely the latest example of military policies designed principally to serve what were considered to be overriding political purposes. Moreover, until recently, no serious moral onus attached to such policies and purposes. We and the British were determined to break Hitler, and the Western world gave its moral approval. Truman, Marshall, and Stimson used atomic bombs on Japanese cities to shorten the war, thereby saving Allied and Japanese lives estimated variously at two hundred and fifty thousand to one million.

These examples, and the confirming response of most civilized peoples at the time, suggest three conclusions. First, it is undeniably true, as Professor DeSaussure and Mr. Glasser make clear, that air warfare has never been subjected to systematic regulation. Second, it is equally clear (as Mr. Tucker notes perceptively in chapter 13) that the morality of decent men on the question of air warfare is a relative matter. When they believe strongly in the justice of a particular war, they develop a partial blindness to the methods employed. But when such conviction is absent, they readily see and deplore the savageries inherent in every act of war. Third, these facts would seem to provide quite fragile underpinnings for assertions regarding legal prohibitions in air warfare, however desirable such prohibitions may be from the standpoint of humanity and morality.

Professor DeSaussure and Mr. Glasser also leave out of their account the West's perception, since 1945, that its safety vis-à-vis Communist expansion (via the vast land armies of Russia and China) depended upon air power, and particularly upon the deterrent threat of air-delivered nuclear weapons. Yet given this assumption regarding the condition of Western democratic survival, it is hardly surprising that attempts to codify international rules for aerial bombing have been consistently tepid, or that manuals on the subject formulated in British and American air staffs have never been brought to fruition. In the simplest terms, nations do not legislate self-denying restrictions on those weapons and techniques that they judge their survival to depend upon. Nuclear counterattack was the ultimate sanction of United States diplomacy during the Truman period. It was elevated to the doctrine of massive retaliation under Eisenhower and Dulles. Today nuclear weapons are still perceived as the ultimate backdrop to diplomacy between and among the nuclear powers. Technology and fear have led to our dependence upon the deterrence provided by "city-busting" policies of nuclear retaliation designed to achieve the "assured destruction" not primarily of enemy military installations, but of enemy populations. Given these compelling facts, it is not easy to understand why Professor DeSaussure and Mr. Glasser find it "amazing" that so little has been done in the direction of regulating air warfare.

So long as the ultimate "security" of major nations or coalitions is perceived to depend on strategic nuclear weapons, it is doubtful whether any meaningful restrictions on the employment of nuclear weapons in war will be accepted by the nuclear powers. Yet what meaning can there be to international law if it is not supported by at least a general consensus of the leading powers?

On the other hand, the prospect for regulation may be brighter in the separable cases of limited-conventional and guerrilla-counterinsurgent war, especially when such wars are fought in areas of peripheral strategic consequence. And, in fairness, such limited conflicts appear to be the real focus of Professor DeSaussure and Mr. Glasser's analysis. It may be possible to persuade high-technology societies that, if they intervene in such conflicts, their self-interest will reside in a military policy of deliberate restraint. This should be apparent if they bear in mind that one main object of limited war is to prevent the conflict from becoming global, and another is to gain or hold the allegiance of the population.

I would argue that, if an advanced society were logical and were governed by a sense of proportion, it would, upon entering into a future insurgent situation, find its political and military actions more effective if it deliberately refrained from using weapons of large-scale destruction, such as bomber aircraft, artillery, and naval gunfire. Unfortunately, it is not clear that technological-industrial society possesses the self-discipline to deny itself available means of large-scale destruction, even in peripheral contests. On the record, we must admit that at least American society seems driven by a political-economic compulsion to fight its wars with high-technology weapons. This is either because we are impatient for quick victory, or because we possess an ingrained preference for substituting metal for men. Or perhaps it is because we can still persuade ourselves that the use of high-cost, powerful weapons will prove less expensive by shortening a war.

Vietnam is the classic example of these national predilections. In that situation, high-technology weapons, applied within the framework of a search-and-destroy strategy, failed to solve either the military or the political problem. Indeed, they produced horrendous side effects. Admittedly, the situation in Vietnam was complicated by the existence of a dual war, one against North Vietnamese regular forces and another simultaneously against guerrillas from South Vietnam. But the record shows that, long before the introduction of North Vietnamese regular forces into South Vietnam, the United States had committed itself to supporting a strategy wholly dependent upon conventional weapons and tactics to fight the insurgents in the South. From 1954 on we created a South Vietnamese army organized entirely in conventional formations. Moreover, we introduced, in late 1961, American-manned bombing aircraft and artillery, even though the guerrilla was still the only enemy.

In view of the Vietnam experience, we should avoid an overly sanguine view of our own capacity to see the advantages of restraint. Nevertheless, we should work seriously toward intelligent, humanitarian restrictions in the context of limited-war situations. It is in that light that Professor DeSaussure and Mr. Glasser's proposed amendment to article 47 of the Draft Protocol I to the 1949 Geneva Conventions for the protection of war victims seems eminently right.

11 Comments

Norman R. Thorpe
*and James R. Miles**

The bombardment of military targets in Hanoi by United States Air Force B-52 aircraft during December 1972 in no way violated international law, the existing laws of war, or the humanitarian principles that these laws reflect. Since only legitimate military objectives were targeted, the sole legal issue that the bombardment raises concerns the applicability of the principle of proportionality. Was the military advantage that the United States sought to gain disproportionate to the North Vietnamese civilian casualties and damage to civilian property that could be expected? We will state unequivocally that, from a military standpoint, the bombardment sought to achieve an important military advantage. The attack was designed to coerce a negotiated settlement by threatening further weakening of the enemy's military effort to maintain and support his armed forces. It is our firm belief that this threat of continued and further destruction of military objectives produced the political settlement.

In their discussion of the December 1972 bombings, Professor DeSaussure and Mr. Glasser have presented an analysis of these air attacks that is confusing and misleading. Based on this account, Professor DeSaussure and Mr. Glasser propose revision of article 47 of the ICRC draft rules, which limits air attacks to purely military objectives. We believe that the proposal by Professor DeSaussure and Mr. Glasser and its weaknesses reach the heart of their legal analysis. But a general discussion of the principles of humanitarian law applicable in armed conflicts should precede comments on the proposal.

International armed conflict arises when two or more sovereign entities that are unable to achieve their political goals through other means resort to force and violence. Their political goals remain substantially the same; only the means for achieving them change. Thus, as Clausewitz has stated in *On War*, war is a continuation of politics by other means. It is the use of military force to achieve particular political objectives. When armed conflict occurs, grave questions arise as to the rules that the participants are obligated to observe in their military

---

*The views expressed in this chapter are those of the authors. Their comments are not an official statement of the Department of Defense.

operations against each other, i.e., the legal limits on the use of force and violence. Although perhaps this is not a unanimous view, we assume for these purposes that the legality or the morality of the political goals of the participants in an international armed conflict has no bearing on the laws applicable to the conduct of hostilities by their military forces.

Sovereigns resort to hostilities when the available peaceful and lawful means for the settlement of international disputes have failed and sometimes before such means are even tried. As a result, efforts to impose a legal regime on parties to a conflict have to take account of the realities of war, including the contemporary origins of armed conflict and the means for its conduct. These factors will vary depending on the resources available to each party and on the method for using such resources in the military effort against the enemy. The war-making capability of the enemy, and the means for rapidly employing this war-making capability in sustaining an armed force engaged in combat with the enemy, constitutes the sum of the military objectives. Thus, for example, military objectives include industrial units and communication and transportation facilities used in the military struggle as well as enemy combatants and military stores, supplies, and installations.

The effort to reduce the savagery of warfare and to apply humanitarian principles as rules of law is somewhat paradoxical. As we have seen, war presupposes a failure or unwillingness to resort to nondestructive means to settle disputes. Nonetheless, we must try to identify humanitarian principles and the consequential limitations that should govern the use of force if the endeavor to apply humanitarian law in armed conflict is to be successful. These principles and limitations should be sought and articulated outside the context of polarized viewpoints, which will only result in their distortion and bias. Very simply, it is our view that the humanitarian principles require provisions in the laws of war to protect innocent victims of war (e.g., civilians, the sick and wounded, and prisoners) and to limit destruction of enemy property to that which would result in significant military advantage in the military struggle.

In chapter 9, Professor DeSaussure and Mr. Glasser suggest that the ICRC should amend its Draft Additional Protocol I to the Geneva Conventions of August 12, 1949, and Relating to the Protection of Victims of International Armed Conflicts, to include in article 47 a prohibition against belligerents attacking admittedly military objectives if it can be shown that the attacks were for *"immediate and predominantly political purposes"* (emphasis added). This proposal is based on Professor DeSaussure and Mr. Glasser's view, expounded throughout their discussion, that it is against the laws of war to launch an attack in order to achieve a political end, even if the attack is directed at military objectives to acquire a military advantage and even if disproportionate civilian damage or civilian casualties do not result.

In order to evaluate the suggested change in the ICRC draft, it is necessary to examine Professor DeSaussure and Mr. Glasser's basic premise that wars, battles, or attacks may not be undertaken for a political end. Some discussion of terminology is also required to resolve what appears to be a semantic problem that has affected their analysis. It is our view that Professor DeSaussure and Mr. Glasser's analysis fails to demonstrate that their suggested change in the ICRC draft would be advisable. Indeed, if their proposal is interpreted as furthering what appears to be the basic premise of their paper, i.e., that wars may not serve political ends but only something called "narrow military objectives," then the suggested amendment of article 47 should be opposed because it runs a real risk of weakening the entire structure of international humanitarian law.

It is widely accepted that war should be viewed as an extension of politics. There may be a good reason for lawyers and political scientists to differ about the precise implications of this axiom. But it is probably not possible to find anyone, in law or political science or in or out of government service, who would accept the obverse principle that seems implicit in Professor DeSaussure and Mr. Glasser's premise. In short, there is no support whatsoever for the proposition that war is (or should be) a lawful end in itself. Those who study why wars occur, how they are fought and otherwise managed, and how they are brought to conclusion have necessarily observed that wars are undertaken to achieve political ends. These students correctly conclude that wars terminate when their ends are attained or are found to be unattainable at acceptable cost.

This situation does not discourage the proponent of international humanitarian law. The fact of political restraint in armed conflict provides a welcome complement to the existing framework of international law. It means that rules of law, which, for example, prohibit attacks directed against civilians, need not stand alone and unrelated to or in contradiction to compelling political interests. Such attacks not only are against the law, but almost certainly are also inconsistent with the political goals that can now be hyopothesized throughout the realistic range of possibilities. Moreover, rules such as the prohibition against attacks on the civilian population are consistent with another persuasive principle that helps to determine the conduct of a belligerent, i.e., the military doctrine of economy of force. It is not easy to imagine a situation in which bombing or firing at civilians would be an economic and efficient use of the limited resources of the attacking party. Thus, attacking civilians, even if it could be justified in terms of operational efficiency or military necessity, which it normally cannot, would be a wholly unacceptable means for achieving any of the political ends that belligerents in the present world are likely to embrace. From the foregoing, it is evident that most attacks that are unlawful are also inefficient, both politically and militarily, in terms of reaching the goals of an armed conflict. Serious violations of the laws of war may make it impossible to reach the political goals of war. However, it does not follow that lawyers may examine the political goals of belligerents in order to determine whether an action is lawful. An aerial attack on enemy military objectives clearly is permitted by the laws of war. This is so regardless of whether political gain is sought by, or whether political gain results from, an attack.

It is difficult to understand Professor DeSaussure and Mr. Glasser's views because of their imprecise and confusing use of the word "objectives" to connote, on the one hand, military targets and, on the other hand, political purposes or motives. It is worse than merely confusing when they impute to public officials of the United States a similar inability to distinguish these separate meanings. Professor DeSaussure and Mr. Glasser seek to prove that improper or unlawful targets were attacked in Hanoi by quoting from public statements of government officials concerning the political objectives of the December 1972 bombing. Such argumentation clearly imputes unintended meaning to those statements. When they proceed further and conclude that a public statement concerning the political objectives of this bombing can be read as a factual statement about the nature of the targets attacked, they have departed from analysis and moved in the direction of polemic.

Professor DeSaussure and Mr. Glasser have cited the Cornell Air War study as a major source of facts concerning United States bombing in Vietnam and of conclusions concerning the effectiveness of that bombing. Any such study that relies on anonymous sources of information and opinion, and that was prepared before the end of the Vietnam War with the evident intention of advocating a particular view as to what United States policy should be, cannot be used uncritically as a source of information or conclusions. It is particularly inappropriate to rely on the Cornell Air War study for guidance concerning the effectiveness of bombing North Vietnam because the study was completed prior to the singularly effective bombing campaign of December 1972, which is the principal subject of Professor DeSaussure and Mr. Glasser's discussion. Moreover, we believe a fair reading of the Cornell Air War study shows that the bombing that they consider politically ineffective was limited by the United States for political reasons.

The ICRC conference, when it reconvenes in 1975, offers the hope of providing agreement on specific and useful legal rules governing the conduct of warfare. But we believe that success in the effort to achieve such rules will be directly proportional to the conferees' ability to avoid extreme and unrealistic proposals that exceed their capacity to legislate in that forum. We regard Professor DeSaussure and Mr. Glasser's recommendation to outlaw the use of force for immediate and predominantly political purposes as such an extreme and unrealistic proposal. They would say that bombardment (whether by air, land, or sea) of otherwise legitimate military targets (i.e., those whose destruction offers military advantage) is rendered unlawful solely because the bombing is for the purpose of forcing the enemy to seek a negotiated political settlement. That approach would not serve humanitarian purposes and would without a doubt result in needless prolongation of the armed conflict.

We submit that the attacking of military objectives, as properly defined in the law, presumptively weakens the military effort of the enemy and is lawful, provided it does not violate any other recognized principle of law. Humanitarian considerations will continue to prevail in the conduct of war to the extent that commanders and others in authority honestly take reasonable precautions when attacking military objectives to avoid injury and damage to civilians and persons taking no part in the hostilities. This will be the case irrespective of the political advantages that may be sought from that attack. Although some proposals may be seen by their authors as having great merit, proponents of humanitarian law should be alert to the real danger of overloading the circuits of the laws of war by asking them to carry too great a burden. We believe that Professor DeSaussure and Mr. Glasser's proposal would have such an undesired effect and would fail to achieve the objectives of promoting the very humanitarian principles that they and we fully support.

Part Two
WEAPONS OF WARFARE

12 *Howard S. Levie*

Any analysis of the legality of using lachrymatories, napalm, and herbicides (defoliants) should not, in my view, be confined to determining their status under the 1925 Geneva Protocol[1] and customary international law. As I have urged elsewhere, we should concern ourselves with the future, not just the past.[2] I will, therefore, attempt here not only to examine the existing law regarding these weapons, but also to look ahead to what this country's policy should be toward their use in armed conflicts.

Lachrymatories

CS,[3] the modern-day lachrymatory or tear gas, is a sensory irritant that harasses and incapacitates by causing a copious flow of tears. While it may sometimes cause irritation, and even blistering, of the skin and, occasionally, nausea and vomiting, the symptoms will usually quickly disappear when the victim is removed from the contaminated area.[4] The incapacity caused by tear gas is said to be "a temporary, reversible disability with few, if any, permanent effects."[5] It is used by most of the police forces of the world for domestic riot-control purposes.[6] Its great advantage over older tear gases, and others currently available such as CN, is the speed with which it incapacitates—about five seconds after exposure. CS is, of course, only a modern version of tear gas, which has long been available in other forms.

Strangely enough, it may truthfully be said that the United States introduced the use of CS in hostilities in Vietnam for humanitarian reasons. One of the first uses of CS, in September 1965, actually accomplished this purpose. A Viet Cong force was holed up in a tunnel. The United States commander believed that there were also quite a few civilian noncombatants, women, and children in the tunnel. He decided to use CS and succeeded in flushing out about four hundred people, including seventeen armed Viet Cong, without inflicting any injuries or causing any deaths.[7] A second use of CS that might be termed "humanitarian" was in helicopter missions to remove the wounded from the field of combat and to rescue downed fliers. In these cases the surrounding area was saturated with CS in order to hold down small-arms fire against the helicopter during the course of its pickup mission.

However, CS proved so effective for these purposes that its use was quickly extended to include numerous methods of delivery, both by air and on the ground, and many types of combat operations. Among the combat uses in Vietnam listed by various students of the matter are:

Defensive operations:

1. Defending perimeters (to repulse attacks on outposts and other fortified areas);

2. Covering the removal of troops by helicopter (an extension to defensive combat operations of the original humanitarian purpose of removing the wounded and rescuing downed fliers); and

3. Responding to the ambush of convoys (the ambushing troops, who, being unseen, were not good targets for small arms, were frustrated by the use of CS covering wide areas on both sides of the road).

Offensive operations:

1. Flushing the enemy from tunnels, caves, bunkers, fortifications, etc. (this considerably reduced the number of friendly casualties);

2. Covering the landing of troops by helicopter (an extension to offensive combat operations of the original humanitarian purpose);

3. Contaminating an area and thus denying its use to the enemy (while CS is not particularly persistent, during dry spells it can be stirred up by the movement of a vehicle for some period of time); and

4. Reconnoitering enemy troop positions (CS forced concealed troops to reveal their position). [8]

Thus we find CS not being employed for humanitarian purposes to reduce the number of casualties, particularly of noncombatants. Instead, it was being used in conjunction with small-arms and artillery fire and with high-explosive and antipersonnel bombs. The individual driven from his place of safety by the tear gas thus became the victim of the conventional weapon. [9] One commentator believes that developing these uses for tear gas, far from having a humanitarian result, actually increased the number of casualties among noncombatants. He concludes that tear gas forced noncombatants from cover, exposing them to weapons from which they would otherwise have been protected. [10]

Was there anything illegal about the use of these combat procedures? Only if there is some norm of international law, either contractual or customary, prohibiting the use of tear gas in international armed conflict. The questions that then arise are: Do the prohibitions of the

1925 Geneva Protocol include a ban on the use of incapacitating gases, such as tear gas? And, if so, has this ban become a part of customary international law, binding on nations such as the United States that were not parties to the Protocol during the hostilities?

On both of these questions there is a sharp difference of opinion among the writers. There are those who believe that, because of the discrepancy in wording between the English and French versions of the Protocol, [11] or for other reasons, tear gases such as CS are not included in the treaty ban. [12] There are others who are just as certain that they are. [13]

Even if one assumes that tear gases are included within the prohibitions of the Protocol, that, of course, merely establishes a contractual ban. It does not necessarily mean that there was a norm of customary international law binding on the United States, then not yet a party to the Protocol. [14] There is just as sharp a division of thought among the experts as to whether there is a norm of customary international law prohibiting the use of tear gas in international armed conflict. [15] The positions taken in the writings on the customary law raise three questions that, in my view, remain unanswered.

1. If the Protocol itself is so indefinite that many articles have been written interpreting it both as banning the use of tear gas in international armed conflict and as not covering incapacitating gases such as tear gas, how can it be said to constitute the basis for, or represent the codification of, a norm of customary international law on the subject?

2. If there is a norm of customary international law banning the use of incapacitating gases, such as tear gas, in international armed conflict, what is the significance of the many reservations to the Protocol making the ratifications applicable only with respect to other parties to the Protocol? Are the reserving states not saying that they are free from any ban on the use of any gas, including incapacitating gases, in hostilities with nonparties? If they are not saying that, what are they saying in the reservations?

3. What do writers such as Lauterpacht [16] and Stone [17] mean when they say that the prohibition on the use of gas (which would presumably include tear gases) is binding upon "practically all States"? How can a rule of customary international law be binding only on practically all states?

Setting aside the unresolved legal problems, what are the practicalities that have motivated nations and international lawyers to find that international law, by treaty and by rule of custom, prohibits the use in international armed conflict of a comparatively harmless gas such as CS? [18] The answer appears to be that there exists a well-founded fear that unless all gases, including the incapacitating gases, are considered barred, nations will build up their production capabilities and their reserves and these will not be limited to incapacitating gases. [19] This did, of course, occur. [20] Furthermore, it is feared that if some gases are not included in the ban, it will be difficult, if not impossible, to draw a clear line between the lawful and the unlawful. [21] If tear gases are allowed because of their nonpermanent effect, why not, for example, a psycho-chemical that gives the victim temporary hallucinations, or a gas that painlessly immobilizes the victim for a number of hours? Finally, there exists the fear that any use of gas, even an agent that is generally admitted to be only temporarily incapacitating, will inevitably escalate into more extensive gas warfare. [22] We have seen that the use of CS in Vietnam started out with a narrow humanitarian purpose and expanded into a major operational combat weapon. While the escalation fortunately did not go any farther, that possibility was always present.

On the basis of the available materials, I am frankly unable to say that the United States was bound during the Vietnam War by any rule of international law prohibiting the use of tear gas in international armed conflict. I am convinced, however, that morally and politically the United States would be well advised to adopt and follow a policy of self-denial. This country should adopt a policy of no first use of tear gas just as it has announced such a policy for other gases. [23] While the original use of CS in Vietnam may have had a humanitarian basis, the varied combat uses subsequently adopted were actually antihumanitarian in nature and result. The United States has isolated itself politically in this area. It has also created the possibility that the use of tear gas in some future conflict will gradually escalate into full-fledged gas warfare. The advantages derived from the use of tear gas in Vietnam, even assuming that such use was completely in accordance with international law, were not worth the price that had to be paid.

Napalm

Fire has, of course, been used as a weapon since time immemorial. Military forces relied heavily on flamethrowers during World War I and even more so during World War II. Similarly, magnesium and white-phosphorous fire bombs were widely employed during World War II both in Europe and in the Far East.

Napalm was first developed and used during World War II. [24] At no time during either world war did a substantial or authoritative voice challenge the legality of using fire as a weapon in international armed conflict. When napalm was used extensively for the first time, in Korea, cries of outrage were heard. But these protests came almost exclusively from the side whose troops were receiving it and were unable to reciprocate in kind. During the Vietnam War these protests grew in volume, and they had support from elements throughout the world.

Napalm is a gelled gasoline. The word itself is an acronym for the two ingredients that were thought to constitute the thickener that is added to the gasoline to produce the gel. [25] It is an extremely effective weapon and undoubtedly the most valuable incendiary now available. Napalm is greatly feared, and its use causes far more panic than other weapons.

For these reasons, the United Nations Group of Consultant Experts on Chemical and Bacteriological (Biological) Weapons stated that napalm should be classified with high-explosive weapons, rather than with asphyxiating or poisonous gases. [26] Resolution XXIII of the International Conference on Human Rights, adopted in Tehran on 12 May 1968, contained a preambulary clause classifying napalm bombing with chemical warfare. [27] This portion of the resolution was omitted from General Assembly Resolution 2444 (XXIII), which resulted from the Tehran conference.

In a report to the International Conference of the Red Cross, held in Istanbul in 1969, the International Committee of the Red Cross (ICRC) noted that napalm is a weapon that "can be very effective, while remaining precise in its consequences"; and that "napalm and incendiary weapons in general are not specifically prohibited by any rule of international law." [28] Some members of the Group of Experts convened by the ICRC expressed the opinion that napalm falls within the coverage of the 1925 Protocol because it can cause asphyxia by air deprivation. Others "considered such an assimilation difficult" and concluded that it is the use to which the weapon is put that determines its legality. [29] Napalm has also been condemned as causing unnecessary suffering in violation of the 1907 Hague Regulations. [30]

I do not believe that, at present, there is any rule of international law that prohibits the use of napalm upon selected targets, but there is, as I have argued previously, a strong humanitarian basis for urging total prohibition. [31] However, as a practical matter, a meaningful agreement probably will not be reached to ban a weapon as effective as napalm has proved itself to be. As an alternative, I concur in the proposal that the Secretary-General of the United Nations have prepared, with the assistance of qualified consultant experts, a report on napalm similar to the one on chemical and bacteriological (biological) weapons. [32] Such a report would examine whether it is necessary to limit or prohibit the use of napalm in international armed conflict. If either of these types of action is agreed upon, the report would serve as a basis for drafting an international convention on napalm.

Herbicides (Defoliants)

Herbicides (defoliants) are agricultural chemicals that poison or desiccate the leaves of plants, causing them either to lose their leaves or to die. When herbicides cause leaf fall, whether they kill the plant or not, they are known as defoliants. While the first actual use of herbicides in armed conflict was probably during the Vietnam War, they are far from a new weapon. In 1945 the United States had already developed herbicides known as LN agents, which were stated to be effective against plants, but not injurious to animals or humans. Some consideration was given to their use against the gardens that supplied food to the Japanese military on Pacific islands that the Allied forces bypassed in their advance toward Japan. [33] But no such action was actually taken. Herbicides have, of course, had considerable use as weed-control agents.

As in the case of CS, the passage of time brought about a major change in the nature of the use of herbicides in Vietnam. While the original use was to defoliate jungle growths in order to open up to view enemy infiltration routes, a number of other uses were soon found. Crop destruction subsequently assumed some importance, although it never displaced defoliation as the primary use. [34] By 1968 the extent of the use of herbicides was limited only by the availability of supplies. [35] Some of the uses to which herbicides were put in Vietnam included:

1. Defoliating enemy infiltration routes—to open them to view; [36]

2. Defoliating friendly base perimeters—to prevent sneak attacks;

3. Defoliating lines of communication, including river banks—to prevent ambushes;

4. Defoliating enemy base areas—to make his troops move; and

5. Destroying crops—to make the enemy divert his combat efforts to food procurement and supply. [37]

Once again, there is a sharp division of opinion among the experts on the applicability of the 1925 Geneva Protocol to herbicides. Some believe that the Protocol includes a ban on antiplant chemicals. They concede that the evidence to support this finding is comparatively weak. [38] Their strongest argument is not the legislative history, which they heavily rely upon. It is rather the practical, not legal, point that, as in the case of incapacitating gases, it is impossible to draw a clear line between what is prohibited and what is not. As a result, unless nations consider all herbicides as banned, the possibility of escalation is ever present. [39]

Other writers find no prohibition in the 1925 Geneva Protocol or in customary international law against the use of herbicides. [40] They are particularly certain of this conclusion if defoliation has a valid military purpose and if crop destruction is limited to crops destined for consumption by the military. [41] It is, perhaps, appropriate to note two arguments that have been advanced in support of this basic thesis. The validity of each has been attacked.

The first is that because herbicides are widely used domestically to control weeds and other unwanted vegetation, the Protocol (and, presumably, customary international law) cannot possibly have been intended to apply to them. [42] This argument is correctly met with the response that evidence of domestic use is irrelevant for these purposes. [43] There is nothing to prevent nations from banning the use as a weapon in international armed conflict of chemicals that may be permitted within the boundaries of many of these same nations. [44] On the other hand, the weakness of this particular argument concerning domestic use of herbicides may not be relied upon to support the view that herbicides are within the reach of the Protocol or of customary international law.

The second argument sometimes advanced against Protocol coverage of herbicides is that it could not have been intended to prohibit the use of herbicides because their military use was unknown in 1925. This is challenged as being of no legal significance if the prohibition falls within the objectives that the parties were attempting to achieve by the Protocol. [45] A similar reply was advanced long ago with respect to Protocol coverage of nuclear weapons. [46] I had difficulty in accepting this view in the context of nuclear weapons. It is equally difficult to support it in this context. The acceptance of such an interpretation could virtually convert a treaty prohibiting the use of certain gases in international armed conflict into a treaty banning war. Salutary as this result might be, I scarcely believe that a legal justification can be found for it. And, of course, if the Protocol is inapplicable, it cannot represent the codification of a norm of customary international law outlawing herbicides.

One of the major practical arguments advanced against the use of herbicides is ecological in character. The report of the United Nations group of consultant experts stated that there had been no scientific evaluation of the long-term ecological changes caused by herbicide spraying. They were able to estimate that twenty years will be needed to regenerate the mangrove forests along the river banks in Vietnam. [47] Another scientist warns that "when we intervene in the ecology of a region on a massive scale we may set in motion an irreversible chain of events." [48] One nonscientist writer in the field coined the word "ecocide" in asserting that a recent scientific study indicated that permanent damage had been done to "future generations [in Southeast Asia] and the very nature of the earth." [49]

The United States heeded the admonitions of the environmentalists and substantially phased out its herbicide-spraying program in Vietnam. When it did so, it sought acceptable substitutes that would accomplish the same missions. Two seemingly noncontroversial methods were adopted: plows that tore up the vegetation along roads and trails to reduce ambushes, and concussion bombs that, by exploding horizontally, destroyed vegetation without cratering. The environmentalists, concerned only with their "thing," attacked the use of these new technologies. [50] Perhaps they will soon make the side effects of war so unpopular that they will succeed where the statesman and the international lawyer have long labored in vain—they will make it impossible for wars to be fought by denying all weapons to their military forces.

I am inclined to conclude that international law does not prohibit the use of herbicides so long as such use does not violate any of the general norms of the laws of war. This means that the destruction caused by herbicides must have a valid military purpose and that a food crop that is sprayed has to be identifiable as being grown for the use of the military. However, this is a weapon the ultimate effects of which are not now really predictable. It is one that may cause a complete upsetting of the life cycle of a treated area. Ultimately, the use of such a weapon may be as destructive to mankind as a nuclear or biological war. It appears not only that the United States was well advised to phase out its use of this weapon, but also that it should cut off the supply to South Vietnam in order to eliminate completely the use of herbicides in that country. With its ratification of the Geneva Protocol of 1925, the United States has now taken the first step by voluntarily renouncing the first use of herbicides, with certain minor exceptions. [51]

13 *Robert W. Tucker*

This chapter examines whether the use of particular weapons or types of technology is permitted by the international laws of war and whether such use is consistent with the purposes for restricting the means for pursuing armed conflicts. It is important, however, to emphasize that the purpose of the laws of war is not to restrict the means as such for pursuing armed conflict. The objective is rather to restrict—or forbid—those means that are treacherous, or that cause unnecessary suffering and destruction (and that, in consequence, are either inhumane or disproportionate), or, finally, that are indiscriminate.

I stress this point at the outset since the view persists that the introduction of a novel weapon or method of war must be regarded as unlawful until such time as it is expressly permitted by a specific rule of custom or convention. To the extent that this view is based upon the alleged principle that what is not expressly permitted in war is thereby prohibited, it must be regarded as unfounded. The essential purpose of the laws of war is to define those means that are forbidden to belligerents. In the absence of restrictions imposed either by custom or by convention, belligerents are permitted to use any means in the conduct of hostilities.

It is another matter to contend that the lawfulness of a weapon must be determined not only by those prohibitions contained in specific rules of custom and convention but also by those customary prohibitions contained in the general principles of the laws of war. Although not expressly forbidden by a rule of custom or convention, a weapon may nevertheless be forbidden if, quite apart from its possible use, it is deemed inhumane, indiscriminate, disproportionate, or treacherous. The difficulty, of course, is not in stating the general principles of the laws of war but in applying them in order to determine the legal status of a weapon (or method) of war to which no more specific rule is applicable.

No such difficulty generally arises when states have agreed upon the regulation of a particular means of war and embodied this agreement in the form of a specific rule of custom or convention. It may then be left in abeyance whether, as is often assumed, the rule in question represents an application of the general principles of the laws of war. The source of the rule is either a practice constitutive of customary law or a treaty. In either case, it becomes largely superfluous to determine whether, and to what extent, the rule forbidding a certain weapon (or method) of war is an application of one or more of the general principles of the laws of war.

When, on the other hand, states have been unable to agree on the status of a particular means of war, the difficulties in applying the general principles of the laws of war are apparent. In part, these difficulties stem from the varying circumstances in which the general principles must be applied. New forms of warfare inevitably create new problems of regulation. It may be true that the changed circumstances attending new forms of warfare do not warrant failure to apply these general principles. But this should not cause us to ignore the considerable obstacles encountered in all such endeavors.

In part, however, the difficulties attending application of the general principles of the laws of war can be found elsewhere. An abundant experience has shown that these principles depend for their application upon standards that are neither self-evident nor immutable. Quite apart, then, from the difficulties encountered in applying them to widely varying circumstances, it is the persistent controversy and uncertainty over the very meaning of the general principles that have limited their utility.

A well-worn illustration presents itself in the case of the principle of humanity. As applied to weapons not already expressly regulated by specific rules, the principle of humanity is used to determine the lawfulness of weapons of war in terms of their military necessity. The principle of humanity thus forbids the employment of any weapon that is unnecessary for the purposes of war or that needlessly or unnecessarily causes human suffering or physical destruction. It should be apparent that the principle of humanity is dependent for its application upon the principle of proportionality. It is not human suffering or physical destruction that the principle of humanity forbids, but such suffering and destruction as are disproportionate to the military utility thereby obtained. Of course, the principle of humanity is not the only principle for determining the legality of a weapon not otherwise regulated by a specific rule. A weapon may be unlawful if it is inherently indiscriminate or if its use is deemed treacherous.

The necessity for a weapon and whether its use is per se illegal must therefore be determined—at least in large measure—by the purposes of war. Even assuming that the purposes of war remain constant, it has seldom been easy to determine whether a particular weapon does cause unnecessary suffering or physical destruction. It is generally agreed that article 23(e) of the Regulations annexed to the Hague Convention

No. IV (1907) has been without substantial effect. By forbidding belligerents "to employ arms, projectiles, or material calculated to cause unnecessary suffering," this provision merely states, in conventional form, the principle of humanity as this principle applies to weapons. Since article 23(e) does not attempt to enumerate any specific weapons falling within this prohibited category, it does not materially improve upon the general prohibition already contained in the principle of humanity. It is for this reason that the United States Army's Field Manual 27-10, *The Law of Land Warfare*, correctly declares, in interpreting the above provision of the Hague Regulations, that "[w]hat weapons cause 'unnecessary injury' can only be determined in light of the practice of States in refraining from the use of a given weapon because it is believed to have that effect."[1] Very nearly the same must be said for the application to weapons of the other general principles of the laws of war.

The distinction between the legality of a weapon, apart from its possible use, and the limitations placed on the use of an otherwise lawful weapon, is, despite its importance, frequently overlooked. Any weapon may be put to an unlawful use. For example, it would be unlawful to use an otherwise legal weapon against the civilian population of any enemy state or as a means for inflicting unnecessary suffering or destruction.[2] The concern here is not with when and how weapons—legitimate in themselves—may be unlawfully used. Rather, we are considering those weapons that were employed by American forces in Vietnam and whose legality, irrespective of their possible use, has been the subject of serious dispute. These weapons include most prominently lachrymatories (the most important of which is CS gas), herbicides, and napalm.

This listing is far from exhaustive. Many critics of the conduct of the war have challenged the legitimacy of a large number of weapons employed by American forces. Thus it has been argued that the M-16 rifle, a standard automatic weapon issued to American troops, may be illegitimate in view of the effect that the projectile it fires has when it makes contact with the human body. The projectile fired by an M-16 enters the body with a tumbling motion and this creates an unusually large wound. Some critics contend that this projectile is the functional equivalent of the prohibited dum-dum bullet. More serious, however, is the charge that many types of antipersonnel bombs are illegitimate weapons because of their indiscriminate and, in some instances, inhumane character. Such weapons are reputedly of little effectiveness against fixed military installations. But it is argued that they are highly effective against personnel in densely populated areas. Their indiscriminate character presumably stems from the relatively large area they may cover; their inhumane character is attributed to the unusual effects many of them have on bone structure, internal organs, and body fluids.

Granted, the antipersonnel bombs used in Vietnam had these technical features. But are they unlawful weapons? They clearly are if their use inevitably causes indiscriminate harm. Yet there are no persuasive reasons for believing that this is the case even after taking into full account the particular circumstances that marked the conflict in Vietnam. Although the radius of effectiveness of some antipersonnel bombs may be upwards of a kilometer, it does not follow that they could not be, and were not, employed in a discriminating manner, i.e., to inflict damage only against combatant forces. Once again, the distinction must be drawn between a weapon and the possible—even the likely—uses to which the weapon may be put.

Whether antipersonnel bombs may be considered unlawful because inhumane is a question that raises considerations touched upon earlier. One must turn chiefly to the practice of states to determine whether a weapon is inhumane by virtue of the unnecessary suffering and injury it causes. Whatever the judgment on the effects of antipersonnel bombs, the practice of states has not been to view the use of these weapons as contravening the principle of humanity. This is only to say that to date the practice of states has been to consider the military utility, or effectiveness, of antipersonnel bombs as outweighing humanitarian claims.

A similar conclusion must be reached with respect to the use of napalm. In an article that deals with "weapons employing fire," the U.S. Army Field Manual 27-10 states that "[t]he use of weapons which employ fire, such as tracer ammunition, flamethrowers, napalm and other incendiary agents, against targets requiring their use is not violative of international law. They should not, however, be employed in such a way as to cause unnecessary suffering to individuals." [3] In view of the known effects of napalm (not to mention flamethrowers), one might almost suspect the authors of intended irony.

In any of its several types, napalm is a severely painful weapon. The more developed types used in Vietnam constituted a marked "improvement" over the simple gelled gasoline used in World War II. The new versions are more combustible and adhere more effectively to the flesh as they burn. The most advanced form of napalm used by American forces, which is combined with white phosphorus, not only generates an intense heat, thereby permitting deep penetration of the flesh, but may cause poisoning of the liver and kidneys. Despite these effects, the current practice of states quite clearly supports the position that napalm is a legitimate weapon of war. It is a striking—and depressing—commentary on the manner in which the principle of humanity may be interpreted that the injury and suffering caused by napalm is nevertheless not considered disproportionate to its military utility. [4]

In the main, controversy over the legal status of the weapons employed in Vietnam has centered on the use by American forces of lachrymatory gases and herbicides. The view that the use of these irritant and antiplant chemicals violates the laws of war rests primarily on the ground that they contravene the provisions of the Geneva Protocol of 1925, which is, in turn, considered as declarative of (or coextensive with) customary international law. The Protocol forbids "the use in war of asphyxiating, poisonous or other gases, and of all analogous liquids, materials or devices," as well as "the use of bacteriological methods of warfare." While the United States had not yet ratified the Protocol, and is only now doing so, it is argued that since the provisions of the Protocol express customary international law, this country was bound by its provisions during the Vietnam War.

Even if the view were accepted that the Protocol is declarative of customary international law, there would remain the problem of determining the prohibitory scope of the Protocol. Whereas the nature of the prohibition against the use of bacteriological weapons is clear, uncertainty has persisted over the scope of the Protocol's provisions respecting chemical weapons other than "asphyxiating" and "poisonous" gases and "all analogous liquids, materials or devices."

In large measure, this uncertainty is the result of the difference between the French and English texts, both of which are authentic. While the English text speaks of "asphyxiating, poisonous or other gases," the French text speaks of "gaz asphyxiantes, toxiques ou similaires." On a broad interpretation, it is contended that the Protocol should be read as prohibiting the use of *all* other gases. On a narrow interpretation, it is argued that only *similar* other gases are forbidden by the Protocol.

If the broad interpretation is accepted, the Protocol prohibits the tear gases used in Vietnam and, though this is less clear, the use of herbicides as well. If the narrow interpretation is accepted—and that is the position that the American government has supported—the irritant and antiplant chemicals used in Vietnam may be considered lawful weapons provided their effects neither destroy human life nor impair health. For the narrow interpretation evidently forbids the use of all other gases—and analogous liquids, materials, or devices—that have harmful effects similar to the effects of poisonous and asphyxiating gases.

It is scarcely possible to resolve this difference in interpretation by appealing to the text of the Protocol, for its terms admit both interpretations. There still remains the need to examine the developments leading up to the Protocol, for they shed light on its object and purpose by revealing what the parties understood of the treaty's terms during this preparatory work. Likewise, the subsequent interpretation of the Protocol by the contracting parties over a period of more than four decades is useful. When these factors are taken into account, there is much to be said for the conclusions reached by Richard R. Baxter and Thomas Buergenthal that the Protocol should be interpreted to prohibit the use in war "of all chemical agents having a direct toxic effect on man that might be used as antipersonnel weapons, including tear gas and other forms of irritant chemicals," and that "the case seems stronger for including anti-plant chemicals within the prohibitions of the Protocol than for excluding them."[5].

Because the United States had not ratified the 1925 Geneva Protocol, its relevance to the use of chemical agents by American forces in Vietnam turns on the relationship of the treaty to customary international law. Thus, even if the broad interpretation of the Protocol is correct, it is still not decisive for assessing the American use of irritant and antiplant chemicals. We still must determine whether the Protocol was declarative of, or coextensive with, customary international law at the time these chemicals were employed in Vietnam.

Those who argue for a broad interpretation of the Protocol and who argue further that the Protocol is declarative of customary international law sometimes take on an unnecessary burden. They often fail to distinguish between the customary law of 1925 and the customary law of 1965.

The relevant customary law at the time of the Protocol's drafting was probably not as sweeping in its prohibitive range as is the broad interpretation of the treaty. For example, the customary rule in 1925 forbidding poison or poisoned weapons does not have the prohibitory scope claimed for a broad interpretation of the Protocol. Let us assume, despite support for the opposite view, that in 1925 the customary rule forbidding poison was applicable either by analogy or by necessary implication to gases and other chemicals. It does not follow that a broad interpretation of the Protocol on this point should be equated with the customary law in 1925. The Protocol can be equated with such prior customary law only insofar as it forbids gases and other chemicals that either are poisonous or—even if not poisonous—inflict unnecessary suffering and injury. If the Protocol were to be equated with the customary international law in 1925, it is not the broad interpretation but, at best, the narrow one that seems appropriate. Indeed, the prohibitions under the Protocol may be broader than those of customary international law in 1925.[6]

It is quite another matter to contend that by the time of the Vietnam War the Protocol, as broadly interpreted, had come to express customary international law in 1965 even though at the time of its conclusion it was not declarative of the customary law. This contention is frequently advanced in the form that the Protocol "created" customary international law. This manner of formulation cannot be taken literally. Neither at the time of its conclusion nor subsequently could the Protocol create customary law. But it could come to express such law if the behavior it prohibits reflects the "constant and uniform practice" and the *opinio juris* required of custom. In support of the position that by 1965 the customary law had become coextensive with the Protocol as broadly interpreted is the almost uniform practice of states over a period of four decades of refraining from the use of all forms of chemical warfare.

Nevertheless, it is still unclear whether this abstention, when taken together with the frequent condemnation by states of the use of "poisonous or noxious gases or other inhumane devices of warfare,"[7] created a presumption by the time of the Vietnam War of a customary norm forbidding all forms of gas—let alone all other forms of chemical warfare. It remains uncertain because the object of almost universal condemnation was gas, rather than all other forms of chemical warfare. In addition, the condemnation of gas was almost invariably made—at least by those states not parties to the Geneva Protocol—in terms of the general principle forbidding the use of inhumane means of warfare.[8]

In view of the foregoing, it is reasonable to maintain that at the time of the Vietnam War there was considerable uncertainty respecting the status of gases, and other chemical weapons, that were neither poisonous, nor asphyxiating, nor inhumane. Nor is it relevant to argue that this uncertainty has now been resolved in favor of the view that the customary law forbids all forms of chemical warfare. The use of lachrymatory gases and herbicides in Vietnam precipitated a reaction—witness, for example, the 1969 resolution of the General Assembly[9]—that might be regarded as clarifying this uncertainty. However, the primary concern here is with the situation that largely preceded the reaction to the American employment of chemical agents in Vietnam. Even now a measure of doubt persists over the status in the customary law of chemical means of warfare that are neither poisonous, nor asphyxiating, nor inhumane. Perhaps this doubt will finally be put to rest by United States accession to the Geneva Protocol and by the formal acceptance by all parties that the Protocol does forbid all forms of chemical warfare.

A much stronger case may be made for the proposition that by the time of the Vietnam War, customary law prohibited the use of all chemical weapons with either lethal or lastingly injurious effects. Once this proposition is accepted—and it would appear as the minimal conclusion to be drawn from the practice of states since World War I—the critical issue raised by the American use of lachrymatory gases and herbicides in Vietnam becomes primarily a factual one, i.e., do these weapons destroy life or impair health?

In the case of the lachrymatories, and notably the extra-strength tear gas CS, it has been argued that the effects may prove lethal to any person exposed to a sufficiently high concentration. Even if this is true, it does not seem a persuasive enough argument for concluding that lachrymatories are consequently forbidden by the customary law. It would be persuasive only if it could be shown that control of the use of such gases is impossible. If this cannot be shown, then the fact that a lachrymatory gas may have lethal effects when administered in high concentrations concerns the method of use rather than the means itself.

More serious, however, is the argument that not all persons react similarly to lachrymatory gases and particularly that babies and children exposed to these gases have a high incidence of fatality. If this is indeed so, and if these gases were routinely used in situations in which babies and children were exposed to them, such use may be considered to have been unlawful. At the same time, the issue here also concerns, at least in part, the method of use rather than the means itself. Presumably, the gases may be used, and predominantly were used, in a discriminating manner against combatants, so that their direct effect would be neither destructive of life nor injurious to health. To be sure, when lachrymatories were used in Vietnam against combatants, the purpose was scarcely the much-advertised one of saving lives. But that is another matter and does not bear on the lawfulness of using such gases against enemy combatants.

In the case of herbicides, a distinction should be drawn between defoliation and crop destruction. The principal aim of defoliation is to increase visibility in dense jungle growth and to deny the enemy the concealment afforded by such growth. The aim of crop destruction—at least, the ostensible aim—is to deny the enemy his sources of food. In either case, the central legal issue raised is whether the effects of spraying can be controlled to prevent effects that are either lethal to, or injurious to the health of, combatant forces or the civilian population. If herbicides can be so controlled, then they are not unlawful means, though of course they may still be used in an unlawful manner. (For example, their use would be unlawful if they were administered in such quantities as to create a health hazard, or directed against a food supply known to be intended exclusively for the civilian population, or employed in such a manner that the damage to crops and, perhaps, to the environment generally is disproportionate to the military advantage gained.)

Although the evidence is still far from complete, and still very much in dispute, there appear to be increasingly persuasive reasons for believing that at least the more effective of the crop-destroying herbicides do create a distinct and serious health hazard. And it is not a sufficient reply to argue that there is as yet a lack of conclusive evidence to this effect. Belligerents are not at liberty to use an antiplant chemical on the grounds that it may not be poisonous to man or even on the grounds that it is probably not poisonous. Instead, there must be solid assurance that the chemical in question is not poisonous to man. To the extent that crop-destroying herbicides were used in Vietnam in circumstances in which this assurance simply could not be given (and there is little question but that some herbicides were so used), one must presume that such use was forbidden by the customary laws of war.

These views have been directed almost exclusively at the legal issues raised by the American use of tear gases and herbicides. They are made without implying any judgment as to whether these means ought ever to have been employed in the Vietnam War in the sense that, irrespective of their legal status, their military utility outweighed any and all countervailing considerations. In retrospect, it seems clear that their use was a mistake in policy, even if it was not a crime. This conclusion seems warranted because the political loss to the United States as a result of the outcry against their use alone outweighed whatever slight military utility they may have served. To the onus incurred by a war that could not ultimately be justified at home or abroad, and one the tactics of which from the outset raised serious question and criticism, was added the use of means that were bound to provoke additional criticism.

It does not really matter from this viewpoint that a reasonable case may be made in law for the American use in Vietnam of lachrymatories and at least some herbicides. In the broader political context the decision to use these weapons has to be regarded as deplorable in its apparent disregard of a reaction that was surely predictable. In part, this reaction was undoubtedly the likely response of those who sought any and every possible reason for discrediting a war they did not approve of for other, broader reasons. However, it was also an expected response to the use of a broad category of means that even in its mildest forms men have long regarded with a special distaste.

It is not the weapons, but the methods employed in Vietnam that go to the heart of the debate over the conduct of the war. Indeed, as compared with the issues raised by the methods or tactics, the issues raised by the weapons per se seem no more than peripherally significant. If the conduct of the war reveals—as many critics now insist—not merely those departures from lawful behavior that we have come to accept as unavoidable in war, but rather a pervasive pattern of unlawful conduct, it is because of the methods or tactics employed.

Among the many lessons of Vietnam, one is surely the difficulty that men have in separating their attitude toward the justice of war in general, or the justice of a particular war, from their evaluation of the conduct of war. When men are convinced that a war is necessary and just, they can be relatively indifferent to the issues raised by the conduct of war, and disposed not to scrutinize too closely the methods pursued in that war. When men are not so convinced, they will see what they might otherwise overlook. This is not to suggest that what is "seen" is necessarily exaggerated, or even simply fabricated. It is to suggest that standards may, and in all likelihood will, be applied to the conduct of an unpopular war that could only be satisfied with the greatest difficulty, if at all.

There are some observers who have sought to explain not only the opposition to Vietnam generally, but the criticism of the conduct of the war particularly, primarily in terms of a changed attitude toward war. On this view, the condemnation of the manner in which the war in Vietnam was fought reveals a new and powerful sentiment against war itself. Thus, if the Vietnam War is condemned for the reason that it was "too destructive," this is taken as an indication that men's standards of judgment have changed and not simply that the conflict in Vietnam was inordinately destructive in quantitative terms. Even a small war—that is, small in terms of quantitative destruction—may appear too destructive if men are no longer willing to tolerate war at all. So, too, the charge that American methods in Vietnam frequently blurred, if not ignored altogether, the distinction between combatants and the civilian population is held to be indicative of this change in men's standard of judgment. For even if it is true that the manner in which the war was fought seriously compromised this vital distinction, it may still be argued that it was largely the adversary who created the difficulty. If the argument is nevertheless unpersuasive, it is presumably because of a growing revulsion against war itself.

A more plausible view, it seems, would find a sweeping condemnation of the conduct of the war in Vietnam rooted in an intense opposition to this particular war. On either view, however, one point stands out quite clearly: the conduct of the war has been scrutinized far more closely, and the standards by which this conduct has been judged have been raised far higher, than in earlier wars. Even what formerly passed for the near commonplace in earlier wars has not been exempt from condemnation in the case of Vietnam. Thus the practice of the body count has been seen by many critics as not only an important but indeed a central feature of a plan for conducting war that was bound to result in a pervasive pattern of atrocities. One critic finds in the body count "the perfect symbol of America's descent into evil," the prime characteristic of the "overall American crime of war in Vietnam." [10]

If that is so, we must conclude that America descended into evil some time ago and that the crime of war in Vietnam is only the latest in a series of crimes. For every war has had its body count, though the invention of that singularly infelicitous expression had to await entry of United States forces into Vietnam. During the Korean War, General Ridgeway declared on more than one occasion that his purpose was not to take real estate but to kill Chinese. At the time, few found this statement and the outlook it expressed particularly reprehensible. Progress in Korea was marked largely by enemy casualties, and the same was true of World War II.

In this respect, what distinguished the Vietnam War was not an insistence on finding in enemy casualties an important indication of progress toward the end of securing the enemy's submission. That is inseparable from war itself. But Vietnam was unique in its veritable obsession with finding in the body count *the* indication of progress. It is clear that the obsession partially obscured to the American command the nature of the conflict in Vietnam. It often prompted absurdly inflated reports of enemy casualties. But it is far from clear that the emphasis on body count led to the widespread commission of atrocities, in the desire to obtain the highest possible count.

There are other examples to bear out the general point that much of what appears to appall many critics about the conduct of this war did not have the same impact in earlier conflicts. It scarcely needs emphasizing that the aerial bombardment undertaken in the course of this war—whether in North or South Vietnam—was no more indiscriminate than the aerial bombardment of World War II. In the case of American bombing of North Vietnam, it was far more discriminating than the practices for air attacks during World War II and, perhaps, during the Korean War as well. Even in South Vietnam the bombing did not compare unfavorably, in terms of its indiscriminate effects, with these earlier conflicts.[11] More generally, the death and destruction visited by American arms upon the civilian population of both Vietnams did not appear unusual when compared with earlier conflicts. In Korea the civilian casualties and refugees resulting from the war were roughly comparable to those in Vietnam, and perhaps they were even greater. Certainly, the total physical destruction was no less.

These considerations need not be taken—and should not be taken —as a defense of the manner in which the Vietnam conflict was waged. On the contrary, they may well be taken as a retrospective condemnation of the way in which earlier conflicts were fought. Whether or not they are so taken, the point remains that it was in the course of this war that standards were insistently applied that were not applied—or, at any rate, not nearly so rigorously applied—to earlier conflicts. It was in the course of this war that many not only discovered the laws of war, but insisted that in judging the American conduct of the war these laws be taken with all seriousness. It is one of the ironies of the Vietnam War that this almost unprecedented development was coincident with a conflict whose characteristics made the application of the laws of war far more difficult than in earlier conflicts.

14 Comments

George H. Aldrich *

The basic conclusions of the chapters by Professors Levie and Tucker are not very different, and their analyses proceed along similar lines. However, their discussions might have been more helpful in preparing for future developments in the laws of war if they had dealt with all of the weapons about which questions have been raised and if they had considered them in some technical detail.

There is little that is useful to be added to what has already been said about napalm, tear gas, and herbicides. On the other hand, it might indeed be worthwhile to know precisely what the military uses and values are of cluster bombs and the M-16 rifle. It is equally important to know the technical details of these weapons, particularly the types of injuries they are likely to cause. These issues perhaps go beyond the competence of lawyers and diplomats. However, I was struck during the International Conference of Government Experts on the Humanitarian Law Applicable in Armed Conflicts in Geneva in 1971 by the futility of lawyers and diplomats proposing legal limitations on armaments without having first consulted their military and technical experts.

The basic value of this book is not confined exclusively to reexamining tactics and weapons used in the war in Vietnam (although there may be emotional benefit to some people from airing their concerns about the way that war was fought). Rather, another, and perhaps the most important contribution of these discussions is to give some meaningful guidance to those who are concerned with future developments in the laws of war. For example, I welcome the valuable suggestion that starvation should be outlawed as a weapon of war. This proposal was recently advanced by Dr. Jean Mayer to the Panel on Humanitarian Problems and International Law of The American Society of International Law and is echoed here in the discussion of crop destruction and the use of herbicides. I regret that there have not been more such concrete ideas presented here, particularly in the discussion of questionable weapons.

*The views expressed are those of Mr. Aldrich and do not necessarily reflect those of the United States Department of State.

With respect to napalm, I think there is general agreement that it is not illegal, but that from a humanitarian standpoint it should be illegal. There is also general agreement that it has great military value and, therefore, that it is unlikely to be outlawed at an early date. We should look at where it has been used, what its effects have been, and what the public reaction has been. But it is doubtful that we shall find a clear guide.

I am informed that the United States used napalm in South Vietnam, but not in North Vietnam. In the North, the substitute weapon for suppression of antiaircraft fire was generally the cluster-bomb unit. That indicates something about the anticipation of public criticism if napalm had been used. One possible direction in which further legal efforts may be pursued was indicated at the 1971 ICRC Conference of Government Experts. Several delegations at that meeting proposed not to ban napalm, but to restrict its use to situations in which it is reasonably thought that noncombatants are unlikely to be affected.

On herbicides and tear gas, the issues are quite different. Speaking personally, I think their future is extremely limited. It seems clear that the world is moving rather quickly in the direction of prohibiting their use in warfare. In my view we will see that prohibition become effective in reasonably short order. However, any prohibition is going to leave unclear areas. For example, the use of herbicides to keep underbrush and foliage down around military installations is not likely to be prohibited. There will probably be several grey areas between the legal and illegal uses. Similarly, with tear gas, what about its use to control a riot in a prisoner-of-war camp? It seems doubtful that that would be considered a prohibited use. But on the surface even this question is unclear.

It is fair to note that, when the issue of the use of tear gas in Vietnam first arose in 1965, the arguments in favor of its use appeared overwhelming. As other contributors have pointed out, using tear gas to force Viet Cong out of caves, particularly in situations in which there were a number of noncombatants with them, seems clearly preferable to employing high explosives. Nevertheless, a number of us who were within the government and concerned with this question were disturbed at the precedent of the use of gas of any kind in warfare. We were afraid that it would be difficult to prevent the use of increasingly dangerous gases and their use for other than humanitarian purposes. However, we felt that there was a rational basis for drawing a distinction that could result in constructing a kind of firebreak against undesirable escalation.

In 1965 and 1966 some of us in government thought that if the type of gas used in Vietnam could be limited to the type used commonly by democratic governments for the control of riots among their own people, this would provide a built-in restraint against the use of dangerous gases. For example, the only gases that were authorized for use in Vietnam were CS and CN. There existed another gas, somewhat stronger, called DM, but it was thought likely to produce a small, but measurable incidence of fatalities. For that reason, it was not used for domestic riot control in the United States, and we recommended against authorizing its use in Vietnam. On this point our views became the controlling policy of the United States.

We also believed that the use of tear gas in Vietnam should be limited to humanitarian purposes—that is, uses that would be likely to save either enemy or civilian lives. However, we were not able to obtain adoption of that limitation. As others have described, the use of tear gas in Vietnam increased greatly, and the types of uses proliferated to include some that, because of the use of tear gas and lethal fire together, could not be justified as humane. Thus our hope to impose this restriction on escalation proved vain.

Without any further details of our unsuccessful efforts in this regard, I believe that we can see in this experience the extreme difficulty of maintaining distinctions of legal and humanitarian significance under the pressures of combat. Perhaps the greatest value of clear international agreements on the laws of war is to make it more likely that distinctions of this type will be respected. And such accords will help to assure that violations of their provisions will be recognized as violations of the laws of war and will result in punishment.

15 Comments

Anthony D'Amato

My assessment of the chapters by Professors Levie and Tucker can best be organized by the simple geometric diagram below (see figure 1).

Figure 1:

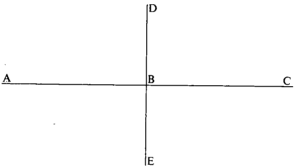

Key:

A = Policy
B = International Legal Obligations of States
C = International Criminal Law Applicable to Persons
D = Geneva Protocol of 1925
E = International Customary Law

This diagram seeks to visualize my understanding of the relationship among national policy, codified and customary international law, and individual responsibility as they impinge upon the rules governing permissible weaponry in armed conflicts. Although I shall treat segments of the diagram one by one, the whole is, in my view, greater than the sum of its parts. I will begin with line ABC and then turn to DBE.

Think of B (International Legal Obligations of States) as a movable point along the line. I believe that Professor Levie clearly and Professor Tucker only slightly less clearly place point B at the right end of the line segment very near, or even coterminous with, point C (International Criminal Law Applicable to Persons). But I think that point B should be moved all the way to the left to be very near, if not superimposed upon, point A (Policy). Before turning to the significance of this difference, I want to assure potential critics that my moving the point from right to left is not simply another reflection of my radicalism.

Professors Levie and Tucker would make a clear separation between policy, or point A, and the requirements of international law, or points B and C at the other end of the line segment (figure 2).

Figure 2:

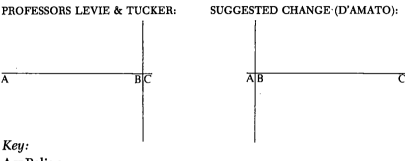

PROFESSORS LEVIE & TUCKER: SUGGESTED CHANGE·(D'AMATO):

Key:
A = Policy
B = International Legal Obligations of States
C = International Criminal Law Applicable to Persons

Professor Levie concludes that tear gas, napalm, and herbicides should as a matter of policy be discontinued without delay, even though their use by American forces in Vietnam did not in his opinion violate any norm of customary international law. Professor Tucker is not quite so sure that tear gas and some herbicides might not have been unlawful weapons as used in Vietnam, but in any event he too deplores their use as a matter of policy even if a reasonable case could be made for them as far as international law was concerned.

However, I draw a much broader conclusion from this case in which international actions of a state so clearly seem to be mistakes of policy within an area traditionally regulated by international customary law. In my view this very clarity of perception of policy has a good statistical probability of testifying to a parallel responsibility under customary law. In this regard there is an analogy from United States tests of hydrogen bombs in the Pacific in 1954. When some Japanese fishing vessels were damaged from the explosions, the United States government paid them full compensation, while at the same time it disclaimed any legal liability. The policy was obviously clear—if by your own actions on the high seas you cause injury to someone else, you should pay compensation. When the policy is that clear, can the legal requirement to pay compensation be absent? Was it persuasive—or even very useful—for the United States to make that disclaimer to the Japanese fishermen? Similarly, if Professor Levie finds it so clear that the use of certain weapons should be discontinued, is it persuasive that discontinuing them would be gratuitous and quite separate from the pressure that norms of customary international law exert upon national decision makers?

Indeed, the very strength of the policy reasons adduced for abandoning these weapons in Vietnam results from having the same policies occur with equal persuasiveness to decision makers in other nations during previous wars not all that dissimilar from Vietnam. Indeed, these policies were in fact responsible for the generation of articulated state practice amounting to customary international law. International norms do not descend upon us out of the blue. Instead they arise out of the policies of nations interacting with other nations.

Any existing norm of international law is the visible top of a pyramid of policies each having great force and conviction. In addition, from a jurisprudential viewpoint, we should not too easily nor too readily separate the *is* from the *ought*—we should not be too positivistic, as Professor Covey Oliver has characterized it. Granted, what ought to be done in the future is not equivalent to present law—here Professor Baxter has put it well in his comments in chapter 3 on Professor Falk's discussion. On the other hand, in law, as Professor Lon Fuller has insightfully written, the *is* and the *ought* intersect in determining the very content of what law is.

Law necessarily includes within its own content certain natural or ethical principles of method and substance—in a way well exemplified by the sort of approach taken by Professor Falk in chapter 1. Professor Falk does not discuss primarily what the law should be in the future as a matter of policy or ethics, but what the legal requirements were with respect to Vietnam. He interprets the *is* of the law in the context of widely held past views or subjective expectations of the *ought*. By this method of interpretation he helps to determine the content of the law in much the same way as a judge would in the context of a real case.

Finally, the working out of customary international law over time entails a certain internal momentum. Incipient customary law itself becomes another policy reason that reinforces the law. In other words, a nation usually finds a strong policy interest in simply obeying international law. This policy interest, added to others, crystallizes and reinforces the emergent norm. This kind of process seems to have taken place, whether subliminally in certain cases or not, within the United States, leading to the almost unanimous conclusion that we really ought to have stopped the use of tear gas, herbicides, and perhaps napalm and antipersonnel bombs in Vietnam long before United States involvement in the war ended. This conclusion is probably not isolable from the requirements of international customary law. Point B in this case is very close indeed to point A.

Perhaps a basic reason for Professors Levie and Tucker separating points A and B is that they do not separate points B and C. They do not distinguish between international legal norms applicable to states and international customary law governing individual conduct. For example, if the use of tear gas violates customary law, then Professors Levie and Tucker would probably say that those Americans in the hierarchy of military command who ordered the use of tear gas in Vietnam would be war criminals. Clearly they are very reluctant to want to be open to such a conclusion, and thus they are impelled to separate policy from law. An even clearer case would be any legal opinion penned by present counsel for the Pentagon or for the State Department. If they were to conclude that the American use of certain weapons and technology in Vietnam contravened international law, they might fear that such a conclusion could be used against their own colleagues in government in any real (or even mock) war crimes trial. Quite naturally they would be likely to conclude with great force that such weaponry should be discontinued immediately as a matter of policy, but not as a matter of international law.

By advocating that point B be moved away from point C and toward point A, I am basically saying that in certain areas of substantive uncertainty individual responsibility for war crimes should not be coterminous with the international obligations of states. A simple violation of international law might be enough to deter a country from using tear gas in warfare without making the governmental advocate of such use a war criminal. Indeed the Geneva Protocol of 1925, like the Hague Conventions of 1899 and 1907, was addressed to states. It was only the Nuremberg trials that picked up some of the substantive provisions of conventions and made criminal legislation out of them. Of course, the Nuremberg tribunals were justified in doing this insofar as grave substantive breaches were concerned.

With respect to certain types of warfare that, as Professors Levie and Tucker have found, are quite controversial as to their inclusion or exclusion from the Geneva Protocol, it might be unfair to hold a decision maker who orders their use criminally liable. Normally, ignorance of the law is no excuse; but perhaps uncertainty of the law should be. For purposes of criminal law, the statute should be very clear and un-ambiguous. I think that even state practice, after some perhaps regret-table excesses at Nuremberg and in the Far East, has come around to this position. In the United States Lieutenant Calley was prosecuted for one of the clearest of all possible war crimes. On the other hand, there is not much support for prosecuting individuals for violation of uncertain rules, such as a pilot who dropped tear gas or a decision maker who ordered the use of herbicides.

If it is accepted that there can be a distinction between laws of war-fare applying to states and those creating war crimes, then we may have resolved the apparent dilemma of counsel for the United States govern-ment. They might have felt free months or even years before now to argue strongly that the use of weaponry and technology such as tear gas and herbicides, and perhaps even napalm, violated international cus-tomary law. Along with their friends outside of government, these counsel might have felt less constrained to distinguish so sharply be-tween policy and law if they knew that their conclusions would not redound to the great personal disadvantage of decision makers within the government. Professor Falk has arrived at this same point by recom-mending a general amnesty for governmental decision makers. My point is that this can be done within the law rather than by resorting to an external device such as amnesty.

I now turn to the vertical line segment DBE. Professors Levie and Tucker have given great attention to the part visible above the horizon-tal line, namely point D (Geneva Protocol of 1925) (see figure 3).

Figure 3:

PROFESSORS LEVIE & TUCKER: SUGGESTED CHANGE (D'AMATO):

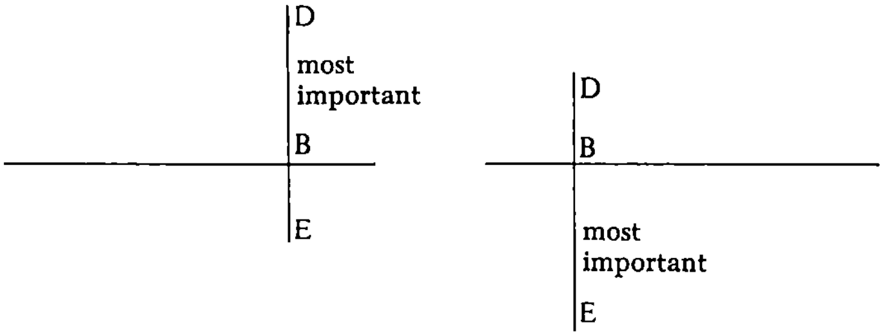

Key:
B = International Legal Obligations of States
D = Geneva Protocol of 1925
E = International Customary Law

They seem to agree with the position taken by Professors Baxter and Buergenthal, in an essay they both cite, that the law of the matter is pretty largely in the Protocol. All of these men seem to agree that the Protocol is broader and more sweeping—and simultaneously, if para- doxically, even more detailed—than customary international law in the absence of the Protocol. This conclusion lets the United States slip out from between the narrow obligation of customary law and the broader shadow of the Protocol, to which the United States as a nonparty was not bound. I find that this view is not supported by a convincing indepen- dent study of the content of customary law. In short, BE (International Customary Law), which is the part of the vertical line segment that is under the horizontal line ABC, may not have been given its due in this collection or in any published book or article to date.

In the first place, I am not as sure as Professor Tucker that the Protocol could not have "created" a goodly amount of customary law relating to the use in warfare of gases and analogous liquids and mater- ials. Certainly one could argue—to take a clear, if extreme, case—that shortly after the passage of the Protocol in 1925 there was, even for non- parties, a rapidly growing international customary law prohibiting the use in war of poisonous gas. Second, we should look very closely at the experience since 1925 (see figure 4). Professors Levie and Tucker, and to a large extent Professors Baxter and Buergenthal, seem to treat the post- 1925 experience as relevant only to the interpretation of the scope of the Protocol, even though they all acknowledge a distinction between the Protocol and customary law.

Figure 4:

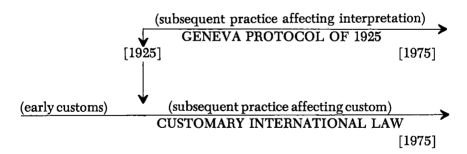

The post-1925 experience, however, might be differently inter- preted depending on whether one is interpreting the provisions of a treaty or the content of customary international law. The two types of interpretations do not follow the same methodology. The provisions of a treaty lean heavily upon analogies with the law of contract even as to subsequent state practice—indeed, here is where Professor Levie's troubles with reservations to the Protocol belong. On the other hand, the interpretation of customary law is more analogous to the common law of judicial decisions (taking articulated state practice to be the rough equivalent of a judicial decision). As a result, contrary to the rather easily adopted assumptions of Professors Levie, Tucker, Baxter, and Buergenthal, customary international law might just possibly have evolved in such a way as to be more immediately relevant and more prohibitory of the use of tear gas and herbicides than any interpretation, broad or narrow, of the Protocol.

To some extent Professor Tucker's discussion may leave this possibility open. By focusing upon certain principles of law—such as weaponry deemed inhumane, indiscriminate, disproportionate, or treacherous—he may be implying that the ambit of customary law could be more particular and immediately relevant to the weapons used in Vietnam than might be the Protocol or the Hague Regulations. The specific trouble with this approach, as Professor Tucker himself seems to recognize, and as Professor Baxter mentions, is that customary law began not with these principles, but rather with the prohibition of specific conduct. The principles came later, interpolated by scholars and governments and, in some cases, tribunals. The principles thus do not constitute the law, although they are relevant factors in interpreting the nature and scope of acts of states that are alleged to constitute precedential situations for customary legal development.

If a definitive study of the customary law pertaining to the use of weaponry and technology in Vietnam is desired, it should be recognized that its preparation will be a time-consuming and costly project. It would include a detailed study of the state papers of many governments and the events of numerous wars. This would be undertaken for five principal purposes. First, it would identify the technologies that were available and were, or were not, employed. Second, if certain technologies were used, the study would determine whether they were relied upon only as reprisals or only to a lesser extent than they effectively could have been. Third, it would uncover what government officials and military officials said among themselves and to each other about the possible and permissible use of such weapons. Fourth, it would discover whether protests were given or received concerning any such actual or threatened use. And, finally, it would pose related questions such as those that the foregoing may have suggested. Until such a study is undertaken, I, for one, would be a little cautious about concluding that the use in Vietnam of tear gas or herbicides clearly did not constitute a violation of customary international law.

16   In Reply

Howard S. Levie

The difficulty that I find with Professor D'Amato's criticisms is that he appears to confuse desirable humanitarian policy with customary international law. Unfortunately, what may have come to be regarded as morally correct does not always constitute, or become, law. For example, as a humanitarian policy I suggest that the use of napalm be expressly outlawed. But it is sophistic logic to assume that the present use of napalm is illegal just because there are many who agree that the use of napalm should be banned.

As has already been pointed out, fire has long been an accepted method of making war. Flamethrowers were used extensively by many of the belligerents during World War I. No claim was advanced that their use was illegal. Flamethrowers, magnesium bombs, phosphorus bombs, napalm, Molotov cocktails, and probably a number of other forms of fire were used by many of the belligerents during World War II. Again there were no claims that their use was illegal. This uncontested practice of states during the two major conflicts of this century certainly seems to testify that there was and is no rule of customary international law outlawing the use of fire in general and napalm in particular. This is the case no matter how desirable such a rule may be from the humanitarian, moral, and ethical points of view.

The intersecting of "the *is* and the *ought,*" to use Professor D'Amato's term, may well be a philosophically valid method of stating how customary international law should develop. But a pragmatic approach to the same subject indicates that the *ought,* no matter how morally valid, does not become customary international law unless and until the practice of states so decrees. As long as the practice of states rejects the *ought,* it remains nothing but a pious desire to be urged by those who believe it to be morally correct. This situation changes only when those who hold these views succeed either in changing the practice of states or in outlawing the conduct in question by appropriate international legislation—in this case, a multilateral convention.

There appears to be a number of individuals interested in the law of armed conflict who assume that their "subjective expectations of the *ought*" determine what that law is. They are correct, in my view, as to the substance of the *ought,* but they are wrong in ascribing binding legislative effect to their personal convictions.

I do not believe that any practical purpose would be served by taking specific issue with the numerous other statements contained in the criticisms made by Professor D'Amato of those portions of my chapter 12 that conflict with his legal philosophy. We apparently agree almost entirely on the *ought;* we appear to disagree nearly as completely on the *is*.

Part Three

INDIVIDUAL RESPONSIBILITY IN WARFARE

17 *Paul C. Warnke*

War raises many questions for which law has no answers. From Saint Augustine to President Nixon, the waging of war has been rationalized as a road to peace. The standards developed for individual behavior have proven to be uneasy analogues in the international regime when resort is made to violence to achieve foreign-policy objectives. Time may show that the use of military force was unwarranted and its objectives unworthy. But history's assessment of national error, and the less remote assessment of the fitness of a nation's wartime leaders to retain or resume high office, must be reviewed as an issue apart from that of combatant conduct.

Books such as Gen. Telford Taylor's document the anomaly of seeking to distinguish degrees of dreadfulness in the context of this most dreadful of human phenomena.[1] What the Vietnam tragedy should have made even clearer, however, is the distinction drawn at the Nuremberg and Tokyo trials between the crime of war and "war crimes." Instead, for some the Vietnam experience has seemed to blur the differences and to require suspension of individual responsibility for crimes in a war that they regard as intrinsically criminal.

The novelty of Nuremberg was the attempt to define and deter as criminal conduct the decisions of national leaders to wage aggressive war. In a world of autonomous national states, this can only be a crime reserved for losers. But the inability to get an objective ruling on the justice of a nation's war effort should not preclude a fair trial for those individuals who engage in, order, or condone acts of calculated cruelty.

Eradication of the crime against peace obviously would put an end to war crimes as well. Those who purposefully cause war are thus the master criminals—guilty, in the Nuremberg judgment's words, of "the supreme international crime differing only from other war crimes in that it contains within itself the accumulated evil of the whole." But the question of responsibility for bringing a war into being is highly resistant to legal resolution. Probably this responsibility can be assessed in the contemporary context only in a tribunal convened by the victor to try the vanquished.

In the case of Vietnam, the United States military participation has been both defended and attacked under the Nuremberg principles of crimes against peace. Opinions have differed on such fundamental issues as whether Vietnam is one or two countries, and thus on whether the United States was defending a small ally against foreign attack or meddling officiously, and illegally, in the internal affairs of another country.

In the past, common perception of the national interest has generally foreclosed domestic attacks on a nation's war effort. As General Taylor has pointed out, the Soviets could thus sit in solemn judgment on Germany's conduct of an aggressive war in which the Soviet Union was for a time its ally.[2] The Vietnam War was perhaps unique, however, in that sizable numbers of Americans have questioned the legitimacy of our country's role.

But no conceivable outcome of the conflict in Vietnam could have made the legitimacy of that role a justiciable question. Military defeat was never in the cards. Thus it is still true that no American President has "lost a war." And, as I have already said, formal charges of crimes against peace are reserved for losers. In another, profounder sense, all the men who occupied the Presidency in the Vietnam War years have been losers from it. Their appreciation of the national interest, or the international interest, has been, at least in hindsight, demonstrably faulty. A heavy political penalty is appropriate and has, in part, already been paid.

But criminal responsibility for personal conduct that transgresses recognized standards is a different, and, I suggest, a far simpler question requiring no novel doctrine and no deep assessment of national motivation and morality.

In an article that appeared in April 1971, Hans Morgenthau asserted: "It is the contrast between the judgment of condemnation handed down by the military court in the case of Lt. Calley and the judgment of acquittal issued by the court of public opinion every day in the case of our leaders and ourselves that deprives the Calley verdict of moral validity."[3] I believe that this confuses quite separate issues. The lack of a national consensus as to the justice of our cause in Vietnam has no bearing on Lieutenant Calley's guilt or innocence. Dr. Morgenthau later maintained that Lieutenant Calley "did what he was ordered to do and what many others did who were lucky enough to escape public attention."[4] To the extent that Lieutenant Calley's superiors may be shown in fact to have ordered what happened at My Lai, their equal responsibility as war criminals would be undeniable—though their complicity would not excuse those who executed an order obviously illegal under the rules of war. Those who sought to ignore or obscure what happened are guilty too—as accessories after the fact and as stimuli to similar atrocities.

But direct involvement in atrocities—whether as actor or director—involves none of the complexities of determining if a conflict should be deemed unwarranted aggression rather than the "collective defense" authorized by article 51 of the United Nations Charter. On this latter issue, the judgment of history may be merciless. I question, however, whether contemporary concern can or should yield penal consequences.

War crimes must continue to be distinguished from crimes against peace. To do otherwise would turn the Nuremberg principles into a shield for those chargeable with the ultimate inhumanity to defenseless human beings. We can, I believe, accept the proposition that mean-minded men can do bad things in the best of wars. I might suggest also that good men in good faith may involve their country in a bad war. But history's assessment is not necessary to support the prosecution and conviction of those responsible for incidents of atrocity. That not all can be found and punished is a failing in the most meticulous attempt at application of criminal law, whether civilian or military.

A war's ultimate justice or injustice is basically irrelevant to the criminality of the actions of an individual combatant. Those who fought in Vietnam and abided by the rules of war should not be subject to prosecution under any construction of the Nuremberg principles. For example, Capt. Howard Levy's contention that war crimes were being committed by others in Vietnam gave him no automatic "Nuremberg defense" for his refusal in this country to obey an intrinsically lawful order to train medical aides.

The ultimate legality of our participation in Vietnam is, as General Taylor has pointed out, not now "susceptible to solution by judicial decree."[5] The resolution of this question, and the fate of those responsible for the American involvement, may—and should—be left for political action. But individual crimes in the Vietnam theater are proper grist for the judicial mill.

Some have argued that the entire idea of war crimes should be abandoned and any personal conduct excused. Their rationale is that war would then become so horrible as to revolt the conscience of the world and lead to its eradication. This is perhaps as misconceived as the argument that soldiers who kill under orders with no colorable military justification should be excused because their military and civilian leaders may be guiltier.

There are significant humanitarian purposes served by the international laws of war. As General Taylor has noted, the rules protecting prisoners of war have saved millions of lives in earlier conflicts. These rules were relied on for protection of United States military personnel held captive in North Vietnam. The scrapping of these restraints would lead directly to the death of countless innocents in current and future armed conflicts.

At the same time it is true, as General Taylor points out, that this has been "a pretty bloody century and people do not seem to shock very easily."[6] This is, as he notes, distressingly confirmed in much of the reaction both to reports of My Lai and to the trial and conviction of an American officer who flatly admitted his role in the slaughter of unarmed civilians—men and women, children and the aged.

The Nuremberg concept of aggressive war as a crime susceptible of legal proof and judicial determination can be regarded as a noble experiment. It could even have some deterrent efficacy, if the combatants, whether they win or lose, could be persuaded to accept the jurisdiction of an international tribunal. Until that millennium, the risk of prosecution is but one small element in the greater risk of total military defeat. But win, lose, or draw, a civilized country with any claim to national morality can and must punish its citizens who violate basic norms of human behavior in contravention either of domestic laws or of the rules of war.

There are those who disagree about whether the personal guilt of combatants can be assessed in the Vietnam context. Not too strangely with respect to this strangest of wars, some of them support the righteousness of the United States cause and others believe the war to have been unjust and immoral. Those who were ardent hawks contend in substance that, because our cause was just, My Lai probably never happened and anyway they were Communists who had it coming. And former doves feel that it is unfair to punish individual soldiers who were caught up in a war that the doves deem itself a far graver crime.

The first argument does not deserve an answer. But as to the second, if the overall injustice of a nation's cause waives individual and personal responsibility on the part of members of its fighting forces, then Lidice, Oradea, and the systematic slaughter of Jewish populations in occupied countries cannot be construed as the acts of war criminals. And if any individual behavior is allowable for those compelled by superior authority to fight in a "bad" cause, then perhaps the unfortunate General Yamashita had a better defense than lack of knowledge and inability to control the conduct of his forces in the Philippines in the closing days of World War II. But we hanged General Yamashita because, in the words of General MacArthur: "The soldier, be he friend or foe, is charged with the protection of the weak and unarmed. It is the very essence and reason for his being." General MacArthur added that when the soldier "violates his sacred trust he not only profanes his entire cult but threatens the very fabric of international society." [7]

There are, of course, the cloudy cases in which arguments of military necessity lead to actions that in less compelling circumstances would earn the condemnation of the civilized world. The bombardment of Coventry and Cologne, of London and Hiroshima, were plainly bound to kill civilians. It is hard to stomach the argument that they were directed at the war-making potential of the other side and intended to bring the war to a close by crippling this potential. Likewise, no one can genuinely believe that in Vietnam air strikes were surgical or that the napalm used by United States military forces distinguished the armed foe from the peasant child. As General Taylor points out, " 'necessity' is a matter of infinite circumstantial variation." [8] But there are, in any war, instances in which discrimination and decision are not difficult; in which casual and deliberate inhumanity can have no arguable effect in bringing further killing to a close. There are, in any war, individuals who allow that war to be an opportunity to satisfy their darkest urges. To excuse them because all wars are dreadful or because a particular one may not be justified by the national interest is, in my view, consonant neither with justice nor with its basic aim of providing and protecting an ordered society.

Perhaps in the grey area, popular wars win readier acceptance of marginal military justification for tactics that cause noncombatant casualties. But there is an area of conduct that is unrelievedly black, and no hand wringing or breast beating about the immorality of the particular conflict or the responsibility of those who brought it about can change this black to white. Some such offenses are sufficiently clear to have been spelled out in the Hague Regulations and Geneva Conventions. Among them is the declaration of article 4 of the annex to the Hague Convention No. IV of 1907, that enemy soldiers who have surrendered are not to be killed. [9] The Geneva Civilians Convention similarly commands safety for enemy civilians. Thus the suggestions that events at My Lai may somehow be excusable because it was a "combat village" and "even the babies might have been booby trapped" are without possible merit. Even if those slaughtered in the huts and ditches of My Lai had previously been armed enemies resisting the attack on their hamlet, their summary execution would still be a clear violation of established international law.

It has been suggested that the tragic peasants of My Lai might not have been "protected persons" within the terms of article 4 of the Geneva Civilians Convention, because they were not enemy civilians but instead "nationals of a co-belligerent state." [10] An open season on "friendlies" might remove legal doubts about some uses of American firepower in Laos, Cambodia, and South Vietnam. It might also decrease enthusiasm for security commitments from the United States. But any such legalism may be countered by the further legalism that under the 1954 Geneva Accords, the seventeenth parallel "should not in any way be interpreted as a political or territorial boundary." [11]

Perhaps a better answer is that, as General Taylor points out, "[t]he laws of war remain a body of what lawyers call 'customary' laws—that is to say, laws that are not created by statutes and enacted by legislators, but develop from societal customs and practices." [12] The Hague Convention No. IV of 1907 stated that questions not covered should be resolved by "the principles of the law of nations, as they result from usages established among civilized people, from the laws of humanity, and from the dictates of the public conscience." Disputed questions of nationality thus cannot control the guilt of those in any way responsible for the massacre.

Some would argue that the responsibility for My Lai extends to any and all who brought about our presence in Vietnam. [13] They contend that the application of massive American military force to put down a native insurgency would become inevitably a war against civilians and that My Lai thus, in the words of its main executioner, was not "any big deal." [14] In antiguerrilla action, in which the people are Mao's sea within which the guerrillas swim and survive, the prospects of widespread civilian suffering are obviously far greater than in the classic clash of front-line forces. This fact should lead to serious reconsideration of the merits of a counterinsurgent policy. It should lead also to more vivid realization that a decision to wage war is a decision to sacrifice an indeterminate number of innocent lives. It should lead to a resolve that military force should be used only on the most compelling showing of imminent danger to our national security.

But from my own experience and from the firsthand reports of those whose word and judgment I trust, I regard My Lai as the exception and believe that hundreds of similar military actions were conducted in Vietnam without the wholesale slaughter of helpless humans.

The inability to bring national leaders to the bar of justice under principles that were novel at Nuremberg cannot excuse failure to prosecute those guilty of committing, ordering, or authorizing actions that the common conscience must recognize as criminal. Close cases may be found. A commander who established a free-fire zone may have done so without considering the ratio of armed enemy to farm families. A pilot may have dropped his bombs with inadequate concern for whether the target was an ammunition cache or a field hospital. An ill-advised war may have multiplied the circumstances in which voiceless noncombatants were sacrificed to poorly perceived aspirations for peace.

A conscientious desire to live by the international and humanitarian standards we espouse would lead to the trial even of the tougher issues. But neither the Nuremberg novelty of war as a crime in itself, nor the problems of proof in close cases, should lead us in clear cases to make bad law.

18 *Richard A. Wasserstrom* *

One way to think about the responsibility of the individual for war crimes is to divide the topic up in two different ways. On the one hand, problems relating to the substantive laws of war can be distinguished from the problems relating to the *mens rea* requirement for the commission of war crimes. On the other hand, different classes of individuals can be held responsible for war crimes: the soldiers in the field who directly commit war crimes, and the military and civilian leaders under whose guidance, direction, or control these soldiers serve. Under these headings I will consider a variety of problems resulting from serious flaws in the prevailing conception of the laws of war and from erroneous interpretations of the way in which this *mens rea* requirement should apply to combat soldiers and military and civilian leaders.

Substantive Laws of War

I am concerned with a particular view of the character of the laws of war and the related notion of a war crime. [1] I believe that this view constitutes an accurate description of the existing laws of war and the dominant conception of a war crime, although I do not insist that it is the only possible explication of the nature and character of the laws of war. But I do claim that this is the view that many, if not most, lawyers, commentators, military tribunals, and courts have had in mind when they have talked about the laws of war and the responsibility of individuals for the commission of war crimes.

This system has certain distinguishing features. There are, to begin with, a number of formal agreements, conventions, and treaties among countries that prescribe how countries (chiefly through their armies) are to behave in time of war. And there are also generally accepted common-law rules and practices that likewise regulate behavior in warfare. Together all of these comprise the substantive laws of war.

For the most part, the laws of war deal with two sorts of problems: how classes of persons are to be treated in war (e.g., prisoners of war) and what types of weapons and methods of attack are permissible or not

*This chapter is a revised and edited version of the one published by Richard Wasserstrom as "The Legal Responsibility of the Individual for War Crimes," in *Philosophy, Morality, and International Affairs,* ed. Virginia Held, Sidney Morgenbesser, and Thomas Nagel, copyright © 1974 by Oxford University Press, which has kindly granted permission for the appearance of this chapter here.

permissible (e.g., the use of poison gas). Some of the laws of war—particularly those embodied in formal documents—are narrow in scope and specific in formulation. Thus, article 4 of the Hague Regulations provides in part that all the personal belongings of prisoners of war, "except arms, horses, and military papers," remain their property. Others are a good deal more general and vague. For example, article 23(e) of the same Regulations prohibits resort to "arms, projectiles, or material calculated to cause unnecessary suffering." Similarly, article 3 of the Geneva Conventions of 1949 provides in part that "[p]ersons taking no active part in the hostilities . . . shall in all circumstances be treated humanely." The reader should also refer to the definition of "war crimes" applied at Nuremberg. [2]

One important feature of this conception of the laws of war is the understanding that only violence and suffering not directly or significantly connected with the waging of war are prohibited. As one commentator has put it, the laws of war have as their objective that "the ravages of war should be mitigated as far as possible by prohibiting needless cruelties, and other acts that spread death and destruction and are not reasonably related to the conduct of hostilities." [3]

This understanding is reflected by the language of many of the laws themselves, but it is demonstrated far more forcefully by the way even relatively unambiguous and absolute prohibitions are to be interpreted. The Nuremberg definition of war crimes, for example, prohibits the "*wanton* destruction of cities, towns or villages." [4] Likewise, article 23(e) of the Hague Regulations prohibits the resort to arms "calculated to cause unnecessary suffering." But "unnecessary suffering" means suffering that is not reasonably related to any military advantage to be derived from its infliction. As Professor Schwartzenberger has noted, "[t]he legality of hand grenades, flame-throwers, napalm, and incendiary bombs in contemporary warfare is a vivid reminder that suffering caused by weapons with sufficiently large destructive potentialities is not 'unnecessary' in the meaning of this rule." [5]

Another way to make the same point is to indicate the way in which the doctrine of military necessity plays a central role in this conception of the laws of war. It, too, is explicitly written into a number of the laws of war to provide a specific exception. Thus, the Nuremberg definition of war crimes prohibits "devastation not justified by military necessity."

The doctrine of military necessity is, moreover, more firmly and centrally embedded in this conception of the laws of war than an illustration of the preceding type would suggest. The doctrine does not merely create an explicit exception, but rather functions as a general justification for the violation of most, if not all, of even the specific prohibitions that constitute a portion of the laws of war. Thus, according to one expositor of the laws of war, Telford Taylor, the unqualified prohibition against the killing of enemy combatants who have surrendered is to be understood to permit the killing of such persons where that is required by military necessity. There may well be times in any war when it is permissible to kill combatants who have laid down their arms and tried to surrender. Professor Taylor states:

Small detachments on special missions, or accidentally cut off from their main force, may take prisoners under such circumstances that men cannot be spared to guard them or take them to the rear, and that to take them along would greatly endanger the success of the mission or the safety of the unit. The prisoners will be killed by operation of the principle of military necessity, and no military or other court has been called upon, so far as I am aware, to declare such killings a war crime. [6]

Similarly, most forms of aerial warfare are legal because of the military importance of bombing. Once more Telford Taylor's analysis is illustrative of this attitude toward the laws of war. The bombing of cities was, he observes, not punished at Nuremberg and is not a war crime. This was so for two reasons. Since it was engaged in by the Allies—and on a much more intensive level than by the Germans or the Japanese—it would have been improper to punish the Germans and the Japanese for what we also did. But more importantly, the bombing of cities is generally permissible becuase bombing is an important instrument of war. [7]

The general test for the impermissibility of bombing is, says Professor Taylor, clear enough. Bombing is a war crime if, and only if, there is no proportionate relationship between the military objective sought to be achieved by the bombings and the degree of destruction caused by it. The importance of bombing as a weapon of war overrides any consideration of its indiscriminate nature. The fact that bombing is an inherently inaccurate undertaking and that bombs cannot discriminate between combatants and noncombatants is overlooked.

The foregoing constitutes a brief sketch of the specific prohibitions, accepted conventions, and general excusing and justifying conditions that comprise that conception of the laws of war with which I am concerned. Two more characteristics of this conception seem to flaw still further the substantive laws of war.

First is the failure of the laws of war to disallow the resort to aerial warfare and the use of weapons of mass destruction. I consider this a serious defect because it obliterates rather completely the distinction between combatants and noncombatants.

Some would doubtless argue that the distinction between combatants and noncombatants is neither an important distinction in theory nor a meaningful one in practice. This seems to me to be a mistake, for the basic distinction reflects, I believe, a concern for two basic considerations—namely, the degree of choice that persons had in getting into the position in which they find themselves and also the likelihood that they are, or are about to be, in a position to inflict harm on anyone else.

To be sure, the distinction between combatants and noncombatants is a relatively crude one. Some noncombatants are able in reasonably direct ways to inflict harm on others, e.g., workers in a munitions factory. And some noncombatants may very well have knowingly and freely put themselves in such a position. Concomitantly, many combatants may have been able to exercise very little choice in assuming the role of a combatant, e.g., soldiers who are drafted into an army under circumstances in which the penalties for refusing to accept induction are very severe.

Difficulties such as the foregoing would make it plausible to argue that the laws of war cannot reasonably be expected to capture these distinctions perfectly. One could thus argue that it is unreasonable to expect anyone or any weapon to be able to distinguish the conscripts from the volunteers in the opponent's army. It would, perhaps, even be plausible to argue (although, in my view, less convincingly) that civilians engaged in activities directly connected with the prosecution of the war can reasonably expect that they will be subject to attack. If the laws of war even preserved a distinction between soldiers, munitions workers, and the like on the one hand, and children, the aged, and the infirm on the other, one might maintain that the laws of war did succeed in retaining—at a low level and in an imprecise way—these distinctions of fundamental moral importance. But, as I understand them, the laws of war relating to aerial warfare and the use of weapons of mass destruction do not endeavor to preserve a distinction of even this crudeness. What is perhaps ruled out, although it is by no means certain after Dresden and Hiroshima, is the deliberate bombing of wholly civilian populations for the sole pupose of destroying those populations. What is clearly permissible is the knowing destruction of civilian populations—women, children, and the like—provided only that a military objective is the purpose of the bombing mission.

I do not think that a plausible justification can be found for regarding such behavior as permissible. I do not see any rational ground by which to distinguish knowingly destroying noncombatants with bombs dropped by a B-52 from shooting them at close range with a machine gun. If the latter is wrong because it does violence to the distinction between combatants and noncombatants, then the former is too. I find quite unpersuasive the two grounds for differentiation that are sometimes advanced.

The first of these alleged distinctions is that a bomb is the kind of weapon that cannot discriminate between combatants and noncombatants, whereas a machine gun, when properly aimed, can. This is doubtless true; but it only seems to me to be a good reason to prohibit the use of weapons like bombs—at least in those cases in which the relevant distinctions cannot be made.

The second defense of aerial bombardment is a particular illustration of a more pervasive defect in the laws of war—namely, that a general exception to almost all of the laws is permitted on grounds of military necessity. This way of thinking justifies the use of bombs and other weapons of mass destruction because they play too central a role in the prosecution of modern warfare. But this is, as I have said, only a particular version of a more pervasive defect that attends the doctrine of military necessity.

That doctrine, it should be noted, is typically employed in an ambiguous and misleading fashion. "Necessity" leads us naturally to think of extreme circumstances that at least excuse, if they do not justify, otherwise impermissible behavior. For example, one exception to the rule about taking prisoners might be a case in which necessitarian language does fit. If the prisoners are taken by the patrol deep in enemy territory, the captors will themselves almost surely be captured or killed. In such circumstances, the capturing forces cannot be held to the rule against killing prisoners because it is "necessary" that the prisoners be killed.

One may not, of course, be convinced that necessitarian language is appropriately invoked even in this case. But what should be apparent is that it is not appropriate to describe the doctrine that justified aerial warfare, submarine warfare, or the use of flamethrowers as one of military necessity. Necessity has nothing whatsoever to do with the legitimacy of the aerial bombardment of cities or the use of other weapons of mass destruction. To talk of military necessity in respect to such practices is to surround the practice with an aura of justification that is in no way deserved. The appeal to the doctrine of military necessity is in fact an appeal to a doctrine of military utility. On this view, the laws of war really prohibit (with only a few minor exceptions) some wrongful practices that also lack significant military value. The laws of war permit and treat as legitimate almost any practice, provided only that there is an important military advantage to be secured.

The more that this interpretation of the doctrine of military necessity permeates the conception of the laws of war, the less intelligible and attractive is the claim that the laws of war are a coherent, complete, or admirable code of behavior—even for the jungle of warfare. For, given the pervasiveness of this doctrine of military utility, the laws of war can be reduced in large measure to the principle that in war it is still wrong to kill (or maim or torture) another person for no reason at all, or for reasons wholly unrelated to the outcome of the war, but that is all. On this view the governing principle is that it is legitimate and appropriate (and sometimes obligatory) to do almost anything to anybody, provided only that what is done is reasonably related to a perceived military objective. It is, in short, to permit almost all possible moral claims to be overridden by considerations of military utility. Whatever else one may wish to claim for such a system of the laws of war, one cannot claim that they deserve either preservation or respect because of the connection these laws maintain with the idea of how persons ought to behave toward other persons.

Nor is it just a matter of abstract, aesthetic concern for coherence that is at stake. Much that is claimed for the laws of war must, I think, be abandoned under this conception of them.[8] In addition, if any persons under any circumstances are to be held to answer for the commission of war crimes, it is important that they be held to answer under a scheme of substantive law that is not fundamentally unfair. This means that they should not be held liable for actions that are indistinguishable in the significant, relevant respects from actions that are not proscribed. Thus, if the bombing of cities cannot be distinguished from other ways of killing civilians, it is hard to justify the punishment of persons who do the latter while people who do the former go unpunished (and even receive medals). Finally, as demonstrated below, this conception of the laws of war makes it very difficult to formulate a defensible *mens rea* requirement and apply it to the typical combat soldier.

Mens Rea *Requirement for the Soldier*

The case that many people consider the easiest in which to justify judgments of culpability and decisions of punishment is that of the soldier in combat who violates the laws of war. I do not think it is at all an easy case, because I do not believe that the *mens rea* requirement that ought to be satisfied before culpability attaches is often satisfied in the case of the ordinary soldier.

These are several considerations that ought to make us uneasy about the application of judgments of criminal responsibility to soldiers in combat, and the most prominent of these is the problem of superior orders. Nuremberg is illustrative of some of the difficulty.[9] The Charter of the Nuremberg International Military Tribunal (IMT) took a hard line with respect to the problems of superior orders. Article 8 said that "[t]he fact that the Defendant acted pursuant to order of his Government or of a superior shall not free him from responsibility, but may be considered in mitigation of punishment if the Tribunal determines that justice so requires."[10]

The IMT, in its judgment, modified (without indicating that it was doing so) the position of the Charter by only half accepting the Charter's rejection of the plea of superior orders as an excuse. The IMT did this by introducing some sort of a defense of duress:

> It was . . . submitted on behalf of most of these defendants that in doing what they did they were acting under the orders of Hitler, and therefore cannot be held responsible for the acts committed by them in carrying out these orders.
> . . . The provisions of . . . article 8 are in conformity with the law of all nations. That a soldier was ordered to kill or torture in violation of the international law of war has never been recognized as a defense to such acts of brutality, though, as the Charter here provides, the order may be urged in mitigation of the punishment. The true test, which is found in varying degrees in the criminal law of most nations, is not the existence of the order, but whether moral choice was in fact possible.[11]

It is difficult to imagine a more obscure way of characterizing the nature of the defense that the IMT was prepared to allow. What is clear, however, is that the IMT accepted superior orders as an excuse (provided "moral choice" was not possible), whereas in the Charter they were at best a mitigating circumstance.

The idea of moral choice is not a clear one, so it is worthwhile to consider a bit more carefully what the IMT might have meant. At least two interpretations come to mind. One would go something like this: The mere fact that an actor has been ordered to do something does not by itself excuse him from responsibility for his actions. This is as it should be because, at a minimum, something should be known about both the stipulated and the likely consequences for disobedience before it can be decided whether a person acting in obedience to orders should therefore be excused.

This is what the talk about the existence of moral choice comes to: Suppose, for instance, that there is a general standing order that soldiers are to kill rather than capture all enemy prisoners. At the very least, a soldier who has complied with such an order and has shot all his prisoners ought not be excused completely until a good deal more is known about the circumstances surrounding such compliance. For example, it would be necessary to determine the announced penalty for disobeying that order, the probable penalty for disobedience, the typical soldier's reasonable beliefs about the penalty, and this particular soldier's belief regarding the penalty. If the announced, probable, and understood penalty for disobedience is summary execution, the case would be very different from one in which the penalty is demotion in rank.

Thus, one interpretation of moral choice would focus heavily on the degree of choice exercisable by the actor. Where the penalty for disobedience is very great, and believed to be such, then one rationale for permitting the defense is that of excuse. In such circumstances a person will naturally, and perhaps inevitably, act so as to avoid the penalty. He does not, we might say, "really have any choice," and so he is for this reason to be exempted from punishment.

A somewhat different rationale would not focus upon the absence of choice so much as upon the poignancy of the dilemma in which the actor finds himself. It is not that he cannot help himself when he seeks to avoid the punishment; it is rather that human beings, when caught up in such circumstances, simply ought not be blamed for opting so as to save their own lives at the cost of other lives. People are not to be blamed, in other words, for failing to behave so heroically or with such altruism that they bring dire consequences upon themselves.

In either case, as I have said, the defense of superior orders would be legitimate provided the accused could show the choice involved to be an illusory or unduly difficult one.

But to say that a soldier in combat is excused from liability only where the consequences of disobedience are perceived by him to be very severe does not, I think, do full justice to the plight of the ordinary soldier. For this account omits the context within which he was trained and within which he finds himself once in combat. His training is likely to have consisted largely of a process designed to inculcate habits of obedience to command. In my view, this is an inevitable part of military training, because an army functions successfully only if habitual, unquestioning obedience is forthcoming on the part of the ordinary soldier. Thus, even if a portion (and it will invariably be a small portion) of basic training is devoted to a discussion of the laws of war, and even if a soldier is instructed that he ought not obey any order that is illegal on its face, the dominant thrust of his training is likely to have consisted of efforts directed toward transforming him into a person who will obey without question and without hesitation. It is not, therefore, sufficient to excuse him only when moral choice was not present; he ought, perhaps, to be excused whenever he does what he is told to do because this is what he will have been trained to do.

But suppose that a soldier's training is not as monolithic with respect to obedience to orders as it has just been described. Suppose instead that a genuine and serious attempt is made to inculcate habits of limited obedience. Suppose soldiers are earnestly encouraged to believe that while obedience to orders is important, it is not all that is important. Suppose, in particular, that soldiers are convincingly taught that an order that is clearly or obviously illegal, one that requires the soldier to do what it is manifestly wrong to do, ought not to be obeyed.

Even if we had such a system of training, and I do not think that we do, there is still a powerful argument that obedience to orders ought to be a complete defense. The argument turns upon the character of the existing laws of war and, concomitantly, upon the soldier's capacity to assess what is and is not a violation of the laws of war. More specifically, two related characteristics of the system of the laws of war are of particular significance to this point.

In the first place, although war crimes are thought to be the most clearly defined of the three sorts of activities with respect to war for which persons are held responsible, they are, as we have seen, often extremely vague and imprecise. Thus, to revert once again to article 23(e) of the Hague Regulations, it seems to me to place an ordinary soldier in an extremely difficult position to require him to decide when he is using a weapon calculated to cause unnecessary suffering. If the "experts" on international law cannot agree, how can the foot soldier be expected to decide? In a more systematic way, moreover, the doctrine of military necessity (conceived of as a general justifying condition) makes it virtually impossible for the soldier to determine from his limited perspective whether an ostensible war crime in fact comes under this exemption. It is, in short, often a fiction that the soldier in the field is in any position to ascertain to which situations the laws of war apply and to which they do not.

In the second place, the problem of knowledge is compounded by the fact that the laws of war are not a rational, coherent scheme of rules and principles. Were there an intelligible rationale to the laws of war, recourse to this rationale might assist the soldier in his attempt to determine which of his actions were war crimes and which were not. For reasons already stated, such a rationale can hardly be derived from the existing laws. As a result, unless the soldier happens to get ordered to do one of those few unambiguously proscribed acts, like firing a projectile filled with glass, there is no readily applicable general principle to which he can appeal for guidance. As the laws of war are constituted at present, he cannot, for instance, appeal in any simple, straightforward way to the idea that the intentional killing of noncombatants is a prohibited act.

So far this discussion has concerned primarily the issue of the soldier who is ordered to do an action that may be a war crime. In this situation there are serious problems of duress and knowledge that ought to be dealt with before criminal liability is fairly imposed. But still, it might be urged, all of this leaves unaffected cases of the gratuitous commission of war crimes. There are cases in which there were no direct superior orders and in which soldiers on their own behaved in ways that were clearly proscribed by the laws of war, and known by them to be such. My Lai is, arguably, one such case; no one ordered the soldiers involved to line up the unarmed women, children, and elderly people and machine-gun them. The laws of war do make it plain that such behavior is forbidden. What are we to say about this kind of case?

There is no question in my mind that there is genuine culpability in such cases. However, the culpability is, in my opinion, diminished by a variety of factors typically present. At the very least I can understand why the ordinary soldier regards this sort of behavior as reasonable and appropriate, even though it is not.

To begin with, all the previously discussed uncertainty and irrationality of the laws of war exists regardless of whether the soldiers in question did what they did because they were ordered to do it or for some other reason. Similarly, as it has already been indicated, the typical combat situation is hardly conducive to a reflective consideration of the application of the laws of war.

In addition, contemporary ideas about warfare have certain consequences of their own. In the first place, in combat it is certainly more plausible than it would be in any other context to regard everyone who is not clearly on your side as your enemy. Because much conduct is permissible in war that is not permissible elsewhere, and because even more actions are performed that would never be performed elsewhere, it is reasonable for the combat soldier to be extremely suspicious of anyone who is not unquestionably his friend or who is not utterly and completely helpless. If the threat to his life as a foot soldeir can so easily and permissibly come from so many sources against which he is defenseless, (e.g., airplanes), apparent cruelty and wanton barbarism often turn out to be nothing more than moderately pursued self-defense. Such is one consequence of the logic of contemporary war.

Moreover, I think that modern warfare is extraordinarily corruptive of the capacity to behave morally. If the distinctions between what is obligatory and what is prohibited appear to rest on no intelligible grounds or persuasive principles, if one is encouraged in war to neglect as morally uninteresting just those distinctions that in any other context are of utmost moral importance, and if one has no reasonable assurance, as one cannot in time of war, that others will behave with a careful regard for the moral point of view, then it is not surprising if persons lose interest in and concern for even the minimum demands of morality. They are somewhat excusable, even when they do terrible things, because war has, in some important ways, made psychopaths of them all. [12]

Once again, the dominant conception of the laws of war has, I submit, a good deal to do with this state of affairs, because it is the laws of war that define what is and is not permissible for the soldier to do in time of war. If we had a different, more rigorous conception of the nature of war crimes, if we had a conception that corresponded more convincingly with fundamental principles, then one could expect more consistent behavior from combatants.

Mens Rea *Requirement for Military and Civilian Leaders*

When we turn to the leaders—both civilian and military—we come to those persons to whom many principles of responsibility most obviously and plausibly apply, and to whom culpability most fairly and appropriately appears to attach. For these are the persons who have substantially more control over their own behavior than do any other combatants. They give orders and formulate battle plans and objectives. They are least subject to formal military discipline. Because they are removed from the heat of combat, they can reflect, deliberate, and more dispassionately assess the consequences of their actions. These conditions satisfy the *mens rea* requirements to a much greater degree than does the combat soldiers' situation.

This truth is, of course, reflected in the principles and the practices of Nuremberg. It was the leaders—both civilian and military—whose culpability seemed easiest to establish and most difficult to deny. In terms of what was done at Nuremberg, as well as what was said, it was leaders and not ordinary soldiers who were most responsible for the commission of war crimes, as well as for the commission of crimes against peace and crimes against humanity.

This does not mean that there are no problems with the standards and principles of responsibility that were applied at Nuremberg to the various leaders. To take just one example, the already described vague and elastic properties of the substantive laws of war create some of the same difficulties for leaders that they do for all other persons. Nonetheless, the problems in respect to culpability of leaders often seem to me too greatly exaggerated. [13] As is more fully discussed below, the only major issues with respect to such culpability appear in my view to center upon any particular leader's knowledge of, and causal connection with, the actual commission of war crimes by others under his supervision, direction, or control.

This is not, however, the way the topic is sometimes discussed. In particular, it is sometimes claimed that there is a special, additional, *mens rea* requirement that must be satisfied before leaders can be held responsible. This claim, which I think is false, is put forth in a well-known article by Townsend Hoopes, in which he said:

> The tragic story of Vietnam is not, in truth, a tale of malevolent men bent upon conquest for personal gain or imperial glory. It is the story of an entire generation of leaders (and an entire generation of followers) so conditioned by the tensions of the Cold War Years that they were unable to perceive in 1965 (and later) that the communist adversary was no longer a monolith, but rather a fragmented ideology and apparatus. . . .
>
> Lyndon Johnson, though disturbingly volatile, was not in his worst moments an evil man in the Hitlerian sense. And his principal advisers were, almost uniformly, those considered when they took office to be among the ablest, the best, the most humane and liberal men that could be found for public trust. No one doubted their honest, high-minded pursuit of the best interests of their country, and indeed of the whole non-communist world, as they perceived those interests. Moreover, the war they waged was conducted entirely within the framework of the Constitution, with the express or tacit consent of a majority of the Congress and the country until at least the autumn of 1967, and without press censorship.
>
> . . . [S]hould we . . . establish a war crimes tribunal . . . and try President Nixon and Dr. Kissinger as 'war criminals'? The absurd questions answer themselves.
>
> . . . above all [we must avoid] the destructive and childish pleasure of branding as deliberate criminals duly elected and appointed leaders who, whatever their human failings, are struggling in good conscience to uphold the Constitution and to serve the broad national interest according to their lights. [14]

This argument is an interesting one, especially Mr. Hoopes's insistence that the state of mind of the leaders of the United States makes their conduct with respect to Vietnam obviously free from culpablity.

We might be tempted to reject the argument out of hand on the ground that the author has confused two notions that the criminal law tries very hard (admittedly with only moderate success) to keep straight —namely, motive and intention. In other words, Mr. Hoopes's argument might be seen as resting on the claim that a person whose motives are good cannot be held accountable by the criminal law, or perhaps even that he should not—or, typically, is not—held accountable. Thus at Nuremberg, according to this view, what was punished was the doing of proscribed acts by persons who had despicable motives in acting.

This is not an accurate account of the requirements of the criminal law generally, nor is it an attractive view of the way the criminal law ought to operate. We might, for example, think that a person who robs a poor widow of her life savings in order to have a wild week in Monaco is worse than a person who robs the same widow in order to give the money to the cancer fund. We might even think it appropriate that the punishment of the two persons should be different. But we would reject the claim that a person ought not be held liable at all merely because his motive for robbing the widow is, in the abstract, a commendable one. [15]

What we, as lawyers, would say is that we are not interested primarily in the criminal's motive or purpose in doing the act. What we want to know is whether the criminal intended to do the act in question, whether he regarded himself as taking by force the money that did not belong to him. If he did, then he has committed the crime of robbery. Similarly, for Nuremberg to be applicable, it would be sufficient for the leaders to have intended to do those acts that are, in fact, prohibited by article 6 of the IMT's Charter. Their motives for so acting are not of central importance to our inquiry.

But this does not put an end to the matter. Someone might reply that the proposed distinction is not always clear. Nor, someone might add, is it obvious that motive ought to be as irrelevant as the criminal law appears at times to make it. Moreover, it might still be claimed, there is something to be said for the original argument that the American leaders seem different from the leaders of the Nazi regime in ways that are of moral, if not legal, significance.

Thus, there is a somewhat more sophisticated defense that might be made of Mr. Hoopes's position. But it, too, does not succeed. To begin with, it might be argued that at least some of the charges established at Nuremberg did mean to include motive as a part of the definition of the offense. For example, it could be maintained that the waging of aggressive war does not mean simply the initiation of war (whatever the motive or purpose), but rather the initiation of war provided there is a certain objective or end in view, namely, to achieve personal gain or the imperial accession of territory. Even more to the point, given the way the definition of war crimes encompasses the notion of military necessity, the separation of motive and intention seems more difficult than it appeared at first. Up to a point, this does seem plausible to me, so that the matter should be considered further.

It is essential, however, to observe that there is nothing about the Nuremberg principles and the judgment of the IMT that supports this sort of interpretation in an unqualified way. It may be true that the German motives for doing some of the things that were done were especially despicable. It is, nonetheless, certainly a mistake to identify the Nuremberg rationale with a condemnation of those motives.

Yet there may be something to be said for this point of view. Perhaps culpability is, and ought to be, limited to those actions that the actor knows to be wrong. This is not quite the same as insisting upon the presence of a malevolent motive. Rather, it emphasizes that serious liability ought not to attach unless the actor had a certain conception of what he was doing—unless he knew or should have known that what he was doing was wrong. And this is a principle that is—at least to some degree—embraced in the operation of our own domestic legal system.

Of course, what has just been said is ambiguous. On the one hand, there is legal wrongdoing—that which the actor knows is forbidden by the legal system. On the other hand, there is moral wrongdoing—that which the actor, if he is concerned with being moral, surely ought to know is morally wrong.

In our domestic legal system the principle generally regarded as operative is that responsibility attaches if the actor knows, or ought to know, that what he is doing is legally wrong.[16] Although there are numerous qualifications that must be made, the general point is clear enough. It is regarded as appropriate to impose criminal liability upon an actor who intended to do an action that he knew to be proscribed by the law. In such a case the actor is not absolved of liability by his belief that it was not morally wrong to do this action.

It is also surely the case that for the conception with which the Nuremberg IMT worked, intention to do an illegal act was sufficient to justify liability. For the IMT was concerned to establish that the actions of the accused were violations of international law and in some cases known to be such by them. The IMT took appreciable pains to demonstrate the preexisting illegality of the acts denominated as crimes against peace and as war crimes. It did so because it deemed it a sufficient basis to justify the imposition of criminal liability that these acts were illegal and either known or capable of being known as such to the defendants.

It is possible, I admit, to fall back to still another position. This would be that, with respect to the kinds of crimes dealt with at Nuremberg, persons are to be held liable only of they knew or should have known that they were violating the relevant law and had bad motives for doing so. At this stage it is not clear how one ought to reply. This is not the standard that was applied at Nuremberg. It is, indeed, quite possible that some of the leaders convicted at Nuremberg—Albert Speer, for example—did not have bad motives. Perhaps, if this is so, such persons ought not to have been convicted. What is plain is that the case for such a new, more stringent *mens rea* requirement has yet to be made. I, for one, do not see why the motives of United States leaders ought to be taken to be decisive in determining their culpability for war crimes in Vietnam.

If we reject the idea that bad motives are an essential requirement for responsibility, we are left with the question of what is the appropriate test for the responsibility of leaders. Anyone thinking about this topic is led sooner or later to the *Yamashita* case, for it deals with the two significant factors of knowledge and causal connection.

As recent discussions of *Yamashita* have brought out, there are two different ways in which the case can be deemed relevant. One approach concentrates upon the situation in which General Yamashita found himself and focuses upon the harshness of holding him responsible for his troops' behavior. The other approach emphasizes the criteria for culpability elaborated in the majority opinion without worrying about whether those criteria were in fact satisfied vis-à-vis General Yamashita.

There is something to be said for the former approach, but not a great deal. If it is the case that General Yamashita was unaware of the brutalities committed by his troops, had no responsibility for having encouraged them to behave as they did, and was in no position to have prevented them from so behaving, then we are tempted, surely, to conclude that he was unjustly held criminally liable for their conduct. As a result, we are also led to conclude that it would be equally unjust to hold American leaders responsible if they were in a similar position with respect to the commission of war crimes in Vietnam.

However, it is not as easy as that. Surely this is not the time to engage in a scrupulous reexamination of the fairness of the treatment by the United States of the German and Japanese leaders after World War II. The point is not that precedents should be mindlessly applied without regard to the fairness of the rule. Rather, it is that having applied rules and principles to others in a certain way, the United States is now in a poor position to object to the fairness of those rules and principles.

As I have indicated, we can acknowledge the force of the argument without being wholly convinced by it. If General Yamashita was treated as badly as he appears to have been, I am inclined to think that this is a good reason for trying to make certain that no one is treated in a similar fashion in the future—even those from the country responsible for his mistreatment.

But to reject this application of *Yamashita* is not, of course, to dismiss the problem with which the case dealt. For there is still the question of the appropriate test for the culpability of leaders for war crimes committed by forces in the field. I will conclude with some thoughts about only one of the main *mens rea* problems in this area.

No one would, I believe, question the appropriateness of holding the military and civilian leaders of the United States responsible for those acts that they ordered United States and South Vietnamese troops to perform and that they knew to be violations of the laws of war. The live issues concern, rather, their culpability in less clear cases. The chief issues can be framed in this way: Is it sufficient to hold leaders responsible if they simply adopted or knowingly permitted the adoption of policies and objectives the realization of which was likely to lead to the commission of war crimes? Under this test, if it is the case that emphasis upon body counts led to the killing rather than the capture of enemy soldiers who wished to surrender, then the leaders who knowingly encouraged or permitted this emphasis are properly held liable for the ensuing war crimes. Or, is it necessary in order to hold the leaders responsible that they, in addition to the previously stated requirement, should have known that such policies and objectives were likely to have such consequences? In other words, is it necessary to ask whether the leaders should have known that an emphasis upon body counts would have this effect? Finally, perhaps the test should be made even more stringent by an inquiry into the leaders' actual state of mind. In that case we might decide that the leaders should be held responsible only if they actually knew that such a policy was likely to have such consequences.

Similar questions can be asked about policies or programs the implementation of which may in fact constitute the commission of war crimes. Thus, if the use of antipersonnel bombs is a war crime, is it sufficient that the leaders directed or knew of the use of this weapon? Or is it necessary to establish that they should have known that the use of such a weapon was a war crime? Or is it necessary to establish that they actually knew that the use of such a weapon was a war crime?

As far as I can tell, actual knowledge in either of these kinds of cases has not usually been required, and was certainly not required with respect to the leaders prosecuted after World War II. On the other hand, strict liability, i.e., holding leaders responsible regardless of what they knew or should have known, is hardly a more attractive notion for war crimes than it is in the American domestic legal system. The appropriate test in this regard appears, therefore, to be that the leaders should be held responsible only if they should have known or foreseen the consequences of the policies and programs under their authorship, direction, or control. It is upon this question, and not the question of the leaders' motives, that our attention ought to focus far more intensely than it has thus far.

19   *Leonard B. Boudin*

The issue of individual responsibility should be considered from three perspectives: that of the individual serviceman, the so-called low-ranking soldier; that of his superiors; and that of the person who was called upon to enter the armed services during the Vietnam War or who, while in the service during that war, was ordered to Vietnam. I proceed on these premises: only Congress can declare war; a war of aggression or one in violation of the United Nations Charter or of treaty is unlawful as a crime against peace; and other relevant crimes exist, such as war crimes and crimes against humanity. The text for this discussion is the Nuremberg judgment of 1946, the Nuremberg principles adopted by the General Assembly of the United Nations in 1946, the Constitution of the United States, the Uniform Code of Military Justice, *The Law of Land Warfare*, which is Field Manual 27-10 of the United States Army, the treaties of the United States, and the decisions of the courts.

The United States Army, in its Field Manual 27-10 of 1956, explicitly adopted the Nuremberg principles. [1] *The Law of Land Warfare* provides that "every violation of the law of war is a war crime." Moreover, the Army Field Manual makes clear that "[c]onspiracy, direct incitement, and attempts to commit, as well as complicity in the commission of, crimes against peace, crimes against humanity, and war crimes are punishable."

It would be relevant in any consideration of the soldier's duty in Vietnam to know the extent to which the Army's educational program before and after My Lai included more than a *pro forma* reference to the sections of the Field Manual on war crimes. This is not to say that a soldier who engages in a massacre of the type recognized by President Nixon [2] and by the world as having occurred at My Lai can be excused because of the Army's failure to advise him that such clearly criminal acts were in fact criminal. There are, however, less obvious situations in which the educational delinquencies of superior officers may have a bearing on the individual guilt of their subordinates.

The second problem that frequently arises relates to the superior-orders doctrine. Does the soldier have immunity from his illegal conduct because it is the result of an illegal order from a superior? This is a problem that has concerned military and civil courts for centuries. Sir James Stephen, in his 1883 volume on the criminal law of England, referred to "the double necessity of preserving on the one hand the supremacy of the law and on the other the discipline of the Army."[3]

The latest edition of the Army Field Manual provides that "[t]he fact that the law of war has been violated pursuant to an order of a superior authority, whether military or civil, does not deprive the act in question of its character of a war crime, nor does it constitute a defense in the trial of an accused individual, unless he did not know and could not reasonably have been expected to know that the act ordered was unlawful."[4] But the Manual permits the superior-orders defense to "be considered in mitigation of punishment," even if it is rejected as a defense to an alleged war crime.

Courts in the past have occasionally suggested that a soldier who obeyed illegal orders under duress is relieved of criminal responsibility. This, indeed, was the view expressed by Lauterpacht, when he wrote in the pre-1952 editions to Oppenheim's treatise: ". . . such a degree of compulsion as must be deemed to exist in the case of a soldier or officer exposing himself to immediate danger of death as the result of a refusal to obey an order excludes *pro tanto* the accountability of the accused." Lauterpacht changed his view in 1952, when in the seventh edition of the famous treatise he said: "No principles of justice and, in most civilised communities, no principle of law permits the individual person to avoid suffering or even to save his life at the expense of the life—or, as revealed in many war crimes trials, of a vast multitude of lives—or of sufferings, on a vast scale, of others."[5]

There is, of course, no indication that the events at My Lai are excusable under any of the theories thus far advanced: direct orders, reason to believe that they were valid, or duress. It is, therefore, most regrettable that the investigations and prosecutions in those cases occurred only as a result of complaints by persons outside the Army, that the investigations appeared to be limited to the My Lai incident, and that the government, beginning with the Chief Executive, eventually tended to palliate the offense.

The duties of the superior officers who give illegal orders to their subordinates have been well noted by Prof. Telford Taylor: "[T]he greater the indulgence shown to the soldier on the theory that his first duty is to give unquestioning obedience, the greater the responsibility of the officer to see to it that obedience entails no criminal consequences."[6] Moreover, it is clear that the superior officers are not relieved of criminal responsibility merely because they did not give illegal orders to their subordinates.

The responsibility of superior officers for the crimes of their troops, even where they have limited knowledge and control of their behavior, is the subject of the well-known *Yamashita* case. There was little evidence that General Yamashita could have done anything to control his troops. But he was convicted and executed. One must agree not only with his counsel, who has documented the injustice that General Yamashita suffered, [7] but also with the dissenting opinions of Justices Rutledge and Murphy in that case.

The less stringent rule adopted by some legal officers of the Army today is emphasized by the instructions to the court members in the case of *United States* v. *Capt. Ernest L. Medina*. Captain Medina, who was the superior officer responsible for the United States soldiers at My Lai, was found not guilty. The charge to the court members repeatedly emphasized that Captain Medina could be convicted only if he had actual knowledge of illegal conduct by his troops. Unlike the standard applied to General Yamashita, Captain Medina could not have been convicted upon the ground that he, as a superior officer responsible for his troops' conduct, should have known of their blatantly illegal activities. The following excerpt from the *Medina* charge illustrates this retreat from the *Yamashita* standard when a United States officer is on trial:

In relation to the question pertaining to the supervisory responsibility of a Company Commander, I advise you that as a general principle of military law and custom a military superior in command is responsible for and required, in the performance of his command duties, to make certain the proper performance by his subordinates of their duties as assigned by him. In other words, after taking action or issuing an order, a commander must remain alert and make timely adjustments as required by a changing situation. Furthermore, a commander is also responsible if he has *actual* knowledge that troops or other persons subject to his control are in the process of committing or are about to commit a war crime and he wrongfully fails to take the necessary and reasonable steps to insure compliance with the law of war. You will observe that these legal requirements placed upon a commander require actual knowledge plus a wrongful failure to act. Thus mere presence at the scene without knowledge will not suffice. That is, the commander-subordinate relationship alone will not allow an inference of knowledge. While it is not necessary that a commander actually see an atrocity being committed, it is essential that he know that his subordinates are in the process of committing atrocities or are about to commit atrocities. [8]

As serious as the My Lai massacre was so far as the behavior of the troops was concerned, a far more serious problem exists with respect to the Army's review of such incidents. When I spoke on the matter in August 1970, before a panel of the American Bar Association in its St. Louis convention, a brigadier general rose from the audience and advised us that I was in error and that the Army was scrupulous in its investigation of alleged war crimes in Vietnam. [9] He stated that he was one of the persons responsible for such investigations. An official of the American Bar Association also took me to task for not accepting the brigadier general's observations and for relying on what he regarded as hearsay, namely, the written observations of such American journalists as Halberstam, Schell, Hersh, and Hammer.

Both before that occasion and after it, individual American servicemen have come forward before ad hoc Congressional committees and courts to attest to individual war crimes of which they had first-hand knowledge. There is no indication that these charges were made the subject of Army investigations. That a contrary position has been taken appears from a detailed story of the case of Lt. Col. Anthony Herbert, a distinguished professional soldier who suffered severe sanctions within the United States military for refusing to ignore the war crimes being committed in Vietnam. In its editorial on Lieutenant Colonel Herbert's case, the *New York Times* said:

The colonel's downfall stemmed from his involvement with atrocities in Vietnam. His problem . . . was not committing those atrocities but reporting them. No zealot but a soldier convinced of the sanctity of the military's own rules of warfare—he was sickened by the outrages he saw being committed by American and South Vietnamese troops against prisoners as well as defenseless women and children. Prevented from stopping these crimes, he reported them to his superiors, only to be told not to meddle. When he persisted, he was made victim of a fraudulent "efficiency" report, broken, fully exonerated—then told that there was no redress. His career was systematically shattered while those who, the record indicates, had denied him justice were promoted. [10]

It is doubtful whether any other country has more criminal laws than does the United States; it certainly challenges in terms of crime, if not punishment, the criminal statutes of eighteenth-century England. Both our Criminal Code and the Uniform Code of Military Justice contain numerous provisions that have a direct bearing upon the duty of officers to investigate the criminal behavior of their subordinates. [11] I suggest that these are the appropriate provisions for consideration in any review of the investigations of war crimes that have already occurred within the United States military.

I have, however, been discussing more or less individual war crimes such as My Lai rather than the broad structure of the war. The larger problem is whether an undeclared counterinsurgent war of the type in Vietnam is inherently illegal and/or necessarily involved means that violate the rules of war and international treaties. Professor Richard Falk has put the matter well in chapter 1 of this book.

Let us assume, for the purposes of this discussion, that Professor Falk is correct in this and in his other writings and that the engagement in, and conduct of, the war by the United States was in fact in violation of international law. This is not to suggest that the leaders of government be prosecuted, because, as Professor Falk says, the issue of war crimes is "crucially related to the development of a realistic political consciousness." As Professor Falk puts it elsewhere:

. . . especially in relation to war, the identification of leaders as "the criminals" tends to exempt the supporting population. The rulers who fail to resist are part of the criminal process that makes it possible for governments to wage illegal wars. These rulers are representatives whose rulership should be repudiated, if at all possible, as soon as the boundaries of crime are crossed. [12]

Again, there is a larger question directly related to the war crimes issue. Assuming that there is agreement about the unlikelihood of prosecuting those who engage in an illegal war, are we to prosecute those young men who refused to participate in that war either because they reasonably believed that they would be guilty of what is elsewhere called conspiracy or because their consciences forbade their participation in such activity? Remember that we are dealing with the larger issue, not with the question of whether the individual soldier will be directed to shoot a defenseless civilian. But even as to the latter—why should an eighteen-year-old be compelled to make that choice on the battlefield? As Dicey has said in a different context: "The position of a soldier is in theory and may be in practice a difficult one. He may, as it has been well said, be liable to be shot by a court-martial if he disobeys an order, and to be hanged by a judge and jury if he obeys it."

I have previously suggested that there were several possible solutions to this problem. [13] We could have permitted the individual to develop at his criminal trial for resisting induction the thesis of the illegality of the war. At least, we could have recognized that there is a basis for his belief, thus eliminating the required criminal intent. In the alternative, the conscientious-objector provisions of the Selective Service laws could have been expanded to provide for a selective exemption from military service. As Professor Taylor correctly pointed out:

Lawyers called upon to represent young men who refuse [or refused] to serve are abundantly justified in raising both the constitutional and the Nuremberg arguments in their defense. . . . Judges and juries should be made aware of the tenuous basis on which they are asked to attribute criminal guilt to men whose driving motive may be [or have been] that of obedience to a higher law. [14]

Perhaps the war crimes problem resulting from the United States involvement in Vietnam should be resolved by a general amnesty. The beneficiaries of this policy would be both the individuals who resisted induction on the grounds of the Vietnam War's illegality and the government leaders who seem to have resisted the mandates of the Nuremberg principles for which this government deserves credit as a principal author. In my view President Ford's conditional amnesty proclaimed on 16 September 1974 does not solve the problem. [15] It assumes that those who refused service committed a wrong while it ignores those who perpetrated, commanded, or tolerated illegal conduct in the field. The only solution that will heal the nation is a total and unconditional amnesty for all—"draft dodgers," deserters, and active participants, military and governmental, in the war.

20 Comments

Tom J. Farer

The Vietnam War raises many questions concerning individual responsibility for which Mr. Warnke's paper has few finally persuasive answers. His organizing proposition, namely, that "[w]ar crimes must continue to be distinguished from crimes against peace," is both commonplace and essentially irrelevant, since I know of no important claim to the contrary. Moreover, by its implication that the case for diminishing the responsibility of Lieutenant Calley and others of his ilk rests on a failure to recognize the proclaimed distinction, his main proposition manages also to be misleading.

The real case for exculpation rests not on the blurring of the distinction between the crime of aggressive war and war crimes, but rather on the blurring of behavioral standards resulting from the tactics and strategies authorized, tolerated, or ineffectually restrained by our highest military and civilian officials. Exculpation rests on the assumption that, as a consequence of our methods for conducting the war, the distinction between bombs and shells, between napalm and bullets, between earth and sky had lost all meaning for Lieutenant Calley, however coherent that distinction might remain for those who danced in the ballrooms of Washington.

That is certainly the most widely defended case for exculpation of Lieutenant Calley and his kind. It is by no means conclusive. In the end it failed to shift my preliminary conviction that the severest of sanctions, even execution, was justifiable. Yet I cannot help but acknowledge the force of this argument.

The closest allusion to this line of reasoning in Mr. Warnke's discussion is his fleeting reference to the argument that "the application of massive American military force to put down a native insurgency would become inevitably a war against civilians and that My Lai thus, in the words of its main executioner, was not 'any big deal.'" But even there Mr. Warnke fails to relate this explicitly to the question of Lieutenant Calley's punishment. There is only the apparently skeptical footnote reference to an article by Burke Marshall, who, Mr. Warnke says, "eloquently stated the moral paradox of punishing the My Lai murders while continuing national policies 'based on killing civilians.'"

One cannot be sure whether Mr. Warnke accepts this characterization of the war. On the one hand, he concludes that My Lai was an exceptional incident. On the other, he concedes that in antiguerrilla action, civilian suffering is much more likely to occur than in other forms of warfare and that this ought to lead to serious (as opposed to frivolous or facetious, I suppose) reconsideration of the merits of a counterinsurgent policy.

Although he offers Lieutenant Calley short shrift, Mr. Warnke cannot fairly be accused of blatant or effective discrimination in favor of men in high places. While he does imply that they are guiltless, he does not press the point with those powerful resources of advocacy that he normally deploys. Surely, the senior civilian and military officials who have presided over the war will find cold comfort in his observation that "[i]n antiguerrilla action, in which the people are Mao's sea within which the guerrillas swim and survive, the prospects of widespread civilian suffering are *obviously* far greater . . ." (emphasis added). For if that is obvious and if, as Mr. Warnke alleges, its obviousness should lead "to more vivid realization that a decision to wage war is a decision to sacrifice an indeterminate number of innocent lives," then it is hard to maintain a defense based on a reasonable failure to become informed about what occurred in Vietnam. As a consequence, those accused of war crimes would have to rely on a finding that the tactics and strategies employed there by United States armed forces were not legally proscribed. With respect to this defense as well, however, the accused may find more comfort in Mr. Warnke's friendly intentions than in his rhetorical implementation thereof.

In responding to the argument that the responsibility for My Lai extends to any and all who brought about our presence in Vietnam, he offers only the conviction that "hundreds of similar military actions were conducted in Vietnam without the wholesale slaughter of helpless humans." In other words, he wholly ignores most of the categories of crimes charged, including the systematic torture of suspects; the assassination of civilians deemed members of Viet Cong cadres; the massive transplantation of civilian population to camps with subhuman amenities; and the indiscriminate or disproportionate employment of aerial, naval, and land bombardment, of delayed-action antipersonnel ordinance, and of chemical weapons. Surely the reference to "similar military actions" is not sufficiently elastic to cover all of these forms of indicated behavior.

Some deny that these acts occurred on any significant scale. Some also contend that not all of these acts are proscribed by international law. Obviously these factual and normative issues are critical. Because he ignores them, Mr. Warnke's exculpatory implications necessarily lack conviction.

With respect to the issue of aggressive war, it is far easier to accept Mr. Warnke's judgment of not guilty than it is to accept his supporting analysis. Although it is not essential to his case, he seems to claim that, regardless of context, crimes against peace cannot and should not "yield penal consequences." In reaching this conclusion, Mr. Warnke explicitly rejects the Nuremberg judgment, which he dismisses as a "noble experiment."

Unless construed ironically, this characterization of the judgment is hard to reconcile with a principal argument employed in support of Mr. Warnke's basic claim. If, as he appears to argue, the victors are inherently incapable of establishing a tribunal that could "get an objective ruling on the justice of a nation's war effort," how can he characterize Nuremberg as a noble experiment? Perhaps he is asserting that the Nuremberg International Military Tribunal's judgment on this issue, by its manifest unfairness, crumpled a reasonable preexisting belief in the possibility of an objective determination. Does Mr. Warnke believe that the actual judgment cannot bear objective analysis?

Aside from appearing inconsistent with his characterization of Nuremberg, Mr. Warnke's denial to the victor of a capacity for objectivity is a little confusing because it would be as applicable to the trial of war crimes as to crimes against peace. To be consistent, Mr. Warnke must insist that the victors prosecute only themselves, and that they leave to the vanquished exclusive jurisdiction to punish those among them guilty of atrocities.

If Germany's post-World War I experience is any evidence of the norm, one must doubt whether a nation convulsed by the agony and humiliation of defeat will be strongly motivated to prosecute alleged war criminals, however low their rank. Limited prosecutorial action by the victors directed against men in the lower ranks is somewhat more plausible because, among other conceivable reasons, it might seem to add moral allure to martial achievement.

The critical point that Mr. Warnke does not face squarely is that the very thrust of his own logic will restrict indictment to men in the lower ranks. "In a world of autonomous national states," he says, aggressive war "can only be a crime reserved for losers." Since victorious leaders would be no more inclined to indict themselves for the authorization of atrocious acts than they would for the waging of aggressive war, war crimes are also reserved for losers, that is to say, for those who are powerless, regardless of the side on which they fought.

And that brings us back to Lieutenant Calley's defense. If justice requires society to treat like cases alike in dispensing deprivations, as well as benefits, then some ask: Can Calley's conviction be just if other criminals remain at liberty? "Yes!" says Mr. Warnke, because the fact that "not all can be found and punished is a failing in the most meticulous attempt at application of criminal law, whether civilian or military." Surely he misses the point. For we are not speaking of cases in which the other criminals are concealed or beyond the jurisdiction of the criminal law. The case actually before us is one in which the other criminals not only are brazenly at liberty within the jurisdiction but are actually honored for their activities and, while still in office, could participate in the process by means of which their pathetic coconspirators were defined out of civilized society. That is the moral dilemma generated by a refusal to contemplate the condemnation of national leaders.

The main ground cited by Mr. Warnke for treating allegations of aggressive war as nonjusticiable is the complexity of "determining if a conflict should be deemed unwarranted aggression rather than the 'collective defense' authorized by article 51 of the United Nations Charter." Vietnam, his only cited example, does of course illustrate that there are difficult cases here, just as there are difficult cases in the application of the laws of war. But this example alone hardly suffices to establish the radical proposition that the propriety of national recourse to violence is susceptible only to distant historical assessment, a proposition that might be inferred from the totality of Mr. Warnke's paper. By this audacious assertion he purports only to be questioning the wisdom, propriety, and precedential force of the Nuremberg judgment. In fact, he is challenging the normative basis of contemporary international society, namely, the categorical rejection of the nineteenth-century legal conception of war as an admissible means for the enhancement of national power or for the protection of national security short of defense against an imminent armed attack.

Mr. Warnke says that the Nuremberg concept of aggressive war as a crime susceptible of legal proof and judicial determination could have some deterrent efficacy if the combatants could be persuaded to accept the jurisidiction of an international tribunal. This remark suggests a functionally inadequate conception of the decentralized international legal system. National behavior is judged continually by decision makers of other states. This process of judgment is ineluctable, and any rational calculation of national interest must take that process into account. If recourse to force is deemed a clear violation of obligatory norms, then its victims are more likely to receive effective support than those in a situation in which legitimacy of force is regarded as a matter of purely historical concern. This is so because in the former case the attack will be identified as a threat to minimum conceptions of public order. By their existence, norms aggravate the provocative quality of certain acts. The consequent increased likelihood of retaliation is international law's main sanction. Another sanction is the use that domestic constituencies can make of a norm in questioning their government's policies. These phenomena lend deterrent efficacy to legal norms even in the absence of formal tribunals.

Mr. Warnke would probably take the position that the aura of legality surrounding the proscription of aggressive war can be retained even if it functions exclusively as a criterion for evaluating state behavior. This may, however, be difficult to achieve, because the proscription is intimately identified with, and draws powerful precedential support from, the Nuremberg trials at which individuals were tried and convicted.

Professor Wasserstrom's discussion brings to mind the old dictum applied to Learned Hand, or perhaps it was to Justice Holmes (it was equally applicable), to the effect that although he was sometimes clearly wrong, he was always wrong clearly. Of course, in his discussion Professor Wasserstrom is often right in interesting and important ways, but I believe that there is a serious fault in the structure of his argument.

The critical seam in that argument is exposed by the following quotation: "Whatever else one may wish to claim for [the] . . . system of the laws of war [as outlined by Professor Wasserstrom], one cannot claim that they deserve either preservation or respect because of the connection these laws maintain with the idea of how persons ought to behave toward other persons."

The easiest way to begin refuting that proposition is to accept, for purposes of argument, that its characterization of the laws of war is correct. I claim that even in the problematic form imputed to them by Professor Wasserstrom, the laws of war deserve preservation and respect both because of the connection they maintain with the idea of how persons ought to behave toward other persons and for other reasons the existence of which is coyly hinted at by the form of Professor Wasserstrom's proposition. Having stated this antithesis, I will limit my defense of it to the following provocations.

First, in light of the fact that the basic structure of the laws of war is integrated into, and is an expression of, the customary law of nations, will not Professor Wasserstrom agree that prima facie his thesis is not merely implausible but definitionally inconceivable, in that customary international law is the crystallization of the ideas and values shared by the overwhelming majority of peoples? If this account of customary international law is accurate, then how can one contend that the system of the laws of war is inadequately connected with the idea of how persons ought to behave toward other persons? Just whose idea is being referred to, that of aesthetes, philosophers, or divines?

Second, I assume that the idea to which Professor Wasserstrom refers is the idea of proper behavior within a group whose members have eschewed recourse to violence in disputes and competition among themselves and who believe that their intramural differences are less important than the similarities that distinguish them from other groups defined as alien. The modern nation-state is an obvious example of such an integrated group. I propose that from time immemorial (a rash phrase, to be sure, but fortunately one not readily susceptible to empirical assault), these groups have maintained dual moral systems governing the treatment of members and aliens. Surely this is nothing more than an elaborate truism.

The laws of war are, I would further submit, a product of the tension between, on the one hand, the domestic value system, particularly as it begins tentatively to open up and embrace aliens—a process fueled by the increase of transnational identifications—and, on the other hand, the still deeply felt belief that one's state has a right to survive, to prosper, and even perhaps to dominate, however benevolently, where that is feasible. The laws of war may appear incoherent as a projection of the domestic value system. But when perceived as the product of a difficult negotiation between values in severe competition, they are indeed coherent. The laws of war do not draw an absolute distinction between combatants and noncombatants because the vast majority of peoples are prepared in wartime to treat the entire population of an enemy state monolithically if that is deemed essential to the survival, or even the mere success, of their own state.

If one accepts the unidimensional criterion of coherence tendered by Professor Wasserstrom, it is doubtful that even domestic criminal-law systems could pass the test, since they too are the visible products of mediation between divergent values. Thus, the hustlers of Harlem end up in Attica, while those of Madison Avenue find dubious peace in a condominium on Fifth Avenue. Neither group is committed to the value of honesty. Both respond to values such as aggressive acquisitiveness and individual self-assertion that power our industrial system. A society draws lines that are clearly arbitrary when measured against only one of these competing values, i.e., honesty on the one hand, acquisitiveness and self-assertion on the other. Yet most people know what those lines are, and, despite the lack of pure coherence, we at least presume that people know or ought to know on which side of the line planned behavior falls.

Even accepting Professor Wasserstrom's critique and his questionable interpretation of the laws of war, if they have in fact resulted in a net saving of life—and by *net* I refer to the implausible possibility that their existence may in some marginal sense help to legitimate recourse to violence—how can any man endowed with the most modest humanitarian instincts claim that they do not merit preservation?

And, finally, does Professor Wasserstrom believe that there is a high expectation among national elites or, for that matter, ordinarily informed people that weapons of mass destruction—notably nuclear and biological weapons—ought to be and will be employed when their use will be efficient from a military perspective? In fact, there seems to be an intense and widespread conviction that such weapons ought to be and will be employed only as a last resort to prevent the destruction of the state. That conviction is part of the laws of war, and its existence is flatly inconsistent with Professor Wasserstrom's perception that what "many, if not most, lawyers, commentators, military tribunals, and courts have had in mind when they have talked about the laws of war and the responsibility of individuals for the commission of war crimes" is that they prohibit "only violence and suffering not directly or significantly connected with the waging of war." There are, indeed, people who do believe that, but hopefully they represent a violent minority.

21 Comments

Telford Taylor

I am prepared to assume that the content of the chapters by Messrs. Warnke, Wasserstrom, and Boudin is determined, at least in part, by reason, logic, and humanity. But I suggest that, to a very large extent, the content in each case is also the result of the world in which each of them lives—or, to put it perhaps more accurately, the world in which each thinks he lives. My comments approach each paper in those terms.

Mr. Warnke, it seems quite plain, lives in a very dark world, where men are governed by selfish motives; where men are willing to go to war and kill and maim on a very large scale in order to achieve national ends. A very dark world and, I hasten to add, this is the world that I live in, or at least think I live in. And, therefore, I have substantially no quarrel with the general propositions that form the main content of Mr. Warnke's chapter. Whether the application of those principles to particular cases would show us to be in equal agreement is a matter of which I am more doubtful.

Mr. Warnke has caused me to reflect on a topic that I think deserves mention because it looks to the future and to possible improvements in the laws of war. He noted in chapter 17, I think quite rightly, that a great deal of the confusion about individual responsibility, in My Lai and other such episodes in South Vietnam involving American forces, has been due to the very ambiguous nature of the terrain in which that conflict was fought. This was not like Germans in Alsace or French in the Ruhr. American troops were engaged on the territory of a country nominally allied, but where a large part of the population was in fact hostile. The Hague Regulations and the Geneva Conventions were not skillfully drawn with an eye to the difficulties presented by that kind of situation.

For parallels we might go back to the Peninsular Wars of the early nineteenth century. First the French went into Spain on the ostensible invitation of the Spanish government. Then the British entered to repel what looked to them like an aggressive attack by Napoleon against the Spanish people. Thus both France and England were engaged on the soil of a country ambiguously allied and ambiguously hostile, for some of the inhabitants were hostile and others friendly. This situation poses great complications that I think should be considered in connection with proposed revisions of the framework of the Hague Regulations and the Geneva Conventions.

Mr. Wasserstrom's world seems to me to be dominated by abstractions, many of which, I think, bear no relation to the world I see, or to an adequate allowance for human frailty. It is very easy to sympathize with his view that the laws of war are defective in not prohibiting aerial bombardment. Similarly, it is very easy to sympathize with his view that the doctrine of military necessity frequently obstructs the intended effects of the laws of war. And it is easy to be very dissatisfied with what is left, that the laws of war do perhaps only prohibit conduct not reasonably related to military success.

Mr. Wasserstrom's sympathies and dissatisfaction no doubt are right. But I am at a total loss to know what facts of human nature, what characteristics of the species would enable men to go to war, to seek victory, and to confront defeat without using those means that seem likely to achieve military success. Therefore, when he condemns the laws of war as devoid of moral content or logical reason, it seems to me that he is like the person who will not take a little because he cannot have a lot, or like a person who says that, if the vessel is flawed, it is wrong for men to drink from it even though they be thirsty.

Mr. Wasserstrom also discusses the allocation of individual responsibility. He suggests—and I am in general agreement with him on this point—that, given complicity by those at a low level and those at a high level, the responsibility of the latter is greater. But I am really puzzled, because if the laws of war are so flawed and so worthless from a moral standpoint, then it seems to me as unjust to apply them to leaders as it is to followers. Indeed, unless there is some intrinsic value in the content of the laws of war, we will have to forget about both the men in command and the men in the field.

Furthermore, I do not see the utility of his distinction between soldiers and leaders. Was Captain Medina a soldier or a leader? This all depends upon the point of vantage. Viewed from high headquarters, a company commander is not at a very high level. Viewed from the standpoint of the ordinary combat soldier, the captain is seated next to the Lord, and is about as high as the ordinary soldier will see in the course of a good long time. And I find nothing in this vocabulary that Mr. Wasserstrom uses that gives us much help in determining who are the "leaders."

Now we come to Mr. Boudin. Mr. Boudin lives in a world that is a better world than he or I or anyone alive today is likely to see. He has more faith in the possibility of using law and sanctions to improve human behavior than I have. But although his is a better world than I see around me, it still is marked by signposts and standards that to me are recognizable, and I think that of the three presentations, his comes the closest to the issue of what the legal responsibility of the individual is in wartime. How do we allocate individual responsibility when there is an admitted war crime?

Mr. Boudin draws a contrast between the standards of command responsibility in the *Yamashita* case and those in the *Medina* case. But the *Yamashita* case, and what the record shows that it stands for, are highly controversial subjects. In my view we do not need to go to the *Yamashita* case to conclude that the standard stated by the military judge in the *Medina* case is wide of the mark. The judge's charge in the latter case contains, no less than three times, the direction to the jury that they cannot find the defendant guilty unless they show that he actually knew that atrocities were being committed by his troops and did nothing to prevent them.

Now in my opinion that is wrong in law and wrong in common sense. One need go no further than the United States Army Field Manual 27-10, *The Law of Land Warfare*, which was published in 1956. It provides explicitly that a military commander is responsible not only for criminal acts committed in pursuance of his orders, but also if he has "actual knowledge, *or should have* knowledge" of what is happening in his command (emphasis added). Paragraph 501 of the Army Field Manual makes it clear that such constructive knowledge of the commander may result "through reports received by him or through other means." It also specifies that criminal liability exists if the commander having such actual or constructive knowledge "fails to take the necessary and reasonable steps to insure compliance with the law of war or to punish violators thereof."

Quite apart from what is in the Army Field Manual, assume for a moment that this problem applied to a noncriminal case. Suppose the troops entering My Lai had encountered resistance, and suppose that because of improper use or selection of weaponry or improper tactics they had suffered heavy losses. When the batallion commander comes to inquire why this has happened, suppose then that the company commander says, "Major, I didn't know that they were doing it." The immediate, logical answer would have come: "Captain, it's your business to know precisely that—that's what company commanders are for."

Apply this now to war crimes. A hypothetical captain knows that he has poorly trained troops who have suffered casualties, who are in a state of panic, who have come to hate the Vietnamese people, and who have been improperly indoctrinated about the purposes of the war. He thinks to himself: "I'm going into this village and I really don't know what will happen if those troops go in shooting and find themselves among the villagers. I guess I'd better not know too much until the operation has gone beyond the first encounter."

I suggest that the standard just enunciated is indefensibly narrow. I am not concerned about the punishment of Captain Medina. He must know that the deaths of the villagers were very directly due to his failure to control his troops. He must know that the image of the Army and of his country was tarnished by the coverup far beyond anything that could possibly have followed if the rules about reporting atrocities had been followed instead of disregarded. That is a heavy enough burden for anyone to bear.

What I am concerned about is the possible perpetuation of the standard for military officers specified in the *Medina* charge. This would, I think, undermine the very legitimate area of command responsibility.

I do not at all mean to suggest a standard of absolute liability for military leaders. But even in ordinary criminal law we have cases in which people have affirmative responsibility. Certainly command in the military is such a situation. An officer is, and should be, responsible for what he should have known about wrongful conduct of his men that he did nothing to prevent. I suggest in conclusion that in terms of individual responsibility—the problem that has been explored and exposed above all others by the recent succession of trials and nontrials, acquittals and convictions—if we are to rise above the rank of the enlisted man at all, the *Medina* charge is a very inhibiting ruling and an ultimately unsatisfactory solution.

22 Comments

Robert G. Gard, Jr.

A good deal of confusion in discussing war crimes results from consultation of secondary sources and the perpetuation of myths that the primary documents do not support. Secondary sources might be responsible for Professor Wasserstrom's apparent confusion about the meaning of the general principle of military necessity. Near the end of his discussion, he argues that national political leaders should be held accountable for violating specifically prohibited acts under the laws of war. But in the first part of chapter 18, Professor Wasserstrom develops the thesis that rules in the laws of war that prohibit specific conduct are virtually vitiated by military necessity because it excuses such conduct if perpetrated for the purpose of achieving military results.

This thesis would appear to condone any excesses by the soldier or his leaders if the excesses can be related to the conduct of the war. This would encourage the very unrestrained barbarism that the laws of war are designed to prevent. Indeed, much would be abandoned under this permissive interpretation of the concept of military necessity.

Although this may surprise many, we in the military have had a long tradition of exercising restraints in conducting warfare. In fact, Professor Wasserstrom has it just backward. It is military necessity that is limited by prohibited acts under the laws of war, not the other way around. The Army Field Manual, *The Law of Land Warfare*, begins by setting out its basic principles, which include explicitly the provision that "[t]he prohibitory effect of the law of war is not minimized by 'military necessity' which has been defined as that principle which justifies those measures not forbidden by international law which are indispensable for securing the complete submission of the enemy as soon as possible."[1] The Manual, finally, includes the following in its general principles: "The law of war is binding not only upon States as such but also upon individuals and, in particular, the members of their armed forces."[2]

These provisions are consistent with the judgment in the *Hostages* case at Nuremberg that qualified the permissiveness of the doctrine of military necessity as subject to the specific laws of war.[3] Mr. Warnke sums this up effectively: We should punish those who violate basic norms of human behavior in contravention of either domestic law or the laws of war.

My only problem with Mr. Warnke's discussion is that he does not extend the analysis far enough. The Geneva Conventions of 1949, which, after all, have the force of law in the United States, provide that each high contracting party is obligated to search for persons alleged to have committed grave breaches and to bring such persons before its own courts. Now, thus far, this country has limited such trials to persons who are still members of the armed services. The United States has ignored its responsibility to apply the law to those who are protected by having been discharged.[4] From those deeply concerned with the application of the laws of war, we fail to hear sufficient support for extending the jurisdiction of American courts to cover prosecution against discharged individuals.

Individual responsibility certainly extends to leaders as well as to the soldier. Mr. Boudin is correct in saying that if the order to commit an atrocity or a crime is given by a superior, he is as guilty as, or guiltier than, the soldier who commits it. On the other hand, it is necessary to explode one myth perpetuated by the frequent referral to secondary sources concerning the *Yamashita* case. The decision in that case is popularly, but incorrectly, believed to have established a principle of unqualified criminal responsibility for the actions of one's subordinates. Mr. Frank Reel, the defense counsel to General Yamashita, has claimed that his client was found guilty of failing to control the actions of members of his command even though the Japanese general had no personal knowledge of the crimes and atrocities.[5]

However, the findings of the military commission that tried General Yamashita stated unequivocally that the prosecution in that case presented evidence to show that the crimes committed by the Japanese soldiers under Yamashita's command were either willfully permitted by the accused or secretly ordered by him. In addition, a board of review comprised of five military lawyers examined this case for General MacArthur. As a part of their recommendation that General MacArthur sustain the sentence of hanging, they reported that the evidence indicated a deliberate plan of atrocities by the Japanese forces commanded by General Yamashita. The board said that "the conclusion is inevitable that the accused knew about . . . [the atrocities] and either gave his tacit approval to them or at least failed to do anything either to prevent them or to punish their perpetrators."[6]

The review by the United States Supreme Court covered procedural questions. It was there that Mr. Reel claimed that the evidence linking General Yamashita to the war crimes committed by forces under his command was inadmissable. It is, however, a fact that both at

Nuremberg and in the military commission in Tokyo, rules of evidence and other procedures were allowed that are no longer permitted according to the Geneva Conventions of 1949.

But one wonders why those concerned with war crimes have concentrated so much on the misinterpretation of the *Yamashita* case to find the legal restraints applicable to military commanders. At the same time, they have ignored the decisions in the subsequent trials against German military leaders conducted under Allied Control Council Law No. 10 at Nuremberg, which were so ably prosecuted under Prof. Telford Taylor's direction. In the *High Command* case, heard by three civilian judges, the findings stated that "[a] high commander cannot be kept completely informed of the details of military operations of his subordinates. . . . He has the right to assume that the details entrusted to responsible subordinates will be legally executed."[7] To hold a commander liable, the tribunal concluded, "[t]here must be a personal dereliction. That can occur only when the act is directly traceable to him or where his failure to properly supervise his subordinates constitutes criminal negligence on his part. In the latter case it must be a personal neglect amounting to a wanton, immoral disregard for the action of his subordinates amounting to acquiescence."[8]

If Nuremberg does indeed represent law, as Mr. Boudin states, then, contrary to Professor Taylor's claim, the following from the *High Command* case decision is consistent with the judge's charge to the court in the *Medina* trial: "[T]he commander must have knowledge of these offenses and acquiesce or participate or criminally neglect to interfere in their commission, and . . . the offenses must be patently criminal."[9]

As a soldier, I hope that we never disregard the concept of individual responsibility in warfare. War is cruel, and compulsory restraints on individuals in the interest of humanity are essential.

23 In Reply

Paul C. Warnke

The comments on my discussion in chapter 17 are interesting and provocative and persuade me of the validity of my central thesis. General
Taylor suggests that I live in a dark world, and I would agree that a
world at war is dark indeed. Professor Farer purports to recognize the
distinction between war crimes and the crime of war. But though he
characterizes this distinction as commonplace, he proceeds thereafter to
ignore it. The context of the conflict in Vietnam, what General Taylor
calls "the very ambiguous nature of the terrain," may have tragically increased the prevalence of war crimes. Surely this does not excuse the
mawkish hyperbole that the circumstances of the war made Lieutenant
Calley mistake a miserable huddle of girls, babies, and old folk for an
armed and dangerous enemy.

The tactics and strategies authorized for use in Vietnam were the
tactics and strategies of modern war. I sincerely hope that we will never
again use them to put down insurgents in their own country. The consequences of our having done so in Vietnam indeed merit serious (as
opposed to passing or cursory) thought.

But it seems to me inescapable that the criminal law is inappropriate to determine the propriety of national recourse to violence. Those
who have led a nation to victory will find in that victory proof of the
validity of their cause. And I find unacceptable a situation in which
relative might rather than relative merit will determine justiciability.
Like the "noble experiment" of Prohibition, prevention of war by application of the criminal law seems to me doomed to fail. (In using the
term, I might perhaps have recognized that some of the commentators
are too young to remember Prohibition.)

Professor Farer's conclusion, that if victors cannot judge the propriety of their war effort, they are just as incapable of trying their
citizens for war crimes, blurs again the "commonplace" distinction between the two. Reasonable and decent minds should not differ on
atrocities. They can, and tragically do, differ on when and where to use
military force for national security purposes.

Those who engaged in atrocities, and those who authorized or condoned them, should be diligently prosecuted. Any perceived injustice in

Lieutenant Calley's conviction should derive from the sense that far too little effort was made to convict all those who directed, participated in, or excused the particular conduct. As General Gard has reminded us, the Geneva Conventions of 1949 obligate us to apply the law to those who have violated the laws of war even though they have since been discharged. And if events like the My Lai incident were the inevitable and expected result of our military participation in Vietnam, this could warrant the application of the criminal law to the responsible political leaders. But there is no such proof. Their fate can thus be left to the political process and the verdict of history. Lieutenant Calley may get off more lightly.

Abbreviations

Notes

Contributors

Index

Abbreviations

ABBREVIATION	FULL REFERENCE
A.J.I.L.	*American Journal of International Law*
A.J.I.L. Supp.	*American Journal of International Law Supplement*
Bevans	Charles I. Bevans, comp. *Treaties and Other International Agreements of the United States 1776-1949.* 11 vols. to date. Washington, D.C.: Government Printing Office, 1968-74.
Br. and For. St. Papers	Library and Records Department of the Foreign and Commonwealth Office, comp. *British and Foreign State Papers.* London: H.M.S. Stationery Office.
Cornell Air War Study Group, *Air War in Indochina*	Air War Study Group, Cornell University. *The Air War in Indochina.* Edited by Rachael Littauer and Norman Uphoff. New rev. ed. Boston: Beacon Press, 1972.
Draft Hague Air Warfare Rules	Draft Hague Air Warfare Rules of 1923, 17 *A.J.I.L. Supp.* 245 (1923). Also in *Documentary History,* ed. Friedman, p. 437.
Einsatzgruppen case	*United States* v. *Otto Ohlendorf et al.,* 4 *Trials of War Criminals before the Nuernberg Military Tribunals* 3 (1948). Washington, D.C.: Government Printing Office, 1950.
Friedman, ed., *Documentary History*	Leon Friedman, ed. *The Law of War: A Documentary History.* 2 vols. New York: Random House, 1972.

GAOR   United Nations, General Assembly Official
                               Records.

Geneva Civilians   Convention Relative to the Protection of
Convention   Civilian Persons in Time of War, *done* at
                               Geneva on 12 August 1949, 6 U.S.T. 3516,
                               T.I.A.S. No. 3365, 75 U.N.T.S. 287
                               (effective 2 February 1956).

Geneva Prisoners of War   Convention Relative to the Treatment of
Convention   Prisoners of War, *done* at Geneva on
                               12 August 1949, 6 U.S.T. 3316, T.I.A.S.
                               No. 3364, 75 U.N.T.S. 135 (effective
                               2 February 1956).

1925 Geneva Protocol   Protocol for the Prohibition of the Use in
                               War of Asphyxiating, Poisonous or Other
                               Gases and of Bacteriological Methods of
                               Warfare, *done* at Geneva on 17 June 1925,
                               94 L.N.T.S. 65, 25 *A.J.I.L. Supp.* 94
                               (1931).

Greenspan, *Modern Law*   Morris Greenspan. *The Modern Law of*
of Land Warfare   *Land Warfare.* Berkeley: University of
                               California Press, 1959.

Hague Convention   Convention Respecting the Laws and
No. IV   Customs of War on Land, *done* at The
                               Hague on 18 October 1907, 36 Stat. 2277,
                               T.S. No. 539, 1 Bevans 631 (effective
                               26 January 1910).

Hague Cultural Property   Convention for the Protection of Cultural
Convention   Property in the Event of Armed Conflict,
                               done at The Hague on 14 May 1954, 249
                               U.N.T.S. 240 (the United States is not a
                               party).

Hague Regulations   Annex to Hague Convention No. IV.

High Command case   *United States* v. *von Leeb et al.*, 11 *Trials*
                               of War Criminals before the Nuernberg
                               Military Tribunals 1 (1948). Washington,
                               D.C.: Government Printing Office, 1950.

Hostages case	*United States* v. *Wilhelm List et al.,* 11 *Trials of War Criminals before the Nuernberg Military Tribunals* 759 (1948). Washington, D.C.: Government Printing Office, 1950.
ICRC	International Committee of the Red Cross
IMT	International Military Tribunal
Law of Armed Conflicts	Denise Bindschedler-Robert. "A Reconsideration of the Law of Armed Conflicts." Lucius Caflisch, ed. "Summary Record of the Conference on Contemporary Problems of the Law of Armed Conflicts, Geneva: 15-20 September 1969." In *Report of the Conference on Contemporary Problems of the Law of Armed Conflicts, Geneva: 15-20 September 1969.* Conferences on Contemporary Problems of International Law, no. 1. New York: Carnegie Endowment for International Peace, 1971.
L.N.T.S.	*League of Nations Treaty Series.* 205 vols. Geneva: League of Nations Secretariat, 1920-46.
London IMT Charter	Agreement for the Prosecution of the Major War Criminals of the European Axis, *signed* at London on 8 August 1945, 59 Stat. 1544, 3 Bevans 1238, 82 U.N.T.S. 279; 1 *Trial of the Major War Criminals before the International Military Tribunal* 8. Nuremberg, 1947.
Malloy	William M. Malloy, comp. *Senate Documents, Treaties, Conventions, International Acts, Protocols and Agreements between the United States of America and Other Powers 1776-1937.* 4 vols. Washington, D.C.: Government Printing Office, 1910-38.

Martens, ed., *Nouveau receuil*	Georg F. Von Martens, ed. *Nouveau receuil général de traités et autres actes relatifs aux rapports de droit internationale*. 1st series, 1843-75. 2d series, 1876-1908.
Medina case	Court-martial of Captain Ernest L. Medina, Instructions from the Military Judge to the Court Members. In *Documentary History*, ed. Friedman, pp. 1729-37.
Nuremberg Judgment	Decision of 30 September 1946 by the Nuremberg International Military Tribunal, 1 *Trial of the Major War Criminals before the International Military Tribunal* 171. Nuremberg, 1947. 41 *A.J.I.L.* 172 (1947).
Oppenheim, *International Law*, ed. Lauterpacht	Lassa Oppenheim. *International Law*. Edited by Hersh Lauterpacht. Vol. 2, *Disputes, War and Neutrality*. 7th ed. London: Longmans, Green and Co., 1952.
Peleus case	The Peleus Trial. 1 *Law Reports of Trials of War Criminals* 1 (1945). London: H.M.S. Stationery Office for the United Nations War Crimes Commission, 1946.
Pentagon Papers	Mike Gravel, ed. *The Senator Gravel Edition: The Pentagon Papers: The Defense Department History of United States Decisionmaking on Vietnam*. 4 vols. Boston: Beacon Press, 1971.
Reel, *General Yamashita*	A. Frank Reel. *The Case of General Yamashita*. Chicago: University of Chicago Press, 1949.
Senate Subcommittee on Refugees	U.S., Congress, Senate, Committee on the Judiciary, Subcommittee to Investigate Problems Connected with Refugees and Escapees.

Stone, *Legal Controls*

Julius Stone. *Legal Controls of International Conflict: A Treatise on the Dynamics of Disputes—and War—Law.* Rev. ed. New York: Rinehart & Company, 1959.

Taylor, *Nuremberg and Vietnam*

Telford Taylor. *Nuremberg and Vietnam: An American Tragedy.* New York: Quadrangle Books, 1970.

T.I.A.S.

Treaties and Other International Acts Series. Washington, D.C.: Government Printing Office, 1945-.

T.S.

Treaty Series. Washington, D.C.: Government Printing Office, 1908-45.

U.N., *CB Weapons*

U.N. Secretary-General. *Report on Chemical and Bacteriological (Biological) Weapons and the Effect of Their Possible Use.* U.N. Doc. A/7575 (S/9292/Rev. 1) (1969).

U.N.T.S.

United Nations Treaty Series. New York: United Nations, 1946-.

U.S. Army Field Manual 27-10

United States Department of the Army. *The Law of Land Warfare: Field Manual 27-10.* Washington, D.C.: Department of the Army, 1956.

U.S.C.

United States Code

U.S.T.

United States Treaties and Other International Agreements. Washington, D.C.: Government Printing Office, 1950-.

Whiteman, *Digest*

Marjorie W. Whiteman. *Digest of International Law.* 15 vols. Washington, D.C.: Government Printing Office, 1963-73.

Yamashita case

In Re Yamashita, 327 *United States Supreme Court Reports* 1 (1946) (6-2 decision, Associate Justices Murphy and Rutledge dissenting, Associate Jackson not taking part). Decision of 7 December 1945 by the United States Military Commission at Manila and Order of 6 February 1946 by General Douglas MacArthur Confirm-Death Sentence. In *Documentary History,* ed. Friedman, pp. 1596-99.

Notes

Introduction

1. Public Law No. 93-148 (vetoed 24 October 1973; veto overridden 7 November 1973), 87 Stat. 555.

2. Plato, *The Republic*, trans. Benjamin Jowett (New York: Random House, n.d.), p. 200.

3. Deut. 20:14-19.

4. References to Sun Tzu's work and to other interesting historical antecedents for the laws of war appear in the valuable introductory essay in *Documentary History*, ed. Friedman, pp. 3-15. See also additional sources mentioned in the discussion of *Documentary history*, ed. Friedman, in Alfred P. Rubin, Book Review, *Harv. Int'l L.J.*, 383, 385 n. 9 (1974).

5. Treaty of Peace and Commerce with The Netherlands, *signed* 8 October 1782, art. 18, 2 Malloy, pp. 1233, 1238-39 (effective 22 January 1783, following ratification by the Continental Congress).

6. Treaty of Amity and Commerce with Prussia, *signed* 10 September 1785, art. 23, 2 Malloy, pp. 1477, 1484 (effective October 1786).

7. The account here is based, in part, on the characteristically lucid essay by Telford Taylor, "Foreword," in *Documentary History*, ed. Friedman, pp. xiii-xxv.

8. Convention for the Amelioration of the Condition of the Wounded in Armies in the Field, *done* at Geneva 22 August 1864, 22 Stat. 940, T.S. 377, 1 Bevans 7 (effective 26 July 1882).

9. See Note, "The International Organization of the Red Cross and the League of Red Cross Societies," 42 *A.J.I.L.* 635 (1948); and George W. David, "The Sanitary Commission—The Red Cross," 4 *A.J.I.L.* 546 (1910), discussing the early history of implementation of the 1864 Red Cross Convention in the United States. See also G. I. A. D. Draper, *The Red Cross Conventions* (New York: Frederick A. Praeger, 1958).

10. James Scott Brown, "The Nobel Peace Prize," 12 *A.J.I.L.* 383 (1918), reviewing the background for the awards to Dunant and the International Red Cross Committee of Geneva, as the ICRC was then known.

11. Convention for the Adaptation to Maritime Warfare of the Principles of the Geneva Convention of 22 August 1864, *signed* at The Hague 29 July 1899, 32 Stat. 1827, T.S. No. 396, 1 Bevans 263 (effective 4 September 1900); Convention for the Amelioration of the Condition of the Wounded of the Armies in the Field, *done* at Geneva 6 July 1906, 35 Stat. 1885, 2 Malloy 2183 (effective 3 August 1907).

12. Convention for the Amelioration of the Condition of the Wounded and Sick of Armies in the Field, *signed* at Geneva 27 July 1929, 47 Stat. 2074, T.S. No. 847, 2 Bevans 965 (effective 4 August 1932).

13. Convention Relative to the Treatment of Prisoners of War, *signed* at Geneva 27 July 1929, 47 Stat. 2021, T.S. No. 846, 2 Bevans 932 (effective 4 August 1932).

14. Convention for the Amelioration of the Condition of the Wounded and Sick in Armed Forces in the Field, *done* at Geneva 12 August 1949, 6 U.S.T. 3114, T.I.A.S. No. 3362, 75 U.N.T.S. 31 (effective 2 February 1956) (hereafter cited as 1949 Geneva First Convention).

15. Convention for the Amelioration of the Condition of the Wounded, Sick and

Shipwrecked Members of Armed Forces at Sea, *done* at Geneva on 12 August 1949, 6 U.S.T. 3217, T.I.A.S. No. 3363, 75 U.N.T.S. 85 (effective 2 February 1956) (hereafter cited as 1949 Geneva Second Convention).

16. Geneva Prisoners of War Convention.

17. Geneva Civilians Convention.

18. For a discussion of the North Vietnamese reservation to article 85 of the Geneva Prisoners of War Convention, which was said to be the basis for the refusal of North Vietnam to apply the Convention during the Vietnam War, see Note, "The Geneva Convention and the Treatment of Prisoners of War in Vietnam," 80 *Harv. L. Rev.* 851 (1967); see also Peter D. Trooboff, "Procedures for Protection of Civilians and Prisoners of War in Armed Conflicts: Southeast Asian Examples—A Comment," *Proc., Am. Soc'y Int'l L.* 228 (1971), and the subsequent debate with Jon Van Dyke, ibid., pp. 232, 234, and 239.

19. 1949 Geneva First and Second Conventions, art. 13.

20. Geneva Prisoners of War Convention, art. 4.

21. See, e.g., 1949 Geneva First Convention, art. 13.

22. See Geneva Prisoners of War Convention, art. 4, para. A(2).

23. Ibid., art. 4, para. A(6).

24. Geneva Civilians Convention, art. 4.

25. Ibid., art. 13.

26. Article 10 of each of the four Geneva Conventions of 1949.

27. Ibid.

28. Declaration Renouncing the Use in Time of War of Explosive Projectiles under 400 Grammes Weight, *done* at St. Petersburg 11 December 1868, 58 *Br. and For. St. Papers* 16; 18 Martens, ed., *Nouveau receuil* (1st series), p. 474; 1 *A.J.I.L. Supp.* 95 (1907).

29. Declaration Covering the Prohibition of the Use of Bullets Which Expand or Flatten Easily in the Human Body, *done* at The Hague 29 July 1899, 91 *Br. and For. St. Papers* 1017; 26 Martens, ed., *Nouveau receuil* (2d series), p. 1002.

30. Declaration Concerning the Prohibition of the Use of Projectiles Which Have as Their Sole Purpose the Spreading of Asphyxiating or Noxious Gases, *done* at The Hague 29 July 1899, 91 *Br. and For. St. Papers* 1014; 26 Martens, ed., *Nouveau receuil* (2d series), p. 998.

31. Declaration Prohibiting the Discharge of Projectiles and Explosives from Balloons, *done* at The Hague 18 October 1907, 36 Stat. 2439; T.S. No. 546; 91 *Br. and For. St. Papers,* 1011; 26 Martens, ed., *Nouveau receuil* (2d series), p. 994.

32. Letter of 18 January 1974 from Leonard Niederlehner, Acting General Counsel, U.S. Department of Defense, to Congressman Donald M. Fraser concerning the legality of the use of the M-16 rifle in armed conflict (68 *A.J.I.L.* 528 [1974]). Mr. Niederlehner also discusses the position of the United States on article 34 of the ICRC Draft Additional Protocol I to the Geneva Conventions of 12 August 1949, which would require parties "in the study and development of new weapons or methods of warfare" to determine whether their use would cause "unnecessary injury."

33. Convention Respecting the Law and Customs of War on Land, *signed* at The Hague 29 July 1899, 32 Stat. 1803, T.S. No. 403, 1 Bevans 247 (effective 9 April 1902).

34. Hague Convention No. IV.

35. Treaty Relating to the Use of Submarines and Noxious Gases in Warfare, *signed* at Washington, D.C., 6 February 1922; Manley O. Hudson, ed., *International Legislation,* 9 vols. (Washington, D.C.: Carnegie Endowment for International Peace, 1931), doc. no. 66, vol. 2, p. 794 (never became effective).

36. The 1925 Geneva Protocol, according to Manley O. Hudson, was separated from the 1922 five-power treaty because of the "reluctance" of states to ratify or adhere to the treaty on submarines (Hudson, "Editor's Note," in *International Legislation,* ed. Hudson, doc. no. 143, vol. 3, p. 1670).

37. U.S., Congress, Senate, Foreign Relations Committee, *Committee Print: Message by President Richard M. Nixon of August 19, 1970, and Report by Secretary of State William P. Rogers,* 91st Cong., 2d Sess., 1970; 63 *Dep't State Bull.* 273, 274 (1970).

The Senate gave its advice and consent to the Geneva Protocol of 1925 after its Committee on Foreign Relations conducted further hearings in December 1974 and issued a report reviewing the history of the Administration's efforts to obtain approval for its ratification by the United States. U.S., Congress, Senate, Foreign Relations Committee, *Hearings on Prohibition of Chemical and Biological Weapons,* 93d Cong., 2d

Sess., 10 December 1974 (hereafter cited as *1974 Hearings*) and S. Exec. Rep. No. 93-35, 93d Cong., 2d Sess., 13 December 1974 (hereafter cited as *1974 Report*). In its report, the Foreign Relations Committee stated that it was recommending advice and consent to ratification of the Protocol after being informed by the Director of the Arms Control and Disarmament Agency, Dr. Fred C. Ikle, that the President

> is prepared, in reaffirming the current U.S. understanding of the scope of the Proto-col, to renounce as a matter of national policy:
> (1) first use of herbicides in war except use, under regulations applicable to their domestic use, for control of vegetation within U.S. bases and installations or around their immediate defensive perimeters;
> (2) first use of riot control agents in war except in defensive military modes to save lives such as:
> (a) Use of riot control agents in riot control circumstances to include controlling rioting prisoners of war. This exception would permit use of riot control agents in riot situations in areas under direct and distinct U.S. military control;
> (b) Use of riot control agents in situations where civilian casualties can be reduced or avoided. This use would be restricted to situations in which civilians are used to mask or screen attacks;
> (c) Use of riot control agents in rescue missions. The use of riot control agents would be permissible in the recovery of remotely isolated personnel such as downed air crews—and passengers;
> (d) Use of riot control agents in rear echelon areas outside the combat zone to protect convoys from civil disturbances, terrorists, and paramilitary organizations.
> *1974 Hearings,* p. 12;
> *1974 Report,* pp. 4-5.

The Senate committee was also assured by Dr. Ikle that the President "intends to conform U.S. policy to this position" and that the Joint Chiefs of Staff "fully support the President's decision." The committee said that it "attaches particular importance" to Dr. Ikle's statement that, although there would be "no formal legal impediment" to a Presidential decision broadening the permissible uses of herbicides and riot control agents,

> the policy which was presented to the Committee will be inextricably linked with the history of Senate consent to ratification of the Protocol with its consent dependent upon its observance. If a future administration should change this policy without Senate consent whether in practice or by formal policy change, it would be inconsis-tent with the history of the ratification, and could have extremely grave political repercussions and as a result is extremely unlikely to happen.
> *1974 Hearings,* p. 29.

The Senate committee expressly conditioned its recommendation that the Senate give advice and consent to ratification "[o]n the basis of this and other Executive Branch assurances reflected in hearing record. . ." (*1974 Report,* p. 5). See especially Dr. Ikle's specification of "illustrative uses" of herbicides and riot control agents prohibited under the newly announced national policy and the responses of the Arms Control and Disarmament Agency (*1974 Hearings,* pp. 13, 26-31). See also testimony of Professor Richard R. Baxter (ibid., p. 31).
The Senate promptly gave its advice and consent to ratification of the 1925 Protocol (120 *Congressional Record* S. 21643 [daily edition, 16 December 1974]), and the Presi-dent signed the instruments of ratification on 22 January 1975 (*Washington Post,* 23 Jan-uary 1975, sec. A, p. 15). The United States ratification is subject to a reservation permitting use by it of any prohibited gases if an enemy state or its allies fail to respect the Protocol. Deposit of the instruments of ratification is anticipated during 1975, at which time the Protocol will enter into force for the United States.
    38. Taylor, *Nuremberg and Vietnam,* p. 20.
    39. Friedman, ed., *Documentary History,* p. 798.
    40. William Greider, "The Point Where War Becomes Murder," *Washington Post,* 11 October 1970, p. D-1.
    41. Friedman, ed., *Documentary History,* pp. 776-77, provides a useful account of the World War I experience on which the text is, in part, based.
    42. Taylor, *Nuremberg and Vietnam,* pp. 81-82.
    43. Friedman, ed., *Documentary History,* pp. 776-77; 14 *A.J.I.L.* 95 (1920).

44. Treaty of Peace with Germany, *done* at Versailles 28 June 1919, S. Doc. No. 49, 66th Cong., 1st Sess., arts. 227-30, 13 *A.J.I.L. Supp.* 151 (1919) (not ratified by the United States).

45. London IMT Charter, art. 2. For an excellent analysis of the legal issues raised by the Nuremberg IMT judgment and the tribunal's proceedings, see Quincy Wright, "The Law of the Nuremberg Trial," 41 *A.J.I.L.* 38 (1947).

46. Richard H. Minear, *Victor's Justice: The Tokyo War Crimes Trial* (Princeton: Princeton University Press, 1971), p. 183. Appendix I of Minear's book contains a number of the relevant documents relating to the Far East IMT, including its charter and excerpts from its judgment.

47. London IMT Charter, art. 6.

48. Friedman, ed., *Documentary History*, p. 796.

49. *U.S. Army Field Manual 27-10*, para. 509.

50. According to paragraph 509, the conditions include "the fact that obedience to lawful military orders is the duty of every member of the armed forces; that the latter cannot be expected, in conditions of war discipline, to weigh scrupulously the legal merits of the orders received; that certain rules of warfare may be controversial; or that an act otherwise amounting to a war crime may be done in obedience to orders conceived as a measure of reprisal." "At the same time," paragraph 509 adds, "it must be borne in mind that members of the armed forces are bound to obey only lawful orders." For this last point, the *Field Manual* cites the Uniform Code of Military Justice, art. 92, 10 U.S.C. § 892.

51. Lassa Oppenheim, *International Law*, vol. 1, *Peace*, ed. Hersh Lauterpacht, 8th ed. (London: Longmans, Green and Co., 1955), p. 26. See, generally, Anthony A. D'Amato, *The Concept of Custom in International Law* (Ithaca: Cornell University Press, 1971).

52. Chapter 12, pp. 157-58, and n. 32.

53. Pres. Proc. No. 4313, Announcing a Program for the Return of Vietnam Era Draft Evaders and Military Deserters, 39 Fed. Reg. 33293 (17 Sept. 1974); Exec. Order No. 11803, Establishing Presidential Clemency Board, 39 Fed. Reg. 33297 (17 Sept. 1974).

Chapter 1

1. Paul Ramsey, *The Just War: Force and Political Responsibility* (New York: Charles Scribner's Sons, 1968), esp. pp. 432-40.

2. A more balanced view of comparative merits of incumbent and insurgent positions is developed in Tom J. Farer, "The Law of War 25 Years after Nuremberg," *International Conciliation,* no. 583 (May 1971), pp. 25-35. See, in particular, his rejection of the American view "that humanitarian law does not inhibit full exploitation of firepower superiority regardless of its effect on the civilian population," p. 33; Farer calls this view "a proposition which every decent man will, or course, reject."

3. These ratios are relied upon and explained in Edward S. Herman, *Atrocities in Vietnam: Myths and Realities* (Philadelphia: Pilgrim Press, 1970), pp. 41-88; see esp. pp. 42-46, 54-60. See also Frank Harvey, *Air War: Vietnam* (New York: Bantam Books, 1967); and Cornell Air War Study Group, *Air War in Indochina.*

4. See, e.g., Taylor, *Nuremberg and Vietnam;* Erwin Knoll and Judith Nies McFadden, eds., *War Crimes and the American Conscience* (New York: Holt, Rinehart and Winston, 1970); Richard A. Falk, Gabriel Kolko, and Robert Jay Lifton, eds., *Crimes of War* (New York: Random House, 1971).

5. Philip E. Slater, *The Pursuit of Loneliness: American Culture at the Breaking Point* (Boston: Beacon Press, 1970), p. 32; for a more developed statement see Jean-Paul Sartre, *On Genocide* (Boston: Beacon Press, 1968). Accounts of typical ground combat campaigns also support an inference of genocidal impact. See, e.g., Jonathan Schell's two books, *The Military Half: An Account of Destruction in Quang Ngai and Quang Tin* (New York: Alfred A. Knopf, 1968), and *The Village of Ben Suc* (New York: Alfred A. Knopf, 1967).

6. As E. L. Katzenbach, Deputy Assistant Secretary of Defense for Education and

Manpower Resources in the Kennedy administration, put it in an influential article: "[w]e need not only troops which can strike on the peripheries of the free world, but also troops which can be sent not merely to fight but also to maintain order. We need not only useful troops but usable troops—that is to say, troops which are politically expendable, the kind of troops who can do the job as it is needed without too great a political outcry in a nation like our own which so abhors war . . ." (E. L. Katzenbach, "Time, Space, and Will: The Politico-Military Views of Mao Tse-tung," in *The Guerrilla and How to Fight Him: Selections from the Marine Corps Gazette,* ed. Thomas N. Greene (New York: Frederick A. Praeger, 1962), p. 21. On covertness, see *Pentagon Papers,* esp. vols. 1-3.

7. Cornell Air War Study Group, *Air War in Indochina,* esp. pp. 167-73. Even if some decline from peak-level bombing occurred, the level of firepower was kept out of all proportion to claims. In addition, of course, the arena of active combat violence expanded to include all of Indochina after President Nixon took office.

8. The American involvement in the Cambodian War beginning in 1970 supplied an example of the Nixon Doctrine in operation. Cornell Air War Study Group, *Air War in Indochina,* pp. 87-90.

9. See Introduction, p. 23.

10. Ibid., pp. 21-23.

11. See ibid., p. 23. For a persuasive case on the basis for considering the American involvement in Vietnam as a crime against peace, see Ralph Stavins, Richard J. Barnet, and Marcus G. Raskin, *Washington Plans an Aggressive War* (New York: Random House, 1971), esp. Ralph Stavins, "Washington Determines the Fate of Vietnam, 1954-1965," part 1, pp. 3-195. Note also that under the Charter for the Nuremberg International Military Tribunal the dependence of "crimes against humanity" on an underlying "war crime" or "crime against peace" was based on the concern in 1945 about retroactivity with respect to crimes against humanity. In the 1970s such concern, of course, no longer has a valid legal foundation.

12. These four principles sum up the relevance of customary international law to the interpretation of the rights and duties of states with respect to the conduct of war. This general legal framework exists independent of and in addition to treaty obligations, although it is relevant, as well, to the interpretation of treaty rules.

13. See arts. 22, 23, and 25 of the Hague Regulations and Introduction, pp. 15-16.

14. See *Law of Armed Conflicts,* pp. 38-45, 78-91.

15. That is, the brunt of the war crimes allegation concerns the impact of methods and tactics of warfare in Indochina on the civilian population, not on the organized insurgent armed forces. Given the scale and magnitude of military effort, and the degree of international involvement, it hardly seems possible to categorize the war as a conflict that falls outside the protective scope of the laws of war altogether. The most that can be argued, and this argument too seems unpersuasive, is that the insurgent combatants are entitled to only limited protection because of their mode of combat.

16. On asymmetry generally see Herman, *Atrocities in Vietnam,* esp. pp. 41-88.

17. There is a dispute among specialists in warfare about whether to emphasize the political affinities of the population or merely to crush the military capabilities of the insurgent forces and their external backers. Roger Hilsman places great, perhaps undue, emphasis on the distinction between the "political" and "military" approaches to counterinsurgency warfare. See Roger Hilsman, *To Move a Nation* (New York: Dell Publishing Co., 1964), pp. 411-537. The military perspective is expressed by a Marine Corps four-star general in Lewis W. Walt, *Strange War, Strange Strategy: A General's Report on Vietnam* (New York: Funk & Wagnalls, 1970); more wide-ranging, but along the same lines is Hanson W. Baldwin, *A Strategy for Tomorrow* (New York: Harper and Row, 1970). See also *Pentagon Papers,* esp. vol. 3, for an inside view of the disagreement that evolved between advocates of "slow squeeze" and advocates of "quick squeeze" with regard to bombing tactics used against North Vietnam. Note that by 1965 the entire government debate had moved from a consideration of political versus military approaches to counterinsurgency to disagreement about the kind of direct military approach. Among those accounts of the underlying conflict that cast most persuasive doubt on a military approach to "winning" is John T. McAlister, Jr., *Vietnam: The Origins of Revolution* (New York: Alfred A. Knopf, 1969); see, more generally, Eric R. Wolf, *Peasant Wars of the Twentieth Century* (New York: Harper and Row, 1969).

18. See, e.g., John Gerassi, *North Vietnam: A Documentary* (Indianapolis: Bobbs-

Merrill Co., 1968), esp. pp. 95-110, 182-90; see also Cornell Air War Study Group, *Air War in Indochina,* and Harvey, *Air War: Vietnam.* The Cornell Air War Study Group's *Air War in Indochina* is the most reliable and comprehensive available account of the air war, though its data go up only to 1971, thereby omitting heavy periods of American bombing, including the infamous Christmas bombing of Hanoi and Haiphong at the end of 1972 and the world outcry occasioned by evidence in 1972 that the United States was deliberately bombing dikes in North Vietnam.

19. Transcript, "Face the Nation," 3 May 1970, pp. 3, 6.

20. Evidence on Laos bombing, with best available sources cited, is well summarized in Cornell Air War Study Group, *Air War in Indochina,* pp. 67-86. See, in general, Nina S. Adams and Alfred W. McCoy, eds., *Laos: War and Revolution* (New York: Harper and Row, 1970). See also report by Congressman Paul N. McCloskey of official trip to Laos, as presented to Senate Foreign Relations Committee, *Hearings on Legislative Proposals Relating to the War in Southeast Asia,* 92d Cong., 1st Sess., April and May 1971, pp. 611-16.

21. See Fred Branfman, "Presidential War in Laos, 1964-1970," in *Laos: War and Revolution,* ed. Adams and McCoy, pp. 213-80.

22. The general rationale, and its intentional character, is summarized in *The Indochina Story: A Critical Appraisal of American Involvement in Southeast Asia,* an account prepared by Committee of Concerned Asian Scholars (New York: Bantam Books, 1970), pp. 97-102.

23. For a brief account see Cornell Air War Study Group, *Air War in Indochina,* pp. 57-59.

24. See Senate Subcommittee on Refugees, *Hearings on Refugee and Civilian War Casualty Problems in Laos and Cambodia,* 91st Cong., 2d Sess., May 1970; Senate Subcommittee on Refugees, *Hearings on War-Related Civilian Problems in Indochina,* 92d Cong., 1st Sess., April 1971.

25. Reliance on this weaponry is discussed by Herman, *Atrocities in Vietnam,* pp. 70-75; see, in general, *Efficiency in Death: The Manufacturers of Anti-Personnel Weapons,* compiled and prepared by Council on Economic Priorities (New York: Harper and Row, 1970), esp. pp. 1-26.

26. See Committee of Concerned Asian Scholars, *The Indochina Story,* pp. 87-90 and references cited therein.

27. *New York Times,* 1 April 1970, p. 1.

28. *New York Times,* 25 July 1971, sec. 4, p. 2.

29. "The United States Embassy's continuing studies show that the enemy's political organization is intact in most of the country" (ibid.). Peterson estimates that as of his July 1971 article 60,000 Vietnamese had been killed, captured, or had defected under the Phoenix Program. See also Herman, *Atrocities in Vietnam,* pp. 34-40. For further information on the Phoenix Program see testimony by Congressman Paul N. McCloskey before Senate Foreign Relations Committee, McCloskey, *Report,* pp. 617-20.

30. See John D. Constable and Matthew Messelson, Letter to the *New York Times,* 4 August 1971, p. 32; see also Herman, *Atrocities in Vietnam,* and Committee of Concerned Asian Scholars, *The Indochina Story,* pp. 111-15; see also Barry Weisberg, ed., *Ecocide in Indochina: The Ecology of War* (New York: Harper and Row, 1970); see comments by Arthur Galston in *War Crimes and the American Conscience,* ed. Knoll and McFadden, pp. 68-72.

31. *New York Times,* 29 August 1971, p. 8; this report indicated that the South Vietnamese Army already had 1.5 million gallons of Agent Orange available for use.

32. *New York Times,* 29 August 1971, p. 8. Large-scale use of 7 1/2-ton bombs was also reported; these bombs destroy all life within a radius of 760 acres.

33. William L. Calley, Jr., and John Sack, *Lieutenant Calley: His Own Story* (New York: Viking Press, 1971), pp. 40-41.

34. For a general account of Lt. Col. Anthony Herbert's experience since he alleged toleration of extreme war crimes by his superior officers, see James T. Wooten, "How a Supersoldier Was Fired from His Command," in *New York Times Magazine,* 5 September 1971, pp. 10-11, 27-28, 33-34. It is indicative of both national mood and Presidential leadership to note the hue and cry that was provoked by Lieutenant Calley's conviction and the general indifference to Herbert's plight. See also Anthony Herbert with James T. Wooten, *Soldier* (New York: Holt, Rinehart and Winston, 1973). For a well-constructed

narrative of a similar experience with the command structure, see Daniel Lang, *Casualties of War* (New York: McGraw-Hill, 1969)..

35. Calley and Sack, *Lieutenant Calley*, p. 79.

36. For a perceptive account of battlefield conditions in Vietnam as "atrocity-producing situations" see Robert Jay Lifton,.*Home from the War: Vietnam Veterans: Neither Victims nor Executioners* (New York: Simon & Schuster, 1973), esp. pp. 135-59.

37. For analysis see Committee of Concerned Asian Scholars, *The Indochina Story*, pp. 79-85, 217-24; an excellent critique of counterinsurgency theory and practice on these grounds is developed by Eqbal Ahmad, "Winning Hearts and Minds: The Theory and Fallacies of Counterinsurgency," *Nation*, 2 August 1971, pp. 70-85. The most influential advocate of counterinsurgent warfare as a positive response to the Vietnamese conflict is Sir Robert Thompson; see his *No Exit from Vietnam* (New York: David McKay Co., 1969), a book that is said to have influenced President Nixon's approach to the Vietnam War.

38. The entire history of revolutionary warfare confirms the basic proposition that the insurgent can offset its material deficiencies vis-à-vis the incumbent only if it can mobilize a popular base of support.

39. Josef Kunz has made this point persuasively in arguing for giving serious attention to rules of conduct *during* a war, despite the existence of rules prohibiting *recourse* to war. Josef Kunz, *The Changing Structure of International Law* (Columbus: Ohio State University Press, 1969), pp. 831-909. In this regard, the failure of first-order restraints brings into play second-order restraints that may help to moderate conflict and avoid excessive suffering and destruction.

40. A pessimistic assessment of the prospect for a post-Vietnam reorientation of American foreign policy in relation to revolutionary activity in the Third World is the main theme of my chapter, "What We Should Learn from Vietnam," in *After Vietnam: The Future of American Foreign Policy*, ed. Robert W. Gregg and Charles W. Kegley, Jr. (New York: Anchor Books, 1971), pp. 324-39; more generally, see the various views expressed in Richard M. Pfeffer, ed., *No More Vietnams? The War and the Future of American Foreign Policy* (New York: Harper and Row, 1968); for an overall depiction of the counterrevolutionary drift of American foreign policy, see Richard J. Barnet, *Intervention and Revolution: The United States in the Third World* (New York: World Publishing Co., 1967).

41. For some discussion of these issues see Taylor, *Nuremberg and Vietnam*, pp. 92-94, 183-207; Marcus G. Raskin, "From Imperial War-Making to a Code of Personal Responsibility," in Stavins, Barnet, and Raskin, *Washington Plans an Aggressive War*, pp. 253-332; Leonard B. Boudin, "War Crimes and Vietnam: The Mote in Whose Eye?" (Book comment on Telford Taylor, *Nuremberg and Vietnam*) 84 *Harv. L. Rev.* 1940 (1971); Richard Falk, "Nuremberg: Past, Present, and Future," 80 *Yale L.J.* 1501 (1971); see also Karl Jaspers, *The Question of German War Guilt* (New York: Dial Press, 1947).

42. That is, battlefield participants in specific atrocities and command officers who fail to report or fail to act in the face of an accurate report. In the latter instances, responsibility is unlikely unless public pressure is mounted to expose the delinquencies involved.

43. Daniel Ellsberg's decision to disclose the *Pentagon Papers* was motivated, it seems, by his sense of moral and legal duty derived, in part, from his understanding of the Nuremberg tradition. These legal foundations for antiwar resistance also influenced many young Americans and their elders (e.g., the Berrigan brothers) who chose jail or exile rather than participate in the armed forces, or radical activities instead of more traditional forms of political participation. On the other hand, American leadership groups are unresponsive to appeals based on Nuremberg thinking. The main policy makers in the Vietnam War have been given jobs in civilian life that reflect their continued high stature, and opposition to appointments based on these lines of objection are not popular. See John F. Campbell, "The Death Rattle of the Eastern Establishment," *New York Magazine*, 20 September 1971, pp. 47-51.

44. I have in mind here the whole notion of "Fifth Columns" that undermine the foundations of political authority to pave the way for the entry of an external power.

45. For detailed discussion of this see Richard Falk, *Legal Order in a Violent World* (Princeton: Princeton University Press, 1968), pp. 109-55.

46. Such distance is a very pronounced characteristic of both the task-force study and the underlying documents that comprise the *Pentagon Papers;* it is also evident in the principal "insider" accounts of the policy process accompanying the American involvement in the Vietnam War. See, e.g., Townsend Hoopes, *The Limits of Intervention* (New York: David McKay Co., 1969); Chester Cooper, *The Lost Crusade: America in Vietnam* (New York: Dodd, Mead & Co., 1970).

47. See, e.g., Tom J. Farer, "Intervention in Civil Wars: A Modest Proposal," in *The Vietnam War and International Law*, ed. Richard Falk, 3 vols. (Princeton: Princeton University Press, 1967-72), vol. 1, pp. 509-22; Farer's views are further developed, partly in response to criticisms, in "Harnessing Rogue Elephants: A Short Discourse on Intervention in Civil Strife," in *The Vietnam War and International Law*, ed. Falk, vol. 2, pp. 1089-116.

48. Some basic material is contained in Richard Falk, ed., *The International Law of Civil War* (Baltimore: Johns Hopkins University Press, 1971); see also Wolf, *Peasant Wars of the Twentieth Century*, and Barnet, *Intervention and Revolution*.

49. For a sensible discussion of prospects for revision see the excellent report by Denise Bindschedler-Robert, "A Reconsideration of the Law of Armed Conflicts," in *Law of Armed Conflicts*.

50. I have tried to deal with this need for fundamental reorientation in Richard Falk, *This Endangered Planet* (New York: Random House, 1971).

51. For a careful study of earlier American attitudes toward Nuremberg, see William J. Bosch, *Judgment on Nuremberg: American Attitudes toward the Major German War-Crimes Trials* (Chapel Hill: University of North Carolina Press, 1970); for an important critique of the Nuremberg approach in the context of the Tokyo trials after World War II, see Richard H. Minear, *Victor's Justice: The Tokyo War Crimes Trial* (Princeton: Princeton University Press, 1971); for a critical assessment of the failure to apply the Nuremberg idea since the end of World War II, see Eugene Davidson, *The Nuremberg Fallacy: Wars and War Crimes Since World War II* (New York: Macmillan, 1973).

Chapter 2

1. Hague Regulations, Preamble.
2. Hague Regulations, art. 25.
3. *Hostages* case, pp. 1295-98.
4. See, e.g., Howard Levie, "Maltreatment of Prisoners of War in Vietnam," 48 *B.U.L. Rev.* 323 (1968); Note, "The Geneva Convention and the Treatment of Prisoners of War in Vietnam," 80 *Harv. L. Rev.* 851 (1967); and Note, "The Geneva Convention of 1949: Application in the Vietnamese Conflict," 5 *Va. J. Int'l L.* 243 (1965).
5. Geneva Civilians Convention, art. 49.
6. *Hostages* case, pp. 1249-54.
7. Ibid., p. 1249.
8. Oppenheim, *International Law*, ed. Lauterpacht, pp. 415-16.
9. While the full text of the Rules of Engagement is classified, excerpts of those rules in effect at the time of the My Lai incident are printed in the publicly released portion of the so-called Peers Report, U.S., Department of the Army, *Report of the Department of the Army Review of the Preliminary Investigations into the My Lai Incident*, 14 March 1970, vol. 1, pp. 9-5 to 9-22.
10. Hague Regulations, art. 23(g).

Chapter 4

1. Richard R. Baxter, "So-called 'Unprivileged Belligerency': Spies, Guerrillas, and Saboteurs," 28 *Brit. Y.B. Int'l L.* 323, 324 (1951), citing the *Hostages* case, p. 1247.
2. Convention on the Prevention and Punishment of the Crime of Genocide, *adopted* by the U.N. General Assembly on 9 December 1948 and *entered into force* on

12 January 1951, 78 U.N.T.S. 277 (not in force in the United States); U.N. Doc. A/64/ Add. 1; G.A. Res. 260, U.N. Doc. A/760 (1948-49), *Yearbook of the United Nations* (Lake Success: U.N. Department of Public Information, 1950), pp. 953-60.

3. Whiteman, *Digest,* vol. 10, p. 429.

4. Stone, *Legal Controls,* pp. 352-53. The principle of military necessity in the application of force is hedged by the qualification "subject to the laws of war" (*Hostages* case, p. 1253: "There must be some reasonable connection between the destruction of property and the overcoming of the enemy [military] forces").

5. *U.S. Army Field Manual 27-10,* para. 3.

6. G.A. Res. 2444, 23 U.N. GAOR Supp. 18, pp. 50-51, U.N. Doc. A/7218 (1968).

7. Geneva Civilians Convention, art. 28.

8. Hague Regulations, art. 1; Geneva Prisoners of War Convention, art. 4.

9. Geneva Civilians Convention, art. 9; Hague Cultural Property Convention, art. 8.

10. G. I. A. D. Draper, "Intervention at Twenty-First ICRC Convention," as reported in "Humanitarian Rights for Inhumanity?" *The Magen David Adom Quarterly,* February 1970, pp. 3-4.

11. ICRC, *Reaffirmation and Development of the Laws and Customs Applicable in Armed Conflicts* (May 1969), p. 55 (hereafter cited as Report of Experts).

12. *U.S. Army Field Manual 27-10,* para. 42.

13. Geneva Civilians Convention, art. 19.

14. Geneva Civilians Convention, art. 28.

15. Hague Cultural Property Convention, art. 28 (1) (a) and (b).

16. Stone, *Legal Controls,* p. 627.

17. Whiteman, *Digest,* vol. 10, p. 428.

18. *U.S. Army Field Manual 27-10,* paras. 45, 253, and 257.

19. *Einsatzgruppen* case, p. 467.

20. *U.S. Army Field Manual 27-10,* paras. 34 and 36.

21. Stone, *Legal Controls,* p. 550.

22. Hague Regulations, art. 23(b).

23. Greenspan, *Modern Law of Land Warfare,* p. 317.

24. David Welsh, "Pacification in Vietnam," in *Crimes of War,* ed. Richard A. Falk, Gabriel Kolko, and Robert Jay Lifton (New York: Random House, 1971), p. 296.

25. Hague Regulations, art. 23(g); Report of Experts, "Summary Review of International Law Rules Concerning the Protection of Civilian Populations against the Dangers of Indiscriminate Warfare," p. 55.

26. *U.S. Army Field Manual 27-10,* para. 56; Geneva Civilians Convention, art. 53; Greenspan, *Modern Law of Land Warfare,* p. 286.

27. *U.S. Army Field Manual 27-10,* para. 37(b).

28. Greenspan, *Modern Law of Land Warfare,* p. 349, where the difference between blockade and siege is explained.

29. War Office (United Kingdom), "Part III—The Law of War on Land," *Manual of Military Law* (London: H.M.S. Stationery Office, 1958), para. 112.

30. *U.S. Army Field Manual 27-10,* paras. 37 and 41.

31. Hague Regulations, art. 23(g).

32. Hamilton DeSaussure, "The Laws of Air Warfare: Are There Any?" 23 *Navy War College Rev.* 35 (February 1971).

33. See Draft Hague Air Warfare Rules, art. 24(2), setting forth a list of "military objectives" against which bombing is lawful if "directed exclusively" at such objectives.

34. Whiteman, *Digest,* vol. 10, p. 428; Stone, *Legal Controls,* p. 623.

35. United States Department of the Army, "An Analysis of the Evolution of Military Assistance Command—Vietnam Rules of Engagement Pertaining to Ground Operations" (unpublished and undated memorandum) (copy available from Professor DeSaussure on request).

36. Hague Regulations, art. 23(g).

37. Compare *U.S. Army Field Manual 27-10,* para. 3 with the predecessor provision in para. 1 of the 1940 edition of *Field Manual 27-10.*

Chapter 5

1. Hence, I have deliberately chosen the phrase Grotius employed to indicate the morality of his proposals for internationally respected rules of war in order to move the conduct of hostilities away from the savagery of "pre-Westphalia" strife.

2. See Stone, *Legal Controls,* pp. 351-53, summarizing the literature on this German doctrine.

3. *Hostages* case, pp. 1253-54.

4. See *United States v. Holmes,* 26 *Federal Cases* 360 (No. 15383) (C. C. E. D. Pa. 1842) and *Regina* v. *Dudley and Stevens,* [1884] 14 Q.B. 273.

5. The *Peleus* case is discussed in Willard B. Cowles, "Trials of War Criminals (Non-Nuremberg)," 42 *A.J.I.L.* 299, 301 (1948).

6. But see Stone, *Legal Controls,* p. 353, emphasizing the inconsistency between the "right" of states to international law for self-preservation in time of peace and the denial of such right to states at war. Stone urges reassessment of the doctrine of self-preservation.

7. This belief is far from the truth. The conduct and utility of guerrilla operations were discussed in a book written in the fourth century B.C.: Sun Tzu, *The Art of War,* trans. Samuel B. Griffith (Oxford: Oxford University Press, 1971). Insurgency, insurrection, and guerrilla operations have been part and parcel of many wars in all parts of the world since that time.

8. Hague Regulations, art. 1.

9. William Edward Hall, *A Treatise on International Law,* ed. A. Pearce Higgins, 8th ed. (Oxford: Oxford University Press, 1924), pp. 616-17, 619 n. 1.

10. Myres S. McDougal and Florentino P. Feliciano, *Law and Minimum World Public Order: The Legal Regulation of International Coercion* (New Haven: Yale University Press, 1961), pp. 241-42.

11. Judith N. Shklar, *Legalism* (Cambridge: Harvard University Press, 1964), p. 158.

12. George Orwell, *Nineteen Eighty-Four* (New York: Harcourt, Brace & World, 1949), pp. 24-25.

13. Carlos Marighela, "Minimanual of the Urban Guerrilla," in *Urban Guerrilla Warfare,* ed. Robert Moss, Adelphi Paper no. 79 (London: International Institute for Strategic Studies, 1971), p. 36. See also Walter Laqueur, "Guerrillas and Terrorists," 58 *Commentary* 40 (October 1974).

Chapter 6

1. *New York Times,* 24 January 1973, p. 17 and 25 January 1973, p. 21.

2. Ibid.

3. Appendix K to Testimony by William E. Colby, Deputy to the Commander, United States Military Assistance Command—Vietnam, Senate Subcommittee on Refugees, *Hearings on War-Related Civilian Problems in Indochina, Part I: Vietnam,* 92d Cong., 1st Sess., April 1971, p. 62 (hereafter cited as *1971 Hearings*).

4. Orr Kelly, "Pentagon Defends Air War," *Sunday Star,* 25 April 1971, sec. A, p. 4 (discussing a Pentagon study ordered by Dennis J. Doolin, Deputy Assistant Secretary of Defense for International Security Affairs, which determined that "American bombing and strafing [in 1971] endangers far less of the civilian population . . . than it did" two years before).

5. Senate Subcommittee on Refugees, *1971 Hearings,* p. 47.

Chapter 7

1. Chapter 5, p. 82.

2. For a balanced consideration of *jus cogens,* see *The Concept of Jus Cogens in International Law: Papers and Proceedings of a Conference at Lagonissi, Greece, 3-8 April 1966* (Geneva: Carnegie Endowment for International Peace [European Centre], 1967) (hereafter cited as Carnegie Endowment, *Jus Cogens*).

3. Hague Convention No. IV, Preamble (emphasis added).

4. Sydney Bailey's stress on the Martens clause is similar to my own. He refers to it as "the first basic principle of the Hague Conventions." As he puts it, "the code the parties adopted was recognized to be incomplete; it was to be supplemented by rules applied in the interests of humanity and civilization, even when these are not expressed in treaty form." Sydney D. Bailey, *Prohibitions and Restraints in War* (London: Oxford University Press for the Royal Institute of International Affairs, 1972), p. 63.

5. Professor George Abi-Saab has stated that some participants in the Carnegie Endowment for International Peace's conference referred to the Nuremberg principles as among those "interests of international society which are protected by *jus cogens.*" Carnegie Endowment, *Jus Cogens,* p. 13.

6. Article 53 of the Vienna Convention on the Law of Treaties, entitled "Treaties conflicting with a peremptory norm of general international law (*jus cogens*)," provides as follows: "A treaty is void if, at the time of its conclusion, it conflicts with a peremptory norm of general international law. For the purposes of the present Convention, a peremptory norm of general international law is a norm accepted and recognized by the international community of States as a whole as a norm from which no derogation is permitted and which can be modified only by a subsequent norm of general international law having the same character." The Vienna Convention makes no attempt to enumerate what norms qualify as peremptory under current international law. For a convenient text of Article 53, see 63 *A.J.I.L.* 891; 8 *International Legal Materials* 698-99 (1969).

7. For the most thorough, abundantly documented study of charges and counter-charges on both sides, see Noam Chomsky and Edward S. Herman, *Counterrevolutionary Violence: Bloodbaths in Fact and Propaganda,* Module 57 (Andover, Mass.: Warner Modular Publications, 1973); see also D. Gareth Porter, "Hue: A Study of Political Warfare," mimeographed (1972) (copy available from Professor Falk on request).

8. For a scholarly, yet scathing, account of counterinsurgent operations in the South Vietnamese province of Long An, see Jeffrey Race, *War Comes to Long An: Revolutionary Conflict in a Vietnamese Province* (Berkeley: University of California Press, 1971).

9. My own evaluation of that role closely parallels two assessments in the published literature: Eqbal Ahmad, "Revolutionary War and Counter-Insurgency," 25 *J. Int'l Affairs* 1 (1971); Noam Chomsky, *For Reasons of State* (New York: Pantheon Books, 1973), esp. pp. 84-93.

10. *Pentagon Papers,* vol. 2, p. 575.

11. Senate Subcommittee on Refugees, *Hearings on Relief and Rehabilitation of War Victims in Indochina; Part IV: South Vietnam and Regional Problems,* 93d Cong., 1st Sess., August 1973, p. 8.

12. Convention on the Prevention and Punishment of the Crime of Genocide, *entered into force* 12 January 1951, 78 U.N.T.S. 277, 45 *A.J.I.L. Supp.* 7 (1951) (the United States has not ratified this treaty).

13. See Richard A. Falk, Gabriel Kolko, and Robert Jay Lifton, eds., *Crimes of War* (New York: Random House, 1971), for fuller treatment of these issues.

14. For text of Mr. Krogh's statement in federal court see *New York Times,* 1 December 1973, p. 16.

15. Chapter 4, p. 67.

16. Incidentally, UNESCO cancelled its earlier willingness to grant Amnesty International facilities in Paris for its December 1973 meeting on the abolition of torture. In other words, even international institutions backed by idealistic charters of incorporation are not politically able to question the propriety of official torture because it would be embarrassing to member governments. Amnesty International, it should be remembered, is a nonpolitical, private, nongovernmental organization with a high reputation for impartiality and responsible action. The issue that caused the cancellation was evidently a conference document that mentioned some sixty governments believed to have engaged in torture during the last decade. See *New York Times,* 4 December 1973, p. 2.

17. Chapter 4, p. 67.

Chapter 8

1. Since Professor Falk cites two such attacks in chapter 7 (p. 107, and n. 9), let me say that they came from two "experts" who passionately opposed everything the United States did in Vietnam. They also displayed abysmal ignorance of the pacification program. See my reply to Eqbal Ahmad at 25 *J. Int'l Affairs* 335-37 (1971). Noam Chomsky's piece merits no reply.

2. See, for example, testimony of William E. Colby, U.S., Congress, Senate, Committee on Armed Services, 93d Cong., 1st Sess., July 1973, pp. 5-7.

Chapter 9

1. Testimony of Robert S. McNamara, Secretary of Defense, U.S., Congress, Senate, Preparedness Investigating Subcommittee of the Committee on Armed Services, *Hearings on Air War against North Vietnam,* 90th Cong., 1st Sess., 9-29 August 1967, pp. 276-77. But see U.S., Congress, Senate, Preparedness Investigating Subcommittee, "Investigation of the Preparedness Program—Air War Against North Vietnam," 90th Cong., 1st Sess., 31 August 1967, p. 10 ("It is clear from the testimony [by professional military witnesses] . . . that . . . many [air] military actions . . . which have thus far been withheld or restricted can and should be taken which are calculated to have a direct and adverse effect upon Hanoi's ability and willingness to continue to support the war.") For background on the 1967 hearings and the disagreement between Secretary McNamara and the professional military over American air warfare policy in North Vietnam, see Townsend Hoopes, *The Limits of Intervention* (New York: David McKay Co., 1969), pp. 83-91.

2. John C. Meyer, "The 11-Day Air Campaign," *United States Air Force Policy Letter for Commanders,* Supplement no. 6 (1973), p. 23 (hereafter cited as Meyer, "Air Campaign").

3. Jean Thoraval, "White House Says Raiding in the North Will Go On Until There Is an Accord," *New York Times,* 19 December 1972, p. 1.

4. Meyer, "Air Campaign," p. 23.

5. Joseph B. Treaster, "Temporary Halt in Raids on North by United States," *New York Times,* 25 December 1972, p. 1. Meyer, "Air Campaign," p. 24. "American bombers tonight conducted the most violent air attack on Hanoi since the beginning of the war" (Agence France-Presse, "Raid on Hanoi Called Heaviest in War," *New York Times,* 27 December 1972, p. 9).

6. Retaliatory attacks by United States aircraft first began over the southern area of North Vietnam on 7 February 1965. "Retaliatory Attacks against North Vietnam," in *Documents on American Foreign Relations, 1965,* ed. Richard P. Stebbins and Elaine P. Adam (New York: Harper and Row, 1966), p. 129 (hereafter cited as *Doc. on Amer. For. Rel.,* with appropriate year). This area was being actively used by Hanoi for training and infiltration by the Viet Cong. There was a 37-day bombing pause from 25 December 1965 to 31 January 1966 in response to many international appeals to President Lyndon Johnson to cease unilaterally the bombing of North Vietnam in order to create an atmosphere for peaceful settlement of the conflict. "United States Peace Efforts: Letter from Ambassador Arthur J. Goldberg to Secretary-General of the United Nations," 4 January 1966, in *Doc. on Amer. For. Rel., 1966,* p. 195. On 31 January 1966, the pause was terminated by President Johnson because of lack of any peaceful response by North Vietnam. "Resumption of Air Action in North Vietnam," in *Doc. on Amer. For. Rel., 1966,* p. 202.

7. *Pentagon Papers,* vol. 4, p. 229.

8. Ibid., p. 24.

9. Cornell Air War Study Group, *Air War in Indochina,* p. 37.

10. "Broadcast Statement by President Lyndon Johnson," 31 January 1966, *Doc. on Amer. For. Rel., 1966,* pp. 202-4.

11. "The petroleum facilities attacked were located away from the population centers of both Hanoi and Haiphong. The pilots were carefully instructed to take every precaution so that only mililtary targets would be hit. Moreover, to assure accuracy, the

attacks have been scheduled only under weather conditions permitting clear visual sighting" ("Attacks on Petroleum Facilities in North Vietnam: Letter from Ambassador Goldberg to the President of the United Nations Security Council," 30 June 1966, *Doc. on Amer. For. Rel., 1966,* pp. 228-29).

12. *Pentagon Papers,* vol. 4, pp. 107-12.

13. Ibid., p. 124.

14. Ibid., p. 170.

15. Ibid., p. 151.

16. Ibid., p. 170. "There has been a new escalation of the air war against North Vietnam, resulting in the destruction of the few remaining untouched objectives in North Vietnam, with a mounting number of victims" ("Intensification of the War: Statement by U Thant and Ambassador Goldberg," 11 May 1967, *Doc. on Amer. For. Rel., 1967,* pp. 234-35).

17. *Pentagon Papers,* vol. 4, p. 172.

18. "Limitation of Bombing of North Vietnam (San Antonio Declaration): Broadcast Address by President Lyndon Johnson," 31 October 1968, *Doc. on Amer. For. Rel., 1968-1969,* pp. 243-48.

19. See William Beecher, "U.S. Letting Pilots Pursue Foe North of 20th Parallel," *New York Times,* 10 January 1973, p. 1. "Lavelle's Raids Are Held Proper," *New York Times,* 19 December 1972, p. 13.

20. "U.S. Letting Pilots Chase Foe in North," *New York Times,* 10 January 1973, p. 6.

21. Cornell Air War Study Group, *Air War in Indochina,* p. 46, citing the second "Jason study" of December 1967.

22. Terence G. McGee, "Hanoi," in *The New Encyclopedia Britannica: Macropaedia,* ed. Warren E. Preece, 19 vols. (Chicago: Helen Hemingway Benton, 1974), vol. 8, pp. 628-30.

23. Senate Subcommittee on Refugees, *Hearings on Problems of War Victims in Indochina, Part III: North Vietnam,* 92d Cong., 2d Sess., August 1972, pp. 21, 30, 37.

24. Hamilton DeSaussure, "The Laws of Air Warfare: Are There Any?" 5 *Int'l Lawyer* 527, 534-39 (1971).

25. J. M. Spaight, *Air Power and War Rights,* 3d ed. (London: Longmans, Green and Co., 1947), pp. 53-56 (hereafter cited as Spaight, *Air Power*).

26. Retaliation for the enemy's actions may be directed at a lawful target, for example, when the objective of a retaliatory attack is a military installation. On the other hand, reprisal entails attack on an otherwise unlawful target that is lawful solely because of the enemy's prior unlawful conduct. While the United States has engaged in retaliatory raids, it has not sought to justify any of its attacks as authorized exclusively on the ground of reprisal. See Bernard Gwertzman, "Nixon and Kissinger and the Collapse of the Paris Peace Talks," *New York Times,* 20 December 1972, p. 14.

27. Senate Subcommittee on Refugees, *Part III: North Vietnam,* p. 2.

28. Spaight, *Air Power,* pp. 17-27.

29. Ibid., p. 17.

30. Stone, *Legal Controls,* pp. 629-31; see also Gerald J. Adler, "Targets in War: Legal Considerations," in *The Vietnam War and International Law,* ed. Richard A. Falk, 3 vols. (Princeton: Princeton University Press, 1968-72), vol. 3, p. 321; M. W. Royse, *Aerial Bombardment and the International Regulation of Warfare* (New York: Harold Vinal, 1928), p. 192; Myres S. McDougal and Florentino P. Feliciano, *Law and Minimum World Public Order: The Legal Regulation of International Coercion* (New Haven: Yale University Press, 1961), p. 613; but see Spaight, *Air Power,* p. 277; Oppenheim, *International Law,* ed. Lauterpacht, p. 528.

31. Jean Pictet, "The Need to Restore the Laws and Customs Relating to Armed Conflicts," 1 *Rev. Int'l Comm. Jurists* 22 (1969). As to the North Vietnamese, their officials made clear that they regarded the Christmas attacks as terror, not morale, bombings. "Hanoi Reports Successes," *New York Times,* 29 December 1972 (citing a statement by North Vietnam protesting "terror bombings unprecedented in history"), p. 3.

32. Wesley F. Craven and James L. Cate, *The Army Air Forces in World War Two,*

7 vols. (Chicago: University of Chicago Press, 1949-58), vol. 2, *Europe: Torch to Point-blank, August 1942 to December 1943* (1949), p. 278.

33. Ibid., p. 298.

34. McDougal and Feliciano, *Law and Minimum World Public Order*, p. 654.

35. *Law of Armed Conflicts*, p. 24.

36. "Historical Analysis of the 14-15 February 1945 Bombings of Dresden" (unpublished memorandum, U.S. Air Force Historical Office, 12 December 1962) (copy available from Professor DeSaussure on request). See Telford Taylor, who states that "Hanoi and Haiphong [should be] considered not in isolation but in conjunction with other cities that have suffered the same or worse fates—Coventry, Hamburg, Berlin, Dresden, Tokyo, Hiroshima and other memorials to the art of war" (Telford Taylor, "Defining War Crimes," *New York Times*, 11 January 1973, p. 39). For a vivid description of the effect of the Hamburg bombings, see George F. Kennan, *Memoirs 1925-1950* (Boston: Atlantic Monthly Press, 1967), pp. 436-37. ("Here, for the first time, I felt an unshakeable conviction that no momentary military advantage—even if such could be calculated to exist—could have justified this stupendous, careless destruction of civilian life and of material values, built up laboriously by human hands over the course of centuries for purposes having nothing to do with war.")

37. United States Strategic Bombing Survey, "The Attack on German Cities," in *Overall Report (European War)* (Washington, D.C.: Government Printing Office, 1945), p. 71.

38. Ibid., p. 29.

39. Craven and Cate, *Army Air Forces*, vol. 2, p. 278.

40. Craven and Cate, *Army Air Forces*, vol. 3, *Europe: Argument to V-E Day, January 1944 to May 1945* (1951), pp. 638-39.

41. Ibid.

42. McDougal and Feliciano, *Law and Minimum World Public Order*, pp. 653-54. French and Swedish sources have, correctly or not, made the analogy between the British decision in World War II and that of the United States in 1972. See, e.g., "A French Comment," *New York Times*, 27 December 1972, p. 31.

43. "Law of War Regulating Aerial Bombardment," Memorandum for Director of Plans, Deputy Chief of Staff Plans and Operations, United States Air Force (unpublished memorandum, 28 April 1971) (copy available from Professor DeSaussure on request).

44. Robert F. Futrell, *The United States Air Force in Korea: 1950-1953* (New York: Duell, Sloan and Pearce, 1961), p. 626; see also Anthony Verrier, *Bomber Offensive* (New York: Macmillan Co., 1969).

45. Futrell, *United States Air Force in Korea*, p. 623.

46. Ibid., p. 626.

47. Hamilton DeSaussure, "International Law and Aerial Bombing," 5 *Air U. Rev.*, 652-54 (1952).

48. United States Department of the Army, "An Analysis of the Evolution of Military Assistance Command—Vietnam Rules of Engagement Pertaining to Ground Operations" (unpublished and undated memorandum), p. 10 (copy available from Professor DeSaussure on request).

49. Senate Subcommittee on Refugees, *Part III: North Vietnam*, National Security Memorandum No. 1, *U.S. Bombing of North Vietnam, 1965-1969*, pp. 177, 183 (hereafter cited as National Security Memorandum No. 1). Cornell Air War Study Group, *Air War in Indochina*, pp. 46-47.

50. National Security Memorandum No. 1, p. 181.

51. ". . . on October 22 in appreciation of Hanoi's 'goodwill' at the negotiating table, Mr. Nixon suspended raids above the 20th Parallel" (Bernard Gwertzman, "Nixon Orders Halt in Bombing of North above 20th Parallel; Peace Talks Will Resume Jan. 8," *New York Times*, 31 December 1972, p. 1). "The President has ordered that all bombing be discontinued above the 20th Parallel as long as serious negotiations are underway" ("Transcript of White House News Conference on Bombing Halt," *New York Times*, 31 December 1972, p. 3).

52. Cornell Air War Study Group, *Air War in Indochina*, p. 40. James Reston, "Power without Pity," *New York Times*, 27 December 1972, p. 39.

53. Meyer, "Air Campaign," p. 24.

54. National Security Memorandum No. 1, pp. 180-81.

55. Meyer, "Air Campaign," p. 23.

56. Joseph B. Treaster, "Trial by Fire for the North," *New York Times*, 31 December 1972, sec. 4, p. 1. "Largest Hospital in Hanoi Reported Damaged in Raid," *New York Times*, 23 December 1972, p. 1. Joseph B. Treaster, "3 B-52's, 2 Other Planes Lost in Raid on North; Foe Shells a Destroyer," *New York Times*, 20 December 1972, p. 1.

57. But see Craig R. Whitney, "B-52 Is Relied On More Than Troops to Blunt Foe in Offensive in Vietnam," *New York Times*, 19 May 1972; James A. Donovan, *Militarism, U.S.A.* (New York: Charles Scribner's Sons, 1970), pp. 181-84.

58. Telford Taylor, "Hanoi under the Bombing: Sirens, Shelters, Rubble and Death," *New York Times*, 7 January 1973, p. 3.

59. One well-placed military officer is quoted as saying "that the eight-engine bombers, which each carry more than 24 tons of bombs and usually fly in formations of three, had smashed storage areas, rail sidings, and power plants and airfields with emphasis on Hanoi, Haiphong and the region immediately surrounding them. This area constitutes the most developed sector of the country" ("U.S. Renews Raids in North Vietnam After Lull Ends," *New York Times*, 26 December 1972, p. 1). It has been suggested that the B-52s flew in groups of more than three. "Before the Christmas pause in bombing, missions were flown by single B-52s or cells of three. Now, to prevent Hanoi from concentrating its fire on such inviting targets, the planes often swarm out in much larger numbers" (Richard Halloran, "The War Is Suddenly Grim for the B-52 Fliers on Guam," *New York Times*, 30 December 1972, p. 1).

60. Whitney, "B-52 Is Relied On," p. 9.

61. John W. Finney, "B-52 Vindicates Its Role, Air Force Aides Assert," *New York Times*, 24 December 1972, p. 3. It has been argued that the United States should have relied on remote-controlled "smart bombs" during the Christmas bombings rather than on "carpet pattern bombing." 246 *Economist* 23 (6 January 1973).

62. "Hanoi and Haiphong: Industrial City and Chief Port," *New York Times*, 21 December 1972, p. 16. "Largest Hospital in Hanoi Reported Damaged in Raid," *New York Times*, 23 December 1972, p. 1.

63. "Heavy Raids Go On for Seventh Day in North Vietnam—Hospital Deaths," *New York Times*, 24 December 1972, p. 1.

64. "Several informed officers have said privately that the [Gia Lam] International Airport was bombed by mistake. 'We have some allies up there who use the airport, too,' one officer said. . . . 'It was hit by mistake. That's all there was to it and the command isn't about to announce its mistakes' " (Joseph B. Treaster, "U.S. Lists Targets of Heavy Attacks in North Vietnam," *New York Times*, 28 December 1972, p. 1).

65. The Polish cargo ship *Joseph Conrad* was reportedly struck and sunk in Haiphong harbor and at least four persons killed (*New York Times*, 21 December 1972, p. 1 and 28 December 1972, p. 8). One of the captured U.S. Air Force navigators who made a tour of downtown Hanoi stated that "what I saw were not military targets destroyed, but several city blocks—which appeared to be a market place—torn apart, a hospital decimated, and an elementary school entirely levelled to the ground" ("P.O.W. Interviewed in Hanoi," *New York Times*, 2 January 1973, p. 8).

66. National Security Memorandum No. 1, p. 192.

67. According to Capt. Michael J. Heck, one of the B-52 pilots who refused to bomb North Vietnam, "one possibility of going off target is maneuvering to avoid surface-to-air missiles. There are also certain inherent errors in any bombing equipment. You can't be exactly accurate. There are a number of human errors and the more planes, the greater the possibility. There is no doubt that nonmilitary targets were hit, but I don't think it was intentional" (George Esper, "B-52 Pilot Who Refused Mission Calls War Not Worth the Killing," *New York Times*, 12 January 1973, p. 2). "B-52 Pilot Faces Military Inquiry," *New York Times*, 11 January 1973, p. 1. Finney, "B-52 Vindicates Its Role," p. 3.

68. See Richard L. Schoenwald, "Dying and Living Casualties," *New York Times*, 30 December 1972, p. 2. Ramsey Clark, explaining why the North Vietnamese broke up families evacuated from Hanoi, said: "They separate them because they say it is terribly

sad to lose a wife or a child, but to lose a whole family is unbearable, and therefore they have separated the wives and the children" (Senate Subcommittee on Refugees, *War Victims in Indochina, Part III*, pp. 5-6). Clark also said that "an air war, unlike other types of war which may affect you daily, affects you every minute of every day." See Agence France-Presse, "For Residents in Hanoi a Full Night's Sleep," *New York Times*, 1 January 1973, p. 1. Professor Telford Taylor writes that "there were still lots of people left, and on the weekend before the bombing resumed Hanoi was a lively bustle of shoppers and sidewalk vendors, its streets crowded with bicyclists and pedestrians" (Taylor, "Hanoi under the Bombing," p. 3).

69. See also a particularly vivid account by a French newspaperman of the destruction alleged to have been done to "[o]ne of Hanoi's most animated and colorful streets," which was " 'carpet bombed' by planes, including B-52s, that plowed up a strip nearly a mile long and several hundred yards wide" (Jean Leclerc du Sablon, "Newsmen in Hanoi Visit Street of Ruins," *New York Times*, 29 December 1972, p. 1). Deirdre Carmody, "Four Who Visited Hanoi Tell of Destruction," *New York Times*, 2 January 1973, p. 1.

70. At least two B-52 pilots refused to continue bombing in 1972. Captain Heck, one of the pilots, refused because "the goals do not justify the mass destruction and killing" (Esper, "B-52 Pilot," p. 1).

71. "20% of Hanoi Razed, 2 Witnesses Report," *New York Times*, 23 January 1973, p. 8. For the report of, and pictures taken by, a Congressional study mission to North Vietnam in March 1973 that inspected the effects of the Christmas bombings, see Senate Subcommittee on Refugees, *Relief and Rehabilitation of War Victims in Indochina: One Year after the Ceasefire*, 92d Cong., 2d Sess., 27 January 1974, pp. 51-59.

72. North Vietnamese authorities reported that 1,318 persons were killed and 1,261 wounded by U.S. bombing raids on Hanoi in December 1972. Not stated was how many were civilian and how many were military casualties. Given the urban targets, however, one could well expect that a substantial portion of the casualties involved civilians ("North Vietnam Says 1,318 Died in the Raids on Hanoi," *New York Times*, 5 January 1973, p. 3). Agence France-Presse, "Visitors in Hanoi See Craters Where 10,000 Lived," *New York Times*, 28 December 1972, p. 3.

73. Meyer, "Air Campaign," p. 23. "The Long Bien Bridge across the Red River was reopened to road and rail traffic today, two months and three days after the end of the heaviest American bombing" (Agence France-Presse, "Hanoi's Long Bien Bridge, Hit in 1972 Bombing, Is Reopened, *New York Times*, 4 March 1973, p. 12). The Long Bien Bridge was not mentioned specifically by General Meyer. It was an important strategic objective linking the center of Hanoi with the Gia Lam airfield. The U.S. military command in Saigon reported that "nineteen of the targets, including the Hanoi railroad yards, the city's power plant and its port facilities, were within 10 miles of the center of Hanoi" (Sylvan Fox, "2 More B-52's Downed, Bringing the Total to 14," *New York Times*, 29 December 1972, p. 1). "One of the principal bombing targets in Hanoi is the 5600 foot Long Bien Bridge over the Red River. Last September, Air Force jets were reported to have destroyed three of its spans and damaged three others" ("Hanoi and Haiphong," p. 16). Editorial, "Terror from the Skies," *New York Times*, 22 December 1972, p. 30.

74. Transcript of the President's News Conference, *New York Times*, 28 July 1972, p. 10.

75. The critics included United Nations Secretary General Kurt Waldheim; Premier Olaf Palme of Sweden, who compared the bombings with Nazi massacres in World War II; Labor Prime Minister of Australia Gough Whitlam; West German Chancellor Willy Brandt, who was unofficially quoted by friends as finding the bombing policy "disgusting and unfathomable"; and the British parliamentarian Roy Jenkins, who described the bombing as "one of the most cold blooded actions in recent history" (Anthony Lewis, "Vietnam Delenda Est," *New York Times*, 23 December 1972, p. 25).

76. Another White House supporter on the war, Senator Henry M. Jackson, Democrat from Washington, said that Mr. Nixon had made "a serious mistake in not making a public statement explaining the massive bombing" (David E. Rosenbaum, "Senate Democrats, 36-12, Back Action to End War," *New York Times*, 5 January 1973, pp. 1, 13). Bernard Gwertzman, "U.S. to Continue Bombing; Says Next Move Is Hanoi's," *New York Times*, 23 December 1972, p. 1. Whiteman, *Digest*, vol. 10, pp. 426-27.

77. See Anthony Lewis, "Madness in Great Ones," *New York Times*, 30 December 1972, p. 21. One reason the United States refrained from divulging too much information at the time of the peace talks was because "it might hurt chances for successful negotiations" ("U.S. Said to Hold Up Data," *New York Times*, 5 January 1973, p. 2). Craig R. Whitney, "Mystery of Bombing in the North," *New York Times*, 22 December 1972, p. 12.

78. Draft Hague Air Warfare Rules, 1923, which never entered into force.

79. James Brown Scott, *The Hague Peace Conferences of 1899 and 1907*, 2 vols. (Baltimore: Johns Hopkins Press, 1909), vol. 2, p. 439.

80. Draft Hague Warfare Rules, art. 24(1) (emphasis added).

81. Oppenheim, *International Law*, ed. Lauterpacht, p. 523.

82. Ibid.

83. Senator Edward M. Kennedy to Melvin R. Laird, 3 May 1972, Senate Subcommittee on Refugees, *Part III: North Vietnam*, p. 70.

84. Hans Blix, Statement to the Third Committee, U.N. General Assembly, "Human Rights in Armed Conflicts," 25 U.N. GAOR, U.N. Doc. A/C.3/SR 1784 (12 November 1970), p. 2.

85. "Historical Analysis of the 14-15 February 1945 Bombings of Dresden" (unpublished memorandum, 12 December 1962), p. 16.

86. Spaight, *Air Power*, p. 275, citing J. A. Farrer, *Military Manners and Customs* (New York: Henry Holt and Co., 1885), p. 106. The strength of Farrer's and Spaight's view is illustrated by the comments of one pilot after a B-52 raid over Hanoi: "a year ago in Thailand, he had passed around a magazine article that described civilian suffering wrought by B-52's. The article had proved deeply moving to himself and his fellows, all of whom had arrived at a single conclusion. The pilot said, 'we decided that if we could have unrestricted bombing, there'd be no more civilian suffering because the war would be over'" (Daniel Lang, "Going to Work over Ground Zero," *New York Times*, 2 January 1973, p. 35).

87. Meyer, "Air Campaign," p. 24; Transcript of Press Conference of Dr. Henry Kissinger on Paris Peace Agreements of 1973, *New York Times*, 25 Jan. 1973, p. 21. There is strong support for the view that the Christmas bombings may have been for an even deeper political purpose than causing the North Vietnamese to resume serious negotiations. Tad Szulc, a former *New York Times* foreign and diplomatic correspondent, states:

> . . . One is left with the impression that Nixon and Kissinger took advantage of Hanoi's political hesitations in December 1972 to inflict the greatest possible damage on North Vietnam so that Thieu would be able to accept the Agreement.
>   . . . The Christmas bombings, therefore, were designed to induce Thieu to sign the Paris Agreement, the price being the "brutalizing" of the North.

Tad Szulc, "How Kissinger Did It: Behind the Vietnam Cease-Fire Agreement," *Foreign Policy*, No. 15 (Summer 1974), p. 61-63, 67. Mr. Szulc reports that "key officials" in the Nixon Administration thought that without the Christmas bombings the United States could have resolved all major disputed issues with North Vietnam that remained to be settled in mid-December 1972 in order to reach a final peace agreement. And there is doubt as to whether the North Vietnamese made any significant political concession to the United States after the bombing that would have been unobtainable had the attacks not occurred (ibid., p. 63).

88. Lt. Gen. William V. McBride, *United States Air Force Policy Letter for Commanders* (Washington, D.C.: Office of the Secretary of the Air Force, 15 October 1973). During the bombing raids South Vietnam's foreign minister Tram Van Lam echoed the view that "the United States bombing of North Vietnam would force Hanoi's leaders to 'accept serious negotiations'" (Joseph B. Treaster, "Saigon Aide Says the Bombing Will Force Hanoi to Negotiate," *New York Times*, 30 December 1972, p. 5.

89. Bernard Gwertzman, "Kissinger Will Renew His Efforts with Tho, White House Says," *New York Times*, 31 December 1972, p.1. During the news conference at which Gerald L. Warren, a deputy Presidential press secretary, announced an end to the bombing of the Hanoi-Haiphong area and a renewal of the private peace talks, he was

asked, "You are implying then that it [the bombings] wouldn't halt until they [serious negotiations] start and we decide they are serious?" Mr. Warren replied, "No, as soon as it was clear that serious negotiations could be resumed at both the technical level and between the principals, the President ordered that all bombing be discontinued above the 20th Parallel" (*New York Times*, 31 December 1972, p. 3). "Congressional Quarterly, a Washington publication, reported that a poll taken [during the week of 23 December 1972] of 73 Senators showed that 45 opposed the latest bombing, 19 in favor, and 9 with no opinion. The other members could not be reached. Moreover, 45 of the 73 Senators said they would support legislation ending the war, 25 were opposed, and 3 undecided" (Gwertzman, "U.S. to Continue Bombing," p. 1). John W. Finney, "Pentagon Says Bombings Wreck Military Targets; It Denies 'Terror' Raids," *New York Times*, 21 December 1972, p. 1.

90. Taylor, "Defining War Crimes," p. 39.

91. McBride, *United States Air Force Policy Letter for Commanders*, p. 3. "Put briefly, Mr. Nixon ordered out the B-52's for diplomatic reasons, tinged with personal anger. It is true that this was done in the context of an actual, if undeclared, war, still, no one has seriously argued that the Christmas bombing was demanded by the exigencies of the war. Instead, it was necessary—in Mr. Nixon's view—to his diplomacy" (Tom Wicker, "Making War, Not Love," *New York Times*, 14 January 1973, sec. E., p. 17). "Another reason the B-52's were called upon last week, more than one officer has said, is their awesome psychological impact. They fly at very high altitudes and often the very first sound heard by a victim is the ear splitting thunder of hundreds of bombs exploding" ("U.S. Renews Raids in North Vietnam," p. 8).

92. For an account of the negotiations to date at Geneva, see Richard R. Baxter, "Humanitarian Law or Humanitarian Politics? The 1974 Diplomatic Conference on Humanitarian Law," 16 *Harv. Int'l L. J.* 1 (1975).

Chapter 12

1. The United States was not a party to the 1925 Geneva Protocol at the time of the Vietnam War. President Nixon submitted it to the Senate for its advice and consent to ratification on 19 August 1970 (U.S., Congress, Senate, Foreign Relations Committee, *Committee Print: Message by President Richard M. Nixon of August 19, 1970, and Report by Secretary of State William P. Rogers*, 91st Cong., 2d Sess., 1970; 63 *Dep't State Bull.* 273 [1970]). Because of a disagreement as to coverage, the Senate had not acted on the Protocol for four years.

On 5 August 1974, by a 315-70 vote, the House of Representatives passed House Res. No. 1258, declaring the sense of the House that the United States should ratify the 1925 Geneva Protocol and that "the President and the Congress should resolve the position of the United States on the future status of herbicides and tear gas so that the Senate may move toward ratification. . . ." 120 *Congressional Record* H 7651-56, 7673 (daily ed. 5 August 1974). See U.S., Congress, House, Committee on Foreign Affairs, *Ratification of the Geneva Protocol of 1925*, H. Rep. 93-1257, 93d Cong., 2d Sess., 1974. The Protocol has now been ratified by the United States and will soon enter into force for it. For an account of the Senate action leading to its advice and consent to ratification, see Introduction, p. 17 and n. 37.

2. Howard Levie, "Some Major Inadequacies in the Existing Law Relating to the Protection of Individuals During Armed Conflict," in *When Battle Rages, How Can Law Protect?* ed. John Carey, Hammarskjold Forum Series, no. 14 (Dobbs Ferry: Oceana Publications, for the Association of the Bar of the City of New York, 1971), p. 18.

3. Contrary to the statement that appears in Seymour Hersh, *Chemical and Biological Warfare: America's Hidden Arsenal* (New York: Doubleday & Company, 1969) p. 51, the "S" in CS does not stand for "super." The name is derived from its codevelopers, B. B. Corson and R. W. Staughton, as reported in Stewart Blumenfeld and Matthew Meselson, "The Military Value and Political Implications of the Use of Riot Control Agents in Warfare," in *The Control of Chemical and Biological Weapons*, ed. A. Alexander et al. (New York: Carnegie Endowment for International Peace, 1971), p. 68 (hereafter cited as *Control of Chemical and Biological Weapons*).

4. U.N., *CB Weapons*, paras. 44 and 153.

5. Ibid., para. 147. In Blumenfeld and Meselson, "Military Value," in *Control of Chemical and Biological Weapons*, p. 69, the statement is made that "for CS the

difference between an incapacitating exposure and one that might produce serious lasting effects is quite large, a factor of many thousands."

6. A frequently quoted statement is that made by the United States representative (James M. Nabrit, Jr.) during a debate in the United Nations General Assembly on 5 December 1966. He said: "It would be unreasonable to contend that any rule of international law prohibits the use in combat against an enemy, for humanitarian purposes, of agents that Governments around the world commonly use to control riots by their own people" (*Documents on Disarmament* [Washington, D.C.: United States Arms Control and Disarmament Agency, 1966], p. 801). A much-publicized domestic use of CS was in the riot at the Attica Correctional Facility in New York during 1971 (see *New York Times*, 14 September 1971, p. 1).

7. Blumenfeld and Meselson, "Military Value," in *Control of Chemical and Biological Weapons*, pp. 67-68.

8. Ibid., pp. 71-75. See also testimony of Matthew Meselson, Senate Subcommittee on Refugees, *Hearings on War-Related Civilian Problems in Indochina*, 92d Cong., 1st Sess., April 1971, pp. 133-37; Professor Meselson's testimony and preliminary report, Herbicide Assessment Commission, American Association for the Advancement of Science, "The Effects and Use of Herbicides in Vietnam," U.S., Congress, Senate, Foreign Relations Committee, *Hearings on Geneva Protocol of 1925*, 92d Cong., 1st Sess., March 1971, pp. 353-77; and testimony of Admiral Lemos, U.S., Congress, House, Subcommittee on National Security Policy and Scientific Developments of the House Committee on Foreign Affairs, *Hearings on Chemical-Biological Weapons*, 91st Cong., 1st Sess., November and December 1972, pp. 225-28.

9. George Bunn, "Banning Poison Gas and Germ Warfare: Should the United States Agree?" [1969] *Wis. L. Rev.* 405-6. Ann Van Wynen Thomas and A. J. Thomas, Jr., *Legal Limits on the Use of Chemical and Biological Weapons* (Dallas: Southern Methodist University Press, 1970), p. 149, find that "the tear gas remains a nonlethal agent. The actual killer is the fragmentation bomb."

10. Meselson testimony, *Hearings on Geneva Protocol of 1925*, pp. 353-57. The House Committee on Foreign Affairs recommended in its report on H. Res. No. 1258 that the Senate consider exercising its Constitutional prerogative to ratify the 1925 Geneva Protocol without the interpretation made by the Administration that the treaty does not cover herbicides and tear gas (House Foreign Affairs Committee, *Geneva Protocol of 1925*, p. 4). See also testimony of Professor Richard R. Baxter, U.S., Congress, House, Subcommittee on National Security Policy and Scientific Developments, Committee on Foreign Affairs, *Hearings on U.S. Chemical Warfare Policy*, 93d Cong., 2d Sess., 7 May 1974, pp. 139-40.

11. The English version of the Protocol uses the words "asphyxiating, poisonous or other gases." The word "other" has been interpretated by some writers to include gases that are not asphyxiating or poisonous. The French version of the Protocol uses the words "gaz asphyxiants, toxiques ou similaires." The word "similaires" has been interpreted by some writers to limit the coverage to gases that are "asphyxiants" or "toxiques." For an excellent discussion of this problem in semantics see Henri Meyrowitz, *Les Armes biologiques et le droit international* (Paris: Editions A. Pedore, 1968), pp. 38-45.

12. See, for example, "Report by Secretary of State William P. Rogers to President Richard M. Nixon, 11 August 1970," 63 *Dep't State Bull.* 273, 274 (1970); Greenspan, *Modern Law of Land Warfare*, p. 359.

13. See, for example, Oppenheim, *International Law*, ed. Lauterpacht, p. 344, n. 1; Richard R. Baxter and Thomas Buergenthal, "Legal Aspects of the Geneva Protocol of 1925," in *Control of Chemical and Biological Weapons*, p. 14 (also published in 64 *A.J.I.L.* 853, 866 [1970]). In 1930 the British government expressed the opinion that the use of tear gas was banned by the Protocol (Oppenheim, *International Law*, ed. Lauterpacht, p. 344, n. 1). In 1970 it reversed its stand (*New York Times*, 3 Feb. 1970, p. 3).

14. Baxter and Buergenthal, "Legal Aspects," in *Control of Chemical and Biological Weapons*, p. 3.

15. For authorities supporting the existence of such a norm, see ibid., p. 32, n. 8; contrary, see Denise Bindschedler-Robert, "A Reconsideration of the Law of Armed Conflicts," in *Law of Armed Conflicts*.

16. Oppenheim, *International Law*, ed. Lauterpacht, p. 344.

17. Stone, *Legal Controls*, p. 556.

18. While some of the extreme antiwar organizations insisted that they had identi-

fied cases in which individuals had been killed by CS, the more responsible scientists do not agree. See notes 4 and 5 above. Moreover, CS has been used in literally hundreds of cases of domestic disturbances with no deaths being charged to it.

19. Bunn, "Banning Poison Gas," p. 404. Unfortunately, even a specific ban on the use of tear gas in international armed conflict would have no effect in this area because of its use for domestic riot-control purposes throughout the world.

20. Stone, *Legal Controls,* p. 556-57.

21. Bunn, "Banning Poison Gas," p. 404.

22. Matthew Meselson, "Ethical Problems: Preventing CBW," in *CBW: Chemical and Biological Warfare,* ed. Steven Rose (Boston: Beacon Press, 1969) p. 167. In World War I tear gas was used as early as 1914. It did not prove effective and it was followed in 1915 by the more effective lethal gases.

23. 61 *Dep't State Bull.* 541 (1969). With several stated exceptions, the United States has now done this. See Introduction, p. 17 and n. 37.

24. Victor Sidel, "Napalm," in *CBW,* ed. Rose, p. 45.

25. Ibid., p. 44.

26. U.N., *CB Weapons,* para. 19. See also Sidel, "Napalm," in *CBW,* ed. Rose; and Baxter and Buergenthal, "Legal Aspects," in *Control of Chemical and Biological Weapons,* p. 33, n. 10.

27. 8 *Int'l Rev. Red Cross* 473 (1968).

28. ICRC, *Reaffirmation and Development of the Laws and Customs Applicable in Armed Conflict: Report to the Twenty-first International Conference* (Geneva: ICRC, 1969), p. 61. To the same effect see, for example, Ian Brownlie, "Legal Aspects of CBW," in *CBW,* ed. Rose, p. 150, and Van Wynen Thomas and Thomas, *Legal Limits,* p. 185.

29. ICRC, *Reaffirmation and Development,* pp. 61-62.

30. This contention is based upon the provisions of art. 23(e) of the Hague Regulations.

31. I have previously recommended that the use of napalm in international armed conflict be prohibited. See Levie, "Some Major Inadequacies," in *When Battle Rages,* ed. Carey, pp. 20-21. (In so doing, I erroneously classified napalm as a chemical weapon. This was, however, irrelevant to the recommendation.)

32. This suggestion was made in the report of the U.N. Secretary-General, *Respect for Human Rights in Armed Conflict,* U.N. Doc. A/8052 (1970), para. 126. Since the foregoing was written, the U.N. General Assembly has made such a request of the Secretary-General in G.A. Res. 2852, 26 U.N. GAOR Supp. 29, p. 90, U.N. Doc. A/8429 (1971); the Secretary-General appointed a group of government experts, which, incidentally, did not include a representative of the United States, and the experts prepared and filed a Report (Report of the Secretary-General, *Napalm and Other Incendiary Weapons and All Aspects of Their Possible Use,* U.N. Doc. A/8803/Rev. 1 [1973]). The final paragraph of that report states: "193. . . .[I]n view of the facts presented in the report, the group of consultant experts wishes to bring to the attention of the General Assembly the necessity of working out measures for the prohibition of the use, production, development and stockpiling of napalm and other incendiary weapons." A finding of "the necessity of working out measures for the prohibition for the use, production, development and stockpiling of napalm" would appear to confirm the conclusion reached in the text that there is currently no rule of international law that prohibits the use of napalm upon selected targets.

33. Judge Advocate General Myron C. Cramer to the Secretary of War, SPJGW 1945/164, March 1945, Memorandum concerning Destruction of Crops by Chemicals, 10 *Int'l Leg. Mat.* 1304 (1971).

34. Bunn, "Banning Poison Gas," pp. 408-9.

35. David E. Brown, "The Use of Herbicides in War: A Political/Military Analysis," in *Control of Chemical and Biological Weapons,* pp. 39-40.

36. It has been estimated that "vertical visibility improves in sprayed areas by 60 to 90 percent and ground visibility by a lesser amount" (Brown, "Use of Herbicides," in *Control of Chemical and Biological Weapons,* p. 46). See also John Constable and Matthew Meselson, "The Ecological Impact of Large Scale Defoliation in Vietnam," 56 *Sierra Club Bull.* 4 (1971).

37. Testimony of Admiral Lemos, Hearings on "Chemical-Biological Weapons," pp. 229-30.

38. See, for example, Baxter and Buergenthal, "Legal Aspects," in *Control of Chemical and Biological Weapons*, p. 16.

39. Arthur Galston, "Defoliants," in *CBW*, ed. Rose, p. 62.

40. Bunn, "Banning Poison Gas," p. 407; Cramer, SPJGW 1945/164, *supra*.

41. Bindschedler-Robert, "Reconsideration," in *Law of Armed Conflicts*, p. 36. To the same effect see *U.S. Army Field Manual 27-10*, para. 37(b).

42. Continuing with the quotation cited in note 6 above, Mr. Nabrit said: "Similarly, the Protocol does not apply to herbicides, which involve the same chemicals and have the same effects as those used domestically in the United States, the Soviet Union and many other countries to control weeds and other unwanted vegetation" (*Documents on Disarmament*, p. 801).

43. Baxter and Buergenthal, "Legal Aspects," in *Control of Chemical and Biological Weapons*, p. 14.

44. The legality of the use of shotguns in international armed conflict was the subject of controversy during World War I. See Oppenheim, *International Law*, ed. Lauterpacht, p. 340, n. 4. Certainly, no one would contend for their legality in international armed conflict solely because they are legal for hunting in most countries.

45. Baxter and Buergenthal, "Legal Aspects," in *Control of Chemical and Biological Weapons*, p. 15.

46. See, for example, Georg Schwarzenberger, *The Legality of Nuclear Weapons* (London: Stevens & Sons, 1958), pp. 37-38.

47. U.N., *CB Weapons*, para. 311. Of course, had the trees been uprooted and destroyed by high explosive shells or aerial bombs, the regrowth period would probably have been equally long. Strangely, no one wept for the millions of coconut palms destroyed by gunfire and aerial bombs in the Pacific during World War II.

48. Galston, "Defoliants," in *CBW*, ed. Rose, p. 63.

49. Fred Warner Neal, "The Nazis Had Their Nuremberg, Americans Will Have Their—Election," 11 *War/Peace Report* 16 (August-September 1971) (review of Albert Speer, *Inside the Third Reich* [New York: Macmillan, 1970]). The report to which Warner refers is Stanford Biology Study Group, *The Destruction of Indochina* (1970).

50. *New York Times*, 29 August 1971, p. 8.

51. See note 23 above and Introduction, p. 17 and n. 37.

Chapter 13

1. *U.S. Army Field Manual 27-10*, para. 34(b).

2. In this connection, a distinction should be made between weapons and instruments (or technologies) used in support of weapons. The gun that fires a dum-dum bullet may be an integral and indispensable part of an unlawful weapons system, but it is not for that reason unlawful. It would be an unlawful weapon only under the condition that it could fire no other bullets than dum-dums. So too, infrared sensors may be an integral and indispensable part of an unlawful weapons system, but they are not for that reason unlawful, since they could be used lawfully. It is sometimes said of the infrared sensors that, since they cannot distinguish between combatants and noncombatants, they are for this reason an unlawful instrument or technology of war. But the inability of infrared sensors to distinguish between legitimate and illegitimate targets no more makes them an unlawful technology of war than does the inability of a gun to distinguish between dum-dum and other bullets (or the inability of radar to distinguish between legitimate and illegitimate targets). Men may choose to employ infrared sensors in a manner that causes indiscriminate destruction. In that case it is the use of the sensors which is illegal, not the sensors themselves.

3. *U.S. Army Field Manual 27-10*, para. 36.

4. On occasion, the legitimacy of napalm has been challenged on the grounds that, when burning, it emits substantial amounts of carbon monoxide and that many napalm casualties result from this deadly gas rather than from burns. In consequence, it is argued

that napalm should be considered, in the terms of the 1925 Geneva Protocol, an analogous material or device (i.e., analogous to asphyxiating and poisonous gases) forbidden by the Protocol and by customary international law. Although there is much to be said for this view, it has found little if any support in state practice. This practice continues to distinguish between (forbidden) weapons employed because of their direct toxic effects on man and (permitted) weapons the primary effects of which are found in physical force or fire. Despite the fact that napalm is a chemical and that in burning it emits a deadly gas, it is nevertheless considered lawful because its primary effect is—or, at any rate, is held to be—combustion.

5. Richard R. Baxter and Thomas Buergenthal, "Legal Aspects of the Geneva Protocol of 1925," in *The Control of Chemical and Biological Weapons*, ed. A. Alexander et al. (New York: Carnegie Endowment for International Peace, 1971), pp. 14, 16. The use of the term "toxic" in the passage quoted from Professors Baxter and Buergenthal introduces perhaps a needless element of confusion. A clearer formulation would simply have been "of all chemical agents having a direct effect on man . . . ," since this clearly appears to be what the authors had in mind. An alternative formulation might have been "of all chemical agents having a toxic or nontoxic effect on man. . . ." With respect to antiplant chemicals the authors go on to state: "It should be emphasized . . . that the evidence to support this interpretation is by no means as strong as is the evidence for including irritant chemicals within the chemicals prohibited by the agreement." For a contrary view, see the comments by George Bunn, in *Control of Chemical and Biological Weapons*, ed. Alexander et al., pp. 120-21. Also George Bunn, "Banning Poison Gas and Germ Warfare: Should the United States Agree?" [1969] *Wis. L. Rev.* 408. It should be noted that part of the interpretation given the 1925 Geneva Protocol by the contracting parties consists in their subsequent practice of abstaining from the use of any forms of chemical warfare. This record of abstention seems at least as significant in determining the understanding the parties have had of the scope of the Protocol as has been their subsequent inability to reach formal agreement on its prohibitory scope.

6. There is still a good deal of controversy and uncertainty over the origins of the customary rule forbidding the use of poison and poisoned weapons. Whereas some base this rule almost entirely upon the conviction that the use of poison constitutes a form of treachery, others find its roots largely in the conviction that poison is a particularly cruel and inhumane weapon. On the latter view, Article 23(a) of the 1907 Hague Regulations, wherein combatants are forbidden "to employ poison or poisoned weapons," is a special case of the more general rule of Article 23(e), which forbids employment of "arms, projectiles, or material calculated to cause unnecessary suffering." This view finds little support in the historical record, however, which shows that the rule forbidding poison stems from the conviction that poison is a treacherous weapon. It is only in the late nineteenth and early twentieth centuries that poison is found to be an inhumane, as well as a treacherous, weapon. Be that as it may, at the time of the Geneva Protocol it was only the rules forbidding poison and those weapons causing unnecessary suffering that could be applied to gases and other chemical weapons. This is why we say that, at best, it is only the narrow interpretation of the protocol that could be considered coextensive with customary international law.

7. The phrase is taken from the statement made during World War II by President Roosevelt in response to reports that Axis powers were preparing to use gas. The President went on to declare: "Use of such weapons has been outlawed by the general opinion of civilized mankind. This country has not used them, and I hope that we never will be compelled to use them. I state categorically that we shall under no circumstances resort to the use of such weapons unless they are first used by our enemies" ("The Axis Is Warned against the Use of Poison Gas," 8 June 1943, in *The Public Papers and Addresses of Franklin D. Roosevelt—1928-1945*, ed. Samuel I. Rosenman, 13 vols. [New York: Harper & Brothers, 1950], vol. 3, *The Tide Turns* [1943], p. 242 [item 58]).

8. Against these considerations, it may of course be argued that the grounds on which states condemned the use of gas are, strictly speaking, irrelevant, so long as they did (if, indeed, they did) make an apparently absolute condemnation of this means. It may be further argued that although states based their condemnation of gas primarily on

the general principle forbidding inhumane weapons, this cannot be taken to mean that they were thereby excluding gases having no more than a temporarily incapacitating effect. On the latter view, states may wish to condemn as inhumane a weapon that may neither destroy life nor impair health while permitting weapons that burn their victims (napalm, flamethrowers). In that case, the observer can only record this rather curious application of the principle of humanity, but he can scarcely question it in any legally relevant sense. In large measure, we have ourselves in earlier pages endorsed this argument by insisting that what weapons cause "unnecessary suffering," and are therefore to be regarded as contravening the principle of humanity, can only be decided in light of state practice. Even so, the question persists whether the condemnation of gas, particularly by states not parties to the Geneva Protocol, was intended to extend to all forms of gas regardless of their effects.

9. G.A. Res. 2603, 24 U.N. GAOR Supp. 30, p. 16, U.N. Doc. A/7630 (1969) "recognized" in its preamble that the Geneva Protocol "embodies the generally recognized rules of international law prohibiting the use in international armed conflicts of all biological and chemical methods of warfare, regardless of any technical developments . . . ." The operative text of the resolution declares as contrary to generally recognized rules of international law "any chemical agents of warfare—chemical substances, whether gaseous, liquid or solid—which might be employed because of their direct toxic effects on man, animals or plants . . . ." Since eighty states supported the resolution, thirty-six abstained, and three opposed (the United States, Australia, and Portugal), this expression may be indicative of the prevailing view taken today of the Geneva Protocol. Even then the support for the resolution may still be seen to fall rather short of the pervasive *opinio juris* required of customary law. Moreover, it would be obtuse to ignore the impact of events since 1969 on this expression of view by the General Assembly.

10. Robert Jay Lifton, "Beyond Atrocity," in *Crimes of War*, ed. Richard A. Falk, Gabriel Kolko, and Robert Jay Lifton (New York: Random House, 1971).

11. That far more tonnage was dropped in the Vietnam War than in earlier conflicts does not alter this judgment. Whether bombing is discriminate or not does not depend simply upon the number of bombs dropped but also upon where they are dropped.

Chapter 17

1. Taylor, *Nuremberg and Vietnam*, esp. chapter 6, "War Crimes: Son My."

2. Taylor, *Nuremberg and Vietnam*, p. 12.

3. Hans Morgenthau, "Calley and the American Conscience," *New Leader*, 19 April 1971, p. 5.

4. Ibid.

5. Taylor, *Nuremberg and Vietnam*, pp. 120-21.

6. Ibid., pp. 39-41.

7. "Order of General Douglas MacArthur Confirming Death Sentence of General Tomoyuki Yamashita February 6, 1946," in *Documentary History*, ed. Friedman, p. 1598.

8. Taylor, *Nuremberg and Vietnam*, p. 35.

9. Hague Regulations, art. 4; such protection for surrendering enemy soldiers is now provided for under the Geneva Prisoners of War Convention, arts. 13 and 85.

10. Geneva Civilians Convention, art. 4.

11. Agreements between the Commander-in-Chief of the French Union Forces in Indo-China and the Commander-in-Chief of the People's Army of Viet-Nam on the Cessation of Hostilities in Viet-Nam, *signed* at Geneva on 20 July 1954, and Final Declaration of the Geneva Conference on the Problem of Restoring Peace in Indo-China, art. 6, 31 *Dep't State Bull.* 162 (1954); also in Richard Falk, ed., *The Vietnam War and International Law*, 3 vols. (Princeton: Princeton University Press, 1967-72), vol. 1, p. 543.

12. Taylor, *Nuremberg and Vietnam*, pp. 28-29.

13. Burke Marshall eloquently stated the moral paradox of punishing the My Lai murderers while continuing national policies "based on killing civilians," *New York Times,* 10 April 1971, p. 23.

14. Richard Hammer, *The Court Martial of Lieutenant Calley* (New York: Coward, McCann and Geoghegan, 1971), p. 276.

Chapter 18

1. For my purposes I treat all violations of the laws of war as war crimes and do not, therefore, make distinctions between the laws of war and the notion of a war crime that in other contexts would be necessary. See, e.g., Richard A. Falk, "The Question of War Crimes: A Statement of Perspective," in *Crimes of War,* ed. Richard A. Falk, Gabriel Kolko, and Robert Jay Lifton (New York: Random House, 1971), p. 3, and Editors' Note, in *Crimes of War,* ed. Falk, Kolko, and Lifton, p. 33.

2. See Introduction, p. 21. London IMT Charter, art. 6.

3. Taylor, *Nuremberg and Vietnam,* p. 20.

4. Introduction, p. 21 (emphasis added).

5. Georg Schwarzenberger, *The Legality of Nuclear Weapons* (London: Stevens & Sons, 1958), p. 44.

6. Taylor, *Nuremberg and Vietnam,* p. 36 (footnote omitted). There is an ambiguity in this quotation that should be noted. Taylor may not mean that the laws of war permit an exception in this kind of case. He may mean only that the law is uncertain, that he knows of no court decision that authoritatively declares this to be either a war crime or a permitted exception. It is sufficient for my purposes if he means the weaker claim, that it is an open question.

A more serious objection to my assertion that I am accurately characterizing the existing laws of war would call attention to the following from the *U.S. Army Field Manual 27-10,* para. 3(a):

> The law of war places limits on the exercise of a belligerent's power in the interests mentioned in paragraph 2 and requires that belligerents refrain from employing any kind or degree of violence which is not actually necessary for military purposes and that they conduct hostilities with regard for the principles of humanity and chivalry.

> The prohibitory effect of the law of war is not minimized by "military necessity" which has been defined as that principle which justifies those measures not forbidden by international law which are indispensable for securing the complete submission of the enemy as soon as possible. Military necessity has generally been rejected as a defense for acts forbidden by the customary and conventional laws of war inasmuch as the latter have been developed and framed with consideration for the concept of military necessity.

I do not know exactly what this means. It seems to anticipate, on the one hand, that the laws of war and the doctrine of military necessity can conflict. It seems to suppose, on the other hand, that substantial conflicts will not arise either because the laws of war prohibit militarily unnecessary violence or because they were formulated with considerations of military necessity in mind. In substance, I do not think that the view expressed in the quotation is inconsistent with the conception I am delineating.

7. Taylor makes the same points in respect to the Treaty for the Limitation and Reduction of Naval Armament, *signed* at London on 22 April 1930, 46 Stat. 2858, T.S. No. 830, 112 L.N.T.S. 65 (effective 31 December 1930). Article 22(2) in part 4 of that treaty required that no ship sink a merchant vessel "without having first placed passengers, crew and ship's papers in a place of safety." The provisions of the treaty were regularly violated during World War II. Nonetheless, these violations were not punished as war crimes at Nuremberg. Here, too, Taylor gives the same two reasons. First, the doctrine of military necessity made the treaty unworkable. And second, even if considera-

tions of military necessity were not decisive, violations of the treaty would not have been war crimes because the treaty was violated by both sides during World War II. And nothing is properly a war crime, says Taylor (at least in the absence of a genuine international tribunal), if both sides regularly engage in the conduct in question (see, e.g., Taylor, *Nuremberg and Vietnam,* pp. 36-39).

This latter point is ambiguous. Sometimes the point seems to be that it is procedurally unfair for the victor to punish the loser, but not himself, for the same act. This I find a quite unobjectionable principle. But sometimes the point seems to be that there is a different principle at work, one that legitimizes a practice that was previously proscribed once the practice becomes widespread. This principle I find far less attractive and not obviously appropriate.

8. E.g., that there is a rationale, based on moral considerations, for such things as the prohibition upon the bombing of hospitals or the prohibition upon the use of poison gas.

9. Although I tend to draw upon the proceedings at Nuremberg per se, I mean in some of my references to Nuremberg to include all of the war crimes trials that took place after World War II.

10. London IMT Charter, art. 8.

11. Nuremberg Judgment, pp. 223-24. I am not certain how to interpret this passage. The problem is in deciding whether the possibility of moral choice is the "true test" for holding an actor responsible for his actions or whether it is the "true test" even for allowing the mitigation of punishment. Both interpretations seem plausible.

The discussion of the "true test" takes place in response to the claim that the defendants were fully excusable because they were obeying orders. From this perspective it is reasonable to interpret the tribunal's response as a twofold one: (1) the fact that an actor was ordered to do an illegal action is a mitigating circumstance that is properly taken into account in deciding upon the fair punishment; (2) the fact that the actor had no moral choice (in respect, for example, to obedience to the order) does excuse the actor and make it improper to hold the actor responsible.

The discussion of the "true test" also occurs immediately after the Charter is referred to. From this perspective it is reasonable to interpret the tribunal's response as an elucidation of the conditions under which mitigation is appropriate. The fact that an actor was obeying an order does not, by itself, even count in deciding upon the fair punishment. However, if moral choice was not possible in respect to obedience to the order, then this is something that ought to be considered in mitigation of the punishment.

For the purpose of my analysis, which is to consider various criteria of responsibility, I have opted for the former of these two interpretations.

12. I find quite unconvincing the claim that the laws of war enhance persons' capacities to be moral. Thus, Telford Taylor argues that the laws of war are:

> . . . necessary to diminish the corrosive effect of mortal combat on the participants. War does not confer a license to kill for personal reasons—to gratify perverse impulses, or to put out of the way anyone who appears obnoxious or to whose welfare the soldier is indifferent. War is not a license at all, but an obligation to kill for reasons of state; it does not countenance the infliction of suffering for its own sake or for revenge.
>
> Unless troops are trained and required to draw the distinction between military and non-military killings, and to retain such respect for the value of life that unnecessary death and destruction will continue to repel them, they may lose the sense for that distinction for the rest of their lives. The consequence would be that many returning soldiers would be potential murderers.
>
> Taylor, *Nuremberg and Vietnam,* pp. 40-41.

I find this unconvincing because the laws of war do not, as I have tried to show, embody and reflect in a coherent way important moral distinctions or truths.

It is possible, of course, to make the claim on another ground, namely, that teaching persons to obey orders, or even laws—whatever their content may be—is an important constituent of the curriculum of moral education. This is not a view I share.

13. I should make it plain, too, that I am not at all interested in this paper in considering arguments that it would be impractical, nationally divisive, or generally unwise to try to hold the leaders of the United States criminally responsible for their respective roles in the Vietnam War. These arguments, too, seem to me to be often exaggerated, but they are beyond the reach of this paper. Here I am concerned only with the question (or a part of the question) of whether they satisfy the conditions of culpability.

14. Townsend Hoopes, "The Nuremberg Suggestion," in *Crimes of War*, ed. Falk, Kolko, and Lifton, pp. 233-37.

15. Or, to give the example a more contemporary bite: Would a proponent of this argument also concede the nonculpability of a black militant who selflessly risks his life to assist other black militants to escape from prison when he sincerely believes (doubtless reasonably) that they were unjustly convicted and confined there?

16. There are clearly differences between the requirement that the actor *know* and the requirement that he *ought to know*. For the present, I wish to ignore those differences, but I return to them at the very end of the chapter.

Chapter 19

1. *U.S. Army Field Manual 27-10*, para. 499.

2. *New York Times*, 9 December 1969, p. 1.

3. Sir James Fitzjames Stephens, *A History of the Criminal Law of England* (London, Macmillan & Co., 1883), vol. 1, p. 206.

4. *U.S. Army Field Manual 27-10*, para 509.

5. Oppenheim, *International Law*, ed. Lauterpacht, pp. 571-72. For Oppenheim's earlier formulation of the superior-order defense, see Lassa Oppenheim, *International Law*, vol. 2, *War and Neutrality*, ed. Ronald F. Roxburgh, 3d ed. (London: Longmans, Green & Co., 1921), pp. 342-43. ("If members of the armed forces commit violations *by order* of their Government, they are not war criminals, and may not be punished by the enemy. . . . In case members of forces commit violations ordered by their commanders, the members may not be punished, for the commanders are alone responsible, and the latter may, therefore, be punished as war criminals on their capture by the enemy.")

6. Taylor, *Nuremberg and Vietnam*, p. 52. But see the discussion of the limits of leadership responsibility in Jordan J. Paust, "My Lai and Vietnam: Norms, Myths and Leader Responsibility," 57 *Military L. Rev.* 99, 175 (1972).

7. Reel, *General Yamashita*. But see the analysis of the *Yamashita* case in Waldemar A. Solf, "A Response to Telford Taylor's *Nuremberg and Vietnam: An American Tragedy*," 5 *Akron L. Rev.* 43, 56 (1972).

8. *Medina* case, in *Documentary History*, ed. Friedman, p. 1732; Kenneth Reich, "Postcript to the Medina Trial," *Nation*, 1 November 1971, p. 433.

9. Henry T. King, ed., Transcript of Program "Nuremberg Revisited: The Judgment of Nuremberg in Today's World" (International and Comparative Law Section, American Bar Association, 12 August 1970), pp. 28-32; see also Kenneth Reich, "My Lai —Was Justice Carried Out?" *Los Angeles Times*, 1 January 1972, sec. 1-A, p. 1.

10. *New York Times*, 5 September 1971, sec. 4, p. 10. See also Anthony B. Herbert with James T. Wooten, *Soldier* (New York: Holt, Rinehart & Winston, 1973).

11. See, e.g., 18 U.S.C. §4 (misprison—a felony cognizable by a court of the United States); 18 U.S.C.§3 and 10 U.S.C.§878 (accessory after the fact); 10 U.S.C. §881 (conspiracy to commit an offense); 10 U.S.C. §907 (false official statements); 10 U.S.C. §932 (frauds against the United States); and finally those dread provisions, 10 U.S.C. §933 (conduct unbecoming an officer and gentleman) and 10 U.S.C. §934 (the general article). See also the recent statement by Lt. Gen. William R. Peers, who headed the Army's investigation of My Lai, that "[w]e have two forms of justice . . . , one for the enemy and one for our own people. I don't think we showed the same kind of sympathy toward the Germans, for example, or the Japanese, in the case of war crimes, but we turn around and we have an incident like this, which I consider a horrible thing, and we find we have only one man finally convicted and he's set free after doing a relatively small part of his sentence" (Leroy Aarons, "My Lai Prober Sees Injustice, Cover-up," *Washington Post*, 2 December 1974, sec. A, p. 6).

12. Richard A. Falk, "The Question of War Crimes: A Statement of Perspective," in *Crimes of War*, ed. Richard A. Falk, Gabriel Kolko, and Robert Jay Lifton (New York: Random House, 1971), pp. 9-10.

13. Leonard B. Boudin, Review of Telford Taylor, *Nuremberg and Vietnam*, 84 *Harv. L. Rev.* 1940 (1971).

14. Taylor, *Nuremberg and Vietnam*, p. 120.

15. Pres. Proc. No. 4313, Announcing a Program for the Return of Vietnam Era Draft Evaders and Military Deserters, 39 Fed. Reg. 33293 (17 Sept. 1974); Exec. Order No. 11803, Establishing Presidential Clemency Board, 39 Fed. Reg. 33297 (17 Sept. 1974).

Chapter 22

1. *U.S. Army Field Manual 27-10,* para. 3(a).

2. Ibid., para. 3(b).

3. *Hostages* case, p. 1253.

4. See Jordan J. Paust, "After My Lai: The Case for War Crime Jurisdiction over Civilians in Federal District Courts," 50 *Texas L. Rev.* 6 (1971).

5. Reel, *General Yamashita.* But see Franklin A. Hart, "Yamashita, Nuremberg and Vietnam: Command Responsibility Reappraised," 25 *Naval War College Rev.* 19 (1972), and the comment on Hart's article by Jordan J. Paust in "The Barometer-Reader's Comments," 25 *Naval War College Rev.* 103 (1973).

6. General Headquarters, United States Army Forces Pacific, Office of the Theatre Judge Advocate, *Review of the Record of the Trial of Tomoyuki Yamashita, General, Imperial Japanese Army* (26 December 1945) (available at the National Archives, Washington, D.C.).

7. *High Command* case, p. 543.

8. *High Command* case, pp. 543-44; the opinion by Judge Harding on this point added that "[a]ny other interpretation of international law would go far beyond the basic principles of criminal law as known to civilized nations" (ibid.).

9. *High Command* case, p. 545.

Contributors

GEORGE H. ALDRICH is Deputy Legal Adviser in the United States Department of State. He received his B.A. (1954) from DePauw University and his LL.B. (1957) and LL.M. (1958) from Harvard Law School. Mr. Aldrich served as Assistant Legal Adviser for East Asian and Pacific Affairs in the Department of State from July 1965 to October 1969. He was head of the United States delegation to the Diplomatic Conference on International Humanitarian Law (1974).

RICHARD R. BAXTER, Professor of Law at Harvard University, served as a member of the United States delegation to the Conference of Government Experts on International Humanitarian Law in Armed Conflicts both in 1971 and in 1972 and to the Diplomatic Conference on International Humanitarian Law (1974). Professor Baxter is a member of the Permanent Court of Arbitration (The Hague), Editor-in-Chief of the *American Journal of International Law*, and President of the American Society of International Law (1974-75). He served in the United States Army from 1942 to 1946 and 1947 to 1954 (Colonel, USAR-Ret.). Professor Baxter received his B.A. (1942) from Brown University and his LL.B. (1948) from Harvard Law School.

LEONARD B. BOUDIN, a member of the New York State and Federal bars, practices in New York City. Mr. Boudin was a Visiting Professor of Law from Practice at the Harvard Law School in 1970-71 and a Lecturer at Law at Yale Law School during 1974. He is the author of "The Army and the First Amendment" in *Conscience and Command: Justice and Discipline in the Military*, ed. James Finn (New York: Random House, 1971); and "War Crimes and Vietnam: The Mote in Whose Eye?," 84 *Harvard Law Review* 1940 (1971). Mr. Boudin was counsel for the defendants in a number of cases relating to the Vietnam War, including *United States* v. *Spock*, *United States* v. *Ahmad*, and *United States* v. *Russo and Ellsberg*. He graduated with a B.S.S. (1933) from the College of the City of New York and received his LL.B. (1934) from St. John's University School of Law.

ANTHONY D'AMATO is Professor of Law at Northwestern University. He received his B.A. (1958) from Cornell University, his J.D. (1961) from Harvard Law School, and his Ph.D (1968) from Columbia University.

Mr. D'Amato is the author of *The Concept of Custom in International Law* (Ithaca: Cornell University Press, 1971); *The Judiciary and Vietnam*, with Robert M. O'Neil (New York: St. Martin's Press, 1972); and "War Crimes and Vietnam: The Nuremberg Defense and the Military Service Resister," 57 *California Law Review* 1055 (1969).

HAMILTON DESAUSSURE is Associate Professor of Law at the University of Akron, from which he is currently on leave to serve as Associate Director of the Institute of Air and Space Law at McGill University. He was a bomber pilot during World War II and a transport pilot during the Korean War. Professor DeSaussure has served as Chief of the International Law Division, United States Air Force Office of the Judge Advocate General (1963-65, 1968-70); Director of International Law, Headquarters of the United States Air Force in Europe (1959-60); and Legal Adviser to the United States negotiating team, Intermediate Ballistics Missiles Committee (1958-60). Professor DeSaussure received his B.A. (1946) from Yale University, his LL.B. (1948) from Harvard Law School, and his LL.M. (1953) from the University of McGill Institute of Air and Space Law. He is the author of "The Laws of Air Warfare: Are There Any?" 5 *International Lawyer* 527 (1971), and other articles concerning the laws of air and outer space.

RICHARD A. FALK is Albert G. Milbank Professor of International Law and Practice at Princeton University. He received his B.S. (1952) from The Wharton School, University of Pennsylvania, his LL.B. (1955) from Yale Law School, and his J.S.D. (1962) from Harvard Law School. Professor Falk is the author of numerous books and articles, including *Legal Order in a Violent World* (Princeton: Princeton University Press, 1968); *This Endangered Planet* (New York: Random House, 1971); and, with co-editors Robert Jay Lifton and Gabriel Kolko, *Crimes of War*. He has served as Vice-President of the American Society of International Law, as Director of the United States Section of the World Order Models Project, and as co-editor with Cyril E. Black of a series of volumes entitled *The Future of the International Legal Order* (Princeton: Princeton University Press, 1969-72).

TOM J. FARER is Professor of Law at Rutgers-Camden Law School. After receiving his B.A. (1957) from Princeton University and his LL.B. (1961) from Harvard Law School, he served as Special Assistant to the General Counsel, Office of the Secretary of Defense (1962-63). He is the author of numerous articles on the laws of war, including "Humanitarian Law and Armed Conflicts: Toward the Definition of International Armed Conflict," 71 *Columbia Law Review* 37 (1971); "The Laws of War 25 Years after Nuremberg," *International Conciliation* No. 583 (May 1971); and "Law and War," in *The Future of the International Legal Order: Conflict*, vol. 3, ed. Cyril E. Black and Richard A. Falk (Princeton: Princeton University Press, 1970).

ROBERT G. GARD, JR., Major General, United States Army, is Commanding General of the United States Army Military Personnel Center. He received his B.S. (1950) from the United States Military Academy and his M.P.A. (1956) and Ph.D (1961) from Harvard University. General Gard was Military Assistant to the Secretary of Defense from 1966 to 1968 and Commander, Division Artillery, and then Division Chief of Staff, 9th Infantry Division, United States Army in Vietnam, from 1968 to 1969. He is a Master Parachutist and was awarded the Silver Star, Legion of Merit, Distinguished Flying Cross, and the Bronze Star (Valor) (3d Oak Leaf Cluster). General Gard is the author of "Arms Control and National Security," in *Issues of National Security in the 1970's,* ed. Amos A. Jordan, Jr. (New York: Praeger, 1967); "The Military and American Society," 49 *Foreign Affairs* 698 (1971); and "Vietnam and the Nuremberg Principles: A Colloquy on War Crimes," 5 *Rutgers-Camden Law Journal* 1 (1973).

ROBERT GLASSER received his B.A. (1970) and M.A. (1973) from the University of Bridgeport and his J.D. (1974) from the University of Akron School of Law. He was articles editor of the *Akron Law Review* (1972-73). Mr. Glasser is currently a graduate student at the Institute of Air and Space Law at McGill University.

ARTHUR J. GOLDBERG is a member of the Illinois and District of Columbia bars and practices in Washington, D.C. Prior to serving as Secretary of Labor from 1961 to 1962, Justice Goldberg was General Counsel of the CIO, United Steelworkers of America, and the Industrial Union Department of the AFL-CIO. From 1962 to 1965 he was Associate Justice of the United States Supreme Court. Justice Goldberg was the United States Representative to the United Nations from 1965 to 1968. He received his B.S.L. (1929) and J.D. (1930) from Northwestern University. He is the author of *Defenses of Freedom,* ed. Daniel P. Moynihan (New York: Harper & Row, 1966), and *Equal Justice: The Supreme Court in the Warren Era* (Evanston: Northwestern University Press, 1971).

L. F. E. GOLDIE is Professor of Law and Director of the International Legal Studies Program at Syracuse University College of Law. During 1970-71, he served as the Charles H. Stockton Professor of International Law at the United States Naval War College. Professor Goldie was a Lecturer in Law and Usages of War at the Royal Military College, Duntroon, Australia, from 1958 to 1959. He received his LL.B. (1941) from the University of Western Australia School of Law and his LL.B. (1947) and LL.M. (1955) from the Sydney University School of Law. He is the author of numerous books and articles on international law, including "Pollution and Liability Problems Connected with Deep-Sea Mining," in *Environmental Policy: Concepts and International Implications,* ed. Albert E. Utton and Daniel H. Henning (New York:

Praeger, 1973), and "International Law and the World Community—The Meaning of Words, the Nature of Things and the Force of International Order," 23 *Naval War College Review* 8 (1971).

TOWNSEND HOOPES is President of the Association of American Publishers. He received his B.A. from Yale University (1944) and attended the National War College in 1951. From 1948 to 1953, Mr. Hoopes was an assistant to the Secretary of Defense. In 1965 Mr. Hoopes was appointed Deputy Assistant Secretary of Defense for International Security (Near East—South Asia). He served as Principal Deputy Assistant Secretary of Defense for International Security Affairs from 1966 to 1967 and Undersecretary of the Air Force from 1967 to 1969. Mr. Hoopes is the author of *The Devil and John Foster Dulles* (Boston: Little, Brown & Co., 1973), and *The Limits of Intervention* (New York: David McKay Co., 1970).

ROBERT E. JORDAN III is a member of the District of Columbia and Virginia bars and practices in Washington, D.C. He received his B.S. (1958) from the Massachusetts Institute of Technology and his J.D. (1961) from Harvard Law School. Mr. Jordan served as General Counsel of the United States Department of the Army and Special Assistant to the Secretary of the Army for Civil Functions from 1968 to 1971. In 1969 he was given the Arthur S. Flemming Award as "One of the Ten Outstanding Young Men in the Federal Service," and in 1971 he received the Army's Decoration for Distinguished Civilian Service.

ROBERT W. KOMER is with the Rand Corporation in Washington, D.C. He received his B.S. (1942) from Harvard College and M.B.A. (1947) from the Harvard Graduate School of Business Administration. Ambassador Komer was Senior Staff Member, National Security Council (1961 to 1965) and Deputy Special Assistant to the President for National Security Affairs (1966 to 1967). In 1967-68 he was Deputy to the Commander of United States Military Assistance Command—Vietnam for Civil Operations and Rural Development Support. From 1968 to 1969 he was United States Ambassador to Turkey. Ambassador Komer received the Presidential Medal of Freedom in 1967 and the Department of State's Distinguished Honor Award in 1968. He is the author of numerous articles on the Vietnam pacification program and other foreign policy issues.

HOWARD S. LEVIE is Professor of Law at Saint Louis University School of Law. He was a colonel in the United States Army Judge Advocate General Corps, with which he served from 1942 to 1963. In 1971-72 Professor Levie was Charles H. Stockton Professor of International Law, United States Naval War College. He received his A.B. (1928) and his J.D. (1930) from Cornell University and his LL.M. (1957) from George Washington University School of Law. He has written "Some Major Inadequacies in the Existing Law Relating to the Protection of Individuals During Armed Conflict" in *When Battle Rages, How Can Law Protect?*, ed. John Carey (Dobbs Ferry: Oceana Publications, 1971); "Maltreatment of Prisoners of War in Vietnam," 48 *Boston University Law Review* 323 (1968); and "International Law Aspects of Prisoner-of-War Repatriation During Hostilities: A Reply," 67 *American Journal of International Law* 693 (1973).

JAMES R. MILES is a Major in the International Law Division of the United States Air Force Office of the Judge Advocate General. He received his A.B. (1957) and J.D. (1961) from Ohio State University and his LL.M. (1973) from the University of Michigan School of Law. Major Miles has completed advanced studies in political science and public administration at the University of Oklahoma and has prepared research papers on "Napalm and the Laws of War" and "The 'Justice' Trial at Nuremberg."

TELFORD TAYLOR is Nash Professor of Law at Columbia Law School. He served from 1946 to 1949 as Brigadier General and Chief of Counsel for War Crimes, Office of Military Government (United States), in West Germany and in that capacity conducted prosecutions before the Nuremberg military tribunals. He received his A.B. (1928), M.A. (1932), and LL.D. (1949) from Williams College and his LL.B. (1932) from Harvard Law School. He is the author of *Nuremberg and Vietnam: An American Tragedy* (Chicago: Quadrangle Books, 1970), and "Vietnam and the Nuremberg Principles: A Colloquy on War Crimes," 5 *Rutgers-Camden Law Journal* 1 (1973).

NORMAN R. THORPE is a Lieutenant Colonel in the International Law Division of the United States Air Force Office of the Judge Advocate General. From 1969 to 1972 he was Legal Adviser to the United States Embassy in Manila, Philippines. Colonel Thorpe received his A.B. (1956) and his J.D. (1958) from the University of Illinois and his LL.M. (1967) from George Washington University, where his thesis was "Prisoners of Contemporary War: Enforcing Community Standards of Treatment."

PETER D. TROOBOFF is a member of the District of Columbia and New York bars and practices in Washington, D.C. He was a Lecturer in International Organizations at the University of Virginia School of Law in 1974 and Director of Studies for English-speaking students at The Hague Academy of International Law in 1972. Mr. Trooboff received his A.B. (1964) from Columbia College, his LL.B. (1967) from Harvard Law School, and his LL.M. (1968) from the University of London. He is the author of "Procedures for Protection of Civilians and Prisoners of War in Armed Conflicts: Southeast Asian Examples—A Comment," [1971] *Proceedings of the American Society of International Law* 228.

From 1970 to 1973 Mr. Trooboff was a member of the Executive Council of the American Society of International Law and served on its Executive Committee in 1972-73. He is Co-Chairman of the American Bar Association's Committee on Transnational Judicial Procedures of the Section of International Law.

ROBERT W. TUCKER is a Professor at the School of Advanced International Studies, The Johns Hopkins University, and Director of the Washington Center of Foreign Policy Research. He received his B.S. (1945) from the United States Naval Academy and his M.A. (1947) and Ph.D. (1949) from the University of California at Berkeley. Professor Tucker is the author of several books concerning American foreign policy and of *Law of War and Neutrality at Sea* (Washington, D.C.: Government Printing Office, 1957); *The Just War* (Baltimore: Johns Hopkins Press, 1961); and *Force, Order, and Justice,* with Robert E. Osgood (Baltimore: Johns Hopkins Press, 1967).

PAUL C. WARNKE practices law in Washington, D.C. He was General Counsel of the United States Department of Defense from 1966 to 1967 and Assistant Secretary of Defense for International Security Affairs from 1967 to 1969, during the Johnson Administration. Mr. Warnke received his A.B. (1941) from Yale University and his LL.B (1948) from Columbia Law School. He is the author of *Vietnam Settlement: Why 1973, not 1969?* (Washington, D.C.: American Enterprise Institute, 1973), and "Should We Reassess Old Alliances?" 6 *Center Magazine* 74 (1973). Mr. Warnke is a director of the Council of Foreign Relations and Chairman of the Board of Visitors of the Georgetown School of Foreign Service.

RICHARD A. WASSERSTROM is Professor of Law and Professor of Philosophy at the University of California at Los Angeles. He received his B.A. (1957) from Amherst College, his M.A. (1958) and Ph.D. (1960) from the University of Michigan, and his LL.B. (1960) from Stanford Law School. Professor Wasserstrom is the author of "On the Morality of War: A Preliminary Inquiry," 21 *Stanford Law Review* 627 (1969); "The Relevance of Nuremberg," 1 *Philosophy and Public Affairs* 22 (1971); and "The Laws of War," 56 *The Monist* 1 (1972). He edited *War and Morality* (Belmont, Cal.: Wadsworth Publishing Co., 1970).

Index